Heart-beguiling Araby

KATHRYN TIDRICK

CAMBRIDGE UNIVERSITY PRESS

Cambridge
London   New York   New Rochelle
Melbourne   Sydney

Published by the Press Syndicate of the University of Cambridge
The Pitt Building, Trumpington Street, Cambridge CB2 1RP
32 East 57th Street, New York, NY 10022, USA
296 Beaconsfield Parade, Middle Park, Melbourne 3206, Australia

First published 1981

Printed in Great Britain at the
University Press, Cambridge

British Library Cataloguing in Publication Data
Tidrick, Kathryn
Heart-beguiling Araby.
1. Arab countries – Description and travel
I. Title
909'.09'74927   DS36.65   80-41542
ISBN 0 521 23483 2

For my parents
JAMES *and* ELLEN JACKSON

'Dark-browed Sailor, tell me now,
Where, where is Araby?
The tide's aflow, the wind ablow,
'Tis I who pine for Araby.'

'Master, she her spices showers
O'er nine and ninety leagues of sea;
The laden air breathes faint and rare –
Dreams on far-distant Araby.'

'Oh, but Sailor, tell me true;
'Twas Man who mapped this Araby;
Though dangers brew, let me and you
Embark this night for Araby . . .'

Wails the wind from star to star;
Rock the loud waves their dirge: and, see!
Through foam and wrack, a boat drifts back:
Ah, heart-beguiling Araby!

Walter de la Mare

The attraction, the spell of Arabia, as it is so frequently called, is a sickness of the imagination. It was not until I had left Arabia and her doors were closed to me that, while tasting the bitter-sweets of memory, I began to muse unhappily on how such a barren mistress, as that country is, can enslave the heart and mind with so deep an intermingling of yearning and abomination. He is comfortless indeed who has opened the windows of his spirit to her parching breath. And it is true that those who have fully known her wish never to return.

The Master of Belhaven, *The Kingdom of Melchior*, 1949

Contents

Illustrations

Acknowledgments

I would like to thank Stephen Krasner, Elizabeth Monroe and Gene Tidrick for reading and commenting on the manuscript. I would also like to acknowledge the use I made of the following libraries and the help given to me by their staffs: Stetson Library, Williams College; Central Library, Manchester; John Rylands Library, Manchester; the British Museum Library; the library of the University of Dar es Salaam; the Library of Congress; Widener Library, Harvard University. Rhoda Blade-Charest typed the manuscript.

Much of this book was written while I was living in Africa, and I was again in Africa while it was going through the press. I must therefore thank Linda Alwitt for checking a crucial point in Chapter 4, and Andrew Brown of Cambridge University Press for taking on many tasks which I was unable to perform myself.

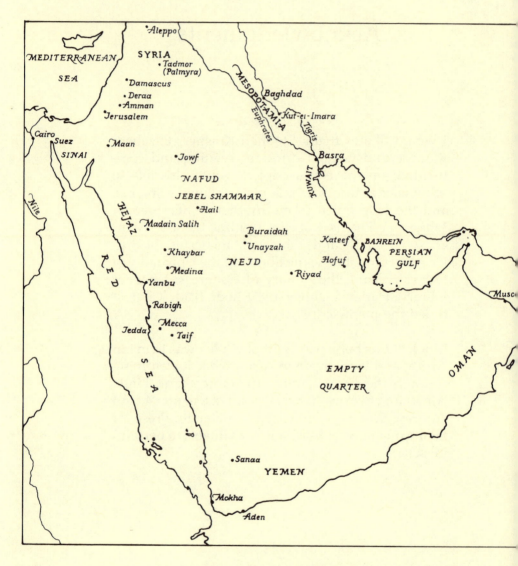

Map 1   The Arabian Peninsula

xii

Prologue

THIS BOOK is concerned with two related phenomena: the fascination exercised upon certain Englishmen by the Arabian desert and its inhabitants, and the development of the notion that Englishmen possessed an intuitive understanding of Arabs which gave them a special right, even an obligation, to interfere in their affairs. 'We call ourselves insular,' wrote John Buchan in *Greenmantle*, 'but the truth is that we are the only race on earth that can produce men capable of getting inside the skin of remote peoples.' The tradition of English expertise on the Arabs was an exceptionally well-developed version of this powerful imperial myth.

It was the writings of four men (Richard Burton, Gifford Palgrave, Wilfrid Blunt and Charles Doughty) which were mainly responsible for the belief that Englishmen knew more about the Arabs than anyone else. They all wrote and travelled in the central decades of the Victorian era, and though they were in most respects utterly different from one another and tended not to get on on the rare occasions when they met, they seem to have left a collective impression. I have tried to find out what lured them to the Arab East and what they found there. The central part of the book is devoted to them.

The first part of the book is an attempt to discover what was the common stock of English ideas about the Arabs by 1855, when the first volume of Burton's *Personal Narrative of a Pilgrimage to Al-Madinah & Meccah* was published. I have tried to describe the context of literate public opinion in which the writings of Burton and the others were received. The last part of the book is concerned with the years from the First World War to the 1950s, when Britain was a power in the Arab world. An epilogue attempts to summarize what those Englishmen whose lot it was to enter into an imperial relationship with the Arabs found satisfying about that relationship.

My interest in the subject of this book began with a copy of Alexander Kinglake's *Eothen*, picked up in a second-hand bookshop when I was sixteen years old. I returned to it years later as a psychologist interested in race relations and the psychology of colonialism, ready to look with a more critical eye at the writers who had charmed me in adolescence. As a psychologist it was natural that my approach should be personal and biographical (the influence of Erik Erikson will be apparent), and individual lives received a large share of my attention. This approach undoubtedly involved some loss of intellectual tidiness, but it also seemed to me to have the advantage of reminding us that the nature of the relationship between members of one culture and members of another cannot be summed up in a few eloquent generalizations. The individual human being, imperfect but intelligent and inquiring, gets in the way. Instead of sweeping him aside I have tried to understand him, placing him in his proper historical context but also setting him off from it. I do not attempt to argue, as Edward Said does in his controversial study, *Orientalism*, published shortly after the present book was completed, that writers on the Middle East are primarily to be understood as prisoners of an institutionalized system of discourse which makes it impossible for them to regard Orientals as human beings like themselves. Their faults were legion, but more various and more interesting.

I have often, of course, had to trespass into the historian's field of expertise. If the result is 'psychohistory', then so be it. The label hardly matters. I have tried, as an amateur historian and a professional psychologist, to show a decent diffidence in drawing conclusions about the thoughts and motives of the dead.

PART ONE

1

A Sometimes Noble Savage

ARABIA was not always an empty desert. Once it contained thriving city states and principalities linked by intricate commercial networks. The most famous of these was Palmyra in the north whose ruins remain to amaze the enterprising tourist, but southern, eastern and western Arabia also had important cities. In late classical times some of these Arabian states were incorporated into the Roman Empire, and then it appears that the nomads who had always inhabited the surrounding desert began their incursions into the weakened cities. The caravan routes were no longer secure, trade declined, and the settlements of the interior began to be deserted. Arabia became the land of the Bedouin.

These Bedouin, who were called by the city folk 'Arabs', were loosely organized into groups claiming descent from a common ancestor. The ancestor's deeds were glorified in epic poems which were both history and literature to the wandering tribes. Their form of government was rudimentary. A leader (sheikh) was chosen from among members of a particular family whose hereditary privilege this was, and he exercised whatever influence he could upon the recalcitrant nomads who considered themselves his equals rather than his subjects. He was advised by a council of elders, the voice of public opinion with the tribe, and this advice he almost invariably followed. The sheikh performed functions which in Western societies have usually been associated with considerable personal power and authority, yet which do not seem to have been so among the Bedouin. He was the tribe's representative in its dealings with other tribes, and guests of the tribe were received in his tent with what lavishness he could command. He possessed prestige, the result of his personal qualities and gentle breeding, but prestige was not associated with the power to coerce. In Bedouin society power resided in the group, not in the individual. The tribesman's loyalty was to his tribe and the force which regulated social life was the force of custom. The sheikh was little more than a symbol of tribal unity, of that group conscious-ness which made survival possible in the desert. Only through such solidarity with his kin could the individual be protected from others, perhaps stronger than he, whose need of the meagre resources of the desert was just as urgent as his.

In the oasis towns, where nomads had settled down and taken to commerce, this group consciousness weakened a little, and it was no longer felt that within the tribe no man was better than his neighbour. Certain families acquired political power along with their control of trade. It was in one of these towns, Mecca in the Hejaz, that the prophet Mohammed was born. He came from a family which, though comfortably off, was not part of the ruling oligarchy, and the new religion which he founded was completely alien to Meccan merchants and pagan tribesmen alike. The tribes-men had their own gods, thought to be resident in particular places, trees and stones. Some of these stones were assembled together in the sanctuary at Mecca, which from early times had been a place of pilgrimage, and a source of profit for the Meccans. The speed and suddenness with which the Moslem religion sup-planted the polytheism of the tribes and was carried forth by them to the rich and civilized countries of the north and west remains one of the most dramatic and enigmatic phenomena of history. The historian can point to patterns of cultural diffusion which prepared the ground for the rise of a monotheistic religion in Arabia, but nothing can diminish the remarkable nature of the conquests made during the seventh century under the banner of Islam. Barely one hundred years after Mohammed's death there was an Arab Empire stretching from the banks of the Indus to the Pyrenees. The Bedouin character of this empire was a transient one. Rude tribal ways rapidly gave way before the demands of administration and contact with civilization, but the Bedouin origin of Arab greatness was never entirely forgotten. Even today Arab townsmen of Egypt and Iraq will boast of some real or imaginary Bedouin ancestor.

By the time of the Crusades, when Northern Europeans found themselves for the first time in prolonged contact with Moslem society, the Bedouin tribes were no longer a central element in that society. The chroniclers of the Crusades describe them waiting like jackals to see the outcome of a battle and then falling on the losers, Christian and Moslem alike.[1] It is difficult to find in the chronicles a single mention of a good deed performed by a nomad. William of Tyre recorded that a Bedouin chief whose wife had been treated kindly by King Baldwin I of Jerusalem helped Baldwin to escape from the beleaguered fortress of Ramlah, but he clearly regarded such behaviour as exceptional; chivalrous actions were the prerogative of the 'Saracens', that is the civilized Arabs, rather than the nomads.[2] Mediaeval Europeans did not regard the savage as noble: they were too recently emerged from barbarism themselves.

The earliest account of the Bedouin by an independent European traveller was that of Sir John Mandeville, of whom little is known, and whose *Travels*, as it has come down to us, is probably very largely a fifteenth-century compilation of travellers' tales from different sources. What Sir John actually saw with his own eyes is impossible to say, but for what it is worth, he found the Bedouin 'right foul folk and cruel and of evil kind'.[3]

By the end of the seventeenth century a few hardy spirits, curious about the lands of the East, had travelled through Egypt and Syria (an area much larger than the modern country of the same name) and had produced accounts of what they had seen. The Arabian peninsula remained unexplored. Their journeys were undertaken in conditions which seem to us extraordinarily dangerous and uncomfortable, though to them it may not have seemed much worse than travelling at home. Filthy inns, robbers, and disease were as prevalent in Europe as in Asia. Bedouin were merely highwaymen on camelback, made perhaps a little more alarming by the unfamiliarity of the terrain. Travellers wrote of how they had been set upon by 'wild Arabs' armed with lances, relieved of their possessions, and abandoned to the mercy of the desert. In such encounters the noble qualities of the Bedouin were not apparent. It was only later, after literary men had begun to take a sentimental and philosophical interest in the inhabitants of what we now call less-developed countries, that a layer of favourable preconceptions was placed between the traveller and his experience. William Lithgow, whose wanderings took him to the Levant around 1612, produced an account of the Bedouin which may stand as typical of this early period.

7

The people generally are addicted to Theft, Rapine, and Robberies: hating all Sciences Mechanicall or Civill, they are commonly all of the second Stature, swift on foot, scelerate, and seditious, boysterous in speech, of colour Tauny, boasting much of their triball Antiquity, and noble Gentry . . . They are not valourous, nor desperate in assaults without great advantage, for a 100 Turkes is truely esteemed to be sufficient to incounter 300 Arabs.[4]

Lithgow took note of the Bedouin's pride of lineage but was not impressed by it. Nor were most of the other Europeans who travelled in the Levant before 1800. They were more likely to complain that the Bedouin were ignorant of the deference 'which is due from inferiors to their superiors'.[5]

Bartholomew Plaisted, an East India Company official travelling overland from Calcutta to England in 1750, had a number of unpleasant experiences at the hands of the Bedouin, from which he drew the obvious conclusions. The first disaster befell his French travelling companion who was robbed while visiting a Bedouin encampment. Animated perhaps by a spirit of philosophical inquiry which seems quite absent from the Englishman, he 'would needs make an excursion out of curiosity to the tents of the Arabs, and was so rash as to enter into one of them'. Later on their Bedouin escort went on strike for higher pay, threatening to leave Plaisted and the Frenchman alone in the desert. Plaisted thought they should compromise by giving the Bedouin a 'loan' repayable at Aleppo, but the Frenchman, a man of principle, refused. The leader of the Bedouin then 'ordered my comrade to be laid hold of, which they did, and stamped him under foot, not forgetting to ply him with blows to force him to a compliance'. The Frenchman parted with the money, but more extortion was to follow later in the journey. Plaisted concluded: 'Therefore let those who shall pass this way hereafter put no trust in any Arab, especially those of the desert, for there is not one of them but is villain enough to cut your throat for ten piasters . . .'[6]

The only early account which came close to portraying the noble Arab of later convention was that of Laurent d'Arvieux, a Frenchman who first went to the Levant on a commercial expedition financed by Louis XIV and then stayed on for the next twenty-five years. In 1664 he visited Palestine on an official mission to the sheikh of Mount Carmel. He was to get an agreement from the sheikh allowing Carmelite monks to resettle on the mountain. D'Arvieux spoke Arabic, and instead of skulking fearfully through the desert as more conventional travellers did, he went boldly forth in Arab dress, returning the salutations of passing Bedouin 'with all the gravity 'twas possible for me'. He was well received by the 'Grand Emir' of Mount Carmel, successfully concluded his business, and spent the remainder of his visit getting to know the Bedouin.

As an honoured guest in Bedouin tents he saw a side of Bedouin life which, as he rather complacently put it,

Common Travellers can inform the Publick nothing of; it being very difficult to discover the Manners of a Nation, whose Acquaintance is so far from being sought after, that it is forever shunn'd. I don't question but that the World will hardly believe that there can be so much Justice and Honesty as there is, found among People whose usual Profession is Robbery, and the Employment of what we call *High-way-men*.[7]

There was much exchanging of compliments between host and guest. The emir is reported to have told d'Arvieux: 'There's no body but would take you for a real *Bedouin*'; and d'Arvieux assured the emir that though 'they believe in *France*, that an *Arabian* has nothing Human about him but his Shape', they would soon change their opinion if they could be received as graciously as he had been.[8]

D'Arvieux's enthusiastic account of Bedouin life, published posthumously in 1718, was received with almost uncritical appreciation by European scholars. It was the only account up to that time by a European who had actually lived with the Bedouin. The English editor of the *Voyage en Palestine* remarked that whatever was known about the Bedouin was due to d'Arvieux.[9] The favourable nature of his account is therefore of the greatest importance. He credited them with being honest in their dealings with each other, hospitable to strangers, polite, patient and sober. He sympathized with their pride of race and was indulgent towards their propensity for robbing travellers, counting it a mere peccadillo when set against their honesty towards each other. He seems to have identified strongly with the Bedouin as an 'in-group' whose conduct towards the 'out-group' (that is, the rest of the world) would naturally be governed by different rules from those prevailing among themselves. He mildly deplored the custom of the blood feud, but also saw it as a beneficial restraint which 'obliges 'em to live friendly together'. Robust merchant adventurer that he was, d'Arvieux could not resist comparing the manly Arabs of

1   The 'Grand Emir' of Mt Carmel, as seen by Laurent d'Arvieux

Mount Carmel with the mincing fops of Paris: he was probably the first European traveller to perceive the Bedouin as offering an instructive contrast to the artificialities of civilized life.[10]

During the seventeenth century the study of Arabic by European scholars began to be freed of the blight of religious bigotry which had marked it since the Middle Ages. A knowledge of Arabic was no longer merely a tool of polemic but an instrument of scholarship in its own right. European Arabists still made ritual obeisance to religious prejudice against Islam, but their work began to show a real interest in and sometimes enthusiasm for Arab history and culture.

Their sources for the Arab character were Arabic literature and the scattered references to Arabs found in the writings of the Greek historians. They seem to have discounted the writings of contemporary travellers until d'Arvieux's *Voyage en Palestine* appeared in 1718. The Arabic literature with which they were familiar included the heroic poetry of pre-Islamic Arabia, in which war, women and honour were eloquently celebrated by the tribal poets, and later Arabic poetry in which the chivalrous life of the desert was nostalgically extolled. Influenced by the glorification of nomad life which they found in their Arabic sources, European Arabists concluded that the Arabs of the desert were superior to those of the town. Bartholomeo d'Herbelot in his *Bibliothèque orientale*, published in 1697, wrote that the Bedouin 'surpassent de beaucoup ceux des villes en bonté et subtilitie d'esprit', though he added that all Arabs, Bedouin and townsmen alike, were 'ingenieux, hardis, genereux, aimans jusqu'à l'excez l'éloquence et la poësie'.[11]

The Greek sources with which scholars were familiar also tended when brought together to produce a rather appealing portrait of a people who were honourable, brave and free. Tacitus's brave, manly Germanii and Herodotus's 'blameless Ethiopians' are better known examples of classical writers' idealization of the savage; but the basic outline of a favourable stereotype of the Arab can also be found in the Greek texts, reflecting the attitude of a highly developed civilization towards savage peoples who seemed to possess the simple virtues which were vanishing at home. Strabo noted that the inhabitants of Arabia were the only people on earth who disdained to send ambassadors to Alexander. Diodorus Siculus wrote that no one had ever enslaved the nomads around Petra; they refused to plant crops or build houses because this would compromise the liberty of which they were exceptionally fond. Herodotus wrote that there were no men who respected pledges more than the Arabians. He was probably the earliest writer to attribute to the Arabs special qualities of fidelity.[12] European Arabists used these Greek references, along with their Arabic sources, to put together a far more sympathetic picture of the Bedouin than that of the hard-pressed traveller whose primary concern was getting himself and his belongings across the desert in one piece.

The writings of scholars and travellers were not totally divergent: on some points they did agree. Scholars deplored the predatoriness and bloodthirstiness of the Bedouin, as of course did travellers who had first-hand knowledge of these qualities; and travellers, learning eventually the rules of desert travel whereby protection could be acquired while travelling through the territory of a particular tribe, sometimes reported that once a promise of protection had been obtained it had been honoured. Nevertheless, the difference in tone between the accounts of early Arabists and early travellers is considerable. The traveller usually neither knew nor cared about the glories of Bedouin poetry. He drew his conclusions from his own limited but vivid experience.

The two most influential English Arabists of the seventeenth and eighteenth centuries were Simon Ockley and George Sale. Ockley, whose *History of the Saracens* was published in 1708 and 1718, was a true scholar who was the first to affirm that Arab history was a legitimate study in its own right. His *History* was finished in Cambridge Castle, where he was imprisoned for debt. George Sale, whose translation of the Koran was published in 1734 and is still to be found in most public libraries, displayed such sympathy with the Arabs and Islam that he earned the reputation of being 'half a Muslim'. Voltaire declared, quite wrongly – Sale never left his native land – that he spent 'twenty-five years among the Arabs'.[13] His encyclopedic knowledge of the Arabs and Arabic apparently made this assertion quite plausible. In his 'Preliminary Discourse' to the Koran he wrote that the inhabitants of Arabia were a remarkable people who had 'preserved their liberty . . . with very little interruption, from the very Deluge'. He gave many examples, in his 'Discourse' and in the articles he contributed to the English edition of Pierre Bayle's *Dictionary*, of Bedouin hospitality and generosity, though he also criticized their 'natural disposition to war, bloodshed, cruelty and rapine'.[14]

Sale used d'Arvieux extensively for a chapter in the 'Preliminary Discourse' entitled 'Of the Arabs before Mohammed', and the way in which he interwove d'Arvieux's contemporary account with material from far older Arabic sources reflected an assumption which was to become an article of faith with Orientalists and travellers alike: that Bedouin society had not changed from time immemorial. Whatever the truth of this assumption, and biblical evidence tends to support it, the idea of social immobility was fascinating to Europeans whose society was in the process of rapid change. Believers in progress deplored it and conservatives admired it, but all found it remarkable that such a society should exist.

Carsten Niebuhr was the first European traveller to penetrate the interior of the Arabian peninsula and produce an articulate account of it. He was a serious and intelligent man who was familiar with the writings of contemporary scholars and the narrative of d'Arvieux. A careful reading of his *Travels in Arabia* suggests that in spite of his careful and observant nature his perceptions were influenced by what he had read.

Niebuhr was the only survivor of a tragic expedition which set out from Denmark in 1761. He was not the leader of the expedition – that honour went to Christian von Haven, an indolent, arrogant and fearful Dane – but he was without doubt the man best suited for the position. He was patient, hardworking, curious about everything, and ready to be flexible in his dealings with the natives. It did not take him long to learn the first and most important lesson that any serious traveller must learn – how to suffer trivial exploitations and importunities with cheerfulness and detachment. Von Haven, ever conscious of his dignity, flew into a rage and refused point-blank when a Bedouin guide in Sinai asked for more money, but Niebuhr, a born traveller, realized instinctively how foolish such tactics were. He was ready to make minor concessions and put up with minor inconveniences in order to avoid major ones. Von Haven accomplished little of what he was sent to do; the modest Niebuhr accomplished that and much more. But Niebuhr was not qualified in the eyes of Danish officialdom to lead an expedition which was intended to reflect great glory on the Danish intelligentsia and the Danish crown. It was the first official expedition to be sent from any country to explore the interior of Arabia, and Niebuhr was only a poor surveyor from the marshes of Friesland, hurriedly promoted to the rank of Engineer-Lieutenant in time for the journey. His job was to make maps, and he did it very well; his map of Yemen was to be praised for its accuracy a hundred years hence.

2 Carsten Niebuhr in his Arabian dress

14

The other members of the expedition were Peter Forsskål, a brilliant and fiery Swedish botanist whom von Haven at one point thought of murdering; Christian Carl Kramer, a Danish doctor; and Georg Wilhelm Baurenfeind, a German engraver. From the beginning there were tensions and jealousies within the group. They were just beginning to be resolved when the members began to drop away one by one, victims of malaria. When the surviving members of the expedition left Arabia Felix, the 'Happy Arabia' they had been sent to explore, Niebuhr was the only one who could stand up. By the time they reached Bombay only Niebuhr and Kramer were still alive, and Kramer died in Bombay. For six months, in an effort to rid himself of the recurring fever, Niebuhr lived on rice, water and a little fruit, but he did not let up on work. He put his journals in order and sent them off to the Danish Academy of Sciences in Copenhagen. They were the only lasting fruit of the great Danish expedition. The immense number of botanical specimens sent back by Forsskål were either lost on the way or destroyed through neglect when they got back to Denmark. The manuscripts sent back by von Haven were few and of little importance; he missed his chance to acquire the great Codex Sinaiticus, the then unknown treasure of St Catherine's monastery in Sinai.

When Niebuhr was well enough to leave Bombay he set off on the last leg of his journey home, overland through Persia and Iraq. From November 1765 to June 1766 he went underground, adopting Arab dress and changing his name to Abdullah. He sent few dispatches home but kept a diary. He seems to have yielded to an impulse which seizes certain travellers in the East, the urge to seek freedom in anonymity, to observe and participate without constraint. At the very beginning of the journey, setting out across the desert from Cairo to Suez, Niebuhr had been the only member of the expedition to ride a camel. When he was left alone like the Ancient Mariner to carry on as best he could he experienced some relief, his son tells us, that he could now 'conform himself without difficulty or hindrance to oriental manners and customs'.[15] He arrived in Copenhagen in November 1767, an almost forgotten man, but his *Travels in Arabia* ensured for him his reputation as the first traveller to produce a coherent and articulate account of the interior of the peninsula.

His account of his journey was remarkable for the restraint with which he recorded the expedition's many vicissitudes and the wretched treatment they received almost without exception from the natives. His most pointed comment on the subject was characteristically oblique and is found in an engraving of himself in Arab dress by Georg Baurenfeind which was printed in his book. We see him arrayed in his oriental finery, serious but not self-conscious, and in the background are two Arabians locked in mortal combat. He wrote glowingly of the Bedouin, though it would not be unfair to say that he hardly knew them. He never had the chance to live with them and encountered them only on his surveying trips out into the desert, when their behaviour tended to be unpredictable. He accepted them at their own valuation, almost without reserve.

He took care to contrast them with the inhabitants of the towns, whose conduct he frequently had cause to deplore. Perhaps in their remoteness he imagined them to be an entirely different order of humanity. As an educated man he was familiar with the then popular idea that primitive peoples retained something of the primeval innocence of mankind and this seems to have coloured his attitude towards the Bedouin. They were an ancient people who had preserved their ancient customs and they displayed certain characteristics ('liberty, independence, and simplicity') which Niebuhr felt illustrated man's natural tendency to goodness away from the destructive influence of civilization. 'Even without adverting to the causes of the pleasure which we feel,' he wrote in his careful way, 'we are always pleased to find some faint traces even of our natural and primary rights, and of the happiness to which we were originally destined.' He also enjoyed the biblical images conjured up by tents and camels: 'We are here tempted to imagine ourselves,' he wrote, 'among the old patriarchs, with whose adventures we have been so much amused in our infant days.'[16]

The poverty of the Bedouin, Niebuhr thought, was clearly voluntary, the noble consequence of their love of freedom. They were unwilling to encumber themselves with the material possessions which inevitably led to servitude. Rather than till the soil like slaves they preferred to be 'uncomfortably lodged, indifferently fed, ill clothed, and destitute of almost all the conveniences of life'. He observed and commented on the limited power of the Bedouin sheikhs and their election on the basis of ability from among members of the ruling family. There seemed much to admire in the system. Dissatisfied subjects could depose their sheikh and replace him with someone more tractable, or they could go off and join another tribe.[17]

The primitive government of the Bedouin, their pride of race and contempt for Turks and townsmen, appealed to a sympathetic disposition in Niebuhr's character. He was a Frieslander, from the province of Hadeln, which had at one time been part of the United Provinces but at the time of Niebuhr's birth was under the sovereignty of Hanover. The peasants of Hadeln were famous for their national spirit and Niebuhr himself, his son tells us, was exceptionally proud of his native province with its republican past and free institutions. Every peasant in Hadeln owned his own farm and the province was administered by elected magistrates. Niebuhr then was predisposed to admire a free people, by upbringing as well as intellectual conviction. His friendship with Peter Forsskål, the Swedish botanist whose death in Yarim had been a great loss to the expedition, perhaps helped to articulate his political ideas. Forsskål had been forced to leave Sweden after speaking out boldly against the tyranny of the Swedish crown. He was a remarkable and ardent man whom Niebuhr greatly admired.

Niebuhr was a peasant all his life: frugal, unimaginative, living only for observation and completely uninterested in abstraction and speculation. In 1778 he returned to Friesland, to a place less than thirty miles from where he was born, and stayed there till his death in 1815. Yet for this sober, modest, careful man the Arabs of the desert possessed a powerful appeal. They exemplified for him that which in his quiet way he held most dear – liberty.

The intellectual character of the Danish expedition and the thorough preparation of its members meant that they arrived in Arabia with more stereotyped preconceptions than most travellers up to that time. Niebuhr knew that the Bedouin were brave, free and unconquerable before he ever set foot in Arabia. He knew also that Arabs were supposed to be polite and was at first disconcerted when they were rude. At Sanaa in Yemen a house was provided for the Danish travellers by the local potentate, but the Europeans had to approach it on foot while their Moslem servants rode. Niebuhr permitted himself a rare display of irritation: 'This humiliating ceremony was what we had not expected to be subjected to among the Arabs, who value themselves upon their politeness.'[18] There had already been a foretaste of Arab rudeness at the Pyramids, a place which was later to become notorious to travellers as a haunt of importunate Bedouin. Forsskål and Niebuhr had attempted to deal with it in a sophisticated, but alas unsuccessful, way. Their Bedouin guide had demanded more money and Forsskål had refused to give it to him, whereupon the Bedouin had begun to threaten Forsskål, going so far as to snatch off his turban.

My friend [wrote Niebuhr] now adopted an admirable attitude. His manner grew quite cold; he turned to the two other Arabs and said: 'You are Bedouin; in our country people say that we Europeans can travel in complete safety so long as we are under the protection of the Bedouin. If you therefore stand by and let me be robbed by this companion of yours, I will go home and tell people that one cannot trust the Bedouin.' These words so roused the Arabs' pride that they at once compelled the third man to give the turban back.

That was as far as he went, however. Having returned the turban he stuck his pistol into Niebuhr's chest and repeated his demand for money, this time successfully.[19]

This was a scene which was to be repeated many times, with minor variations, in the course of European contact with the Arabs. Over the next hundred years or so delinquent Bedouin must have grown used to being upbraided by Europeans for failing to live up to their reputation. Some travellers, such as James Carmichael and James Bruce, were entirely cynical in their appeals to Arab virtue, but others, like a certain Mrs Hill who found herself in difficulties in Syria in the 1880s, were most assuredly sincere.[20]

In the closing decades of the eighteenth century there was a gradual consolidation of the Arabs' literary reputation for independence, faithfulness and hospitality. These were the three qualities which eventually found their way into popular literature as peculiarly Bedouin characteristics.

Edward Gibbon, in the fiftieth chapter of the *Decline and Fall*, produced an elegant summary of all that was known and thought about Arabia. Niebuhr and d'Arvieux were important sources for his opinions on the Arabian character. He praised Bedouin hospitality and love of poetry and commented approvingly on the élan with which the Bedouin defied their Turkish masters. Following Sale, he took it as axiomatic that there had never been any meaningful infringement of Arabian independence, and then went on to say, in the finest eulogy of Arab liberty ever written:

The slaves of domestic tyranny may vainly exult in their national independence; but the Arab is personally free; and he enjoys, in some degree, the benefits of society, without forfeiting the prerogatives of nature . . . If the Arabian princes abuse their power, they are quickly punished by the desertion of their subjects, who had been accustomed to a mild and parental jurisdiction. Their spirit is free, their steps are unconfined, the desert is open, and the tribes and families are held together by a mutual and voluntary compact.[21]

Gibbon's friend Sir William Jones, a brilliant polyglot who was the most accomplished Orientalist of the day, was also a notable Arabophile. The Arabs were a nation, he said, 'who have ever been my favourites'.[22] Of the Hejazi Arabs he met in Calcutta he wrote that 'their eyes are full of vivacity, their speech voluble and articulate, their deportment manly and dignified, their apprehension quick, their minds always present and attentive; with a spirit of independence appearing in the countenance of even the lowest among them'.[23]

Neither Gibbon nor Jones was blind to the faults of the Arabs. They were not simple lovers of the primitive but men of the Enlightenment ready to admire political virtues wherever they found them. Chief among these virtues, in the eyes of both men, was political liberty, and they seized upon its apparent manifestation in a faraway, 'simple' people. Jones was an idealist who had leanings towards republicanism and saw English political life as a crude struggle for power and profit.[24] He saw in the vaunted liberty of the Arabs a happy human condition which had all but disappeared in his own country. But he was also a judge and a constitutionalist and could not wholly approve of a liberty which was unrestrained by law. The seven pre-Islamic odes of Arabia, which he himself had translated into English, showed 'what may be constantly expected from men of open hearts and boiling passions, with no law to control, and little religion to restrain, them'.[25]

In spite of their reservations about their predatoriness and anarchic tendencies, Jones and Gibbon focussed the interest of the reading public on the Bedouin as exemplars of an admirable freedom from external and internal domination. No matter that

Gibbon's 'mutual and voluntary compact' was based on a serious misunderstanding of the nature of tribal society, with its deep subservience to custom, or that the foundations of Arabian independence lay not in valour but in an accident of geography; what mattered was that the Bedouin could be used as a convenient metaphor for the complex of ideas about personal liberty and national independence which were becoming central to European political thought.

With the development of nationalist thought in the eighteenth century a subtle but profound change occurred in the thinking of educated people about the significance of those human groups known variously as 'nations' and 'races'. According to nationalist theory in its purest form there are no subject races; every nation has a 'genius' all its own. National pride, which leads to national independence, is an emotion appropriate to any group of people which might legitimately be said to constitute a nation. Germans ought to be proud of being Germans and Arabs of being Arabs; only thus can they be free. It was an idea of revolutionary significance which developed almost imperceptibly from far older and more limited ideals of patriotism which taught that it was a man's duty to defend his native land and to promote its interests when he could. A man like William Lithgow, proud though he doubtless was of his own nationality (he was a Scot), found the pretensions of the Bedouin unworthy of comment. He was unfamiliar with the Greek sources on which George Sale based his opinion that the Arabs had preserved their independence literally since the Flood; but of equal importance was his ignorance of the notion that national independence was a good in itself.

Lithgow had remarked that the Bedouin were 'seditious' but 'not valourous'. This was a distinction which escaped many later eulogists of Bedouin liberty. The assumption came to be that the desert had never been conquered, therefore the Bedouin must have been brave upholders of their national freedom. It is true that the single Roman expedition into the interior of Arabia was a failure, and it is also true that Alexander the Great, setting out almost as an afterthought to conquer Arabia on his way back from India, narrowly avoided the obliteration of his army, but these failures were not the result of Bedouin valour; they were the result of thirst, disease and treachery. The great powers of the ancient world showed little serious interest in occupying Arabia, and mostly confined themselves to police operations on the desert marches. The Romans aspired to little more than control of the spice route from Yemen. The fact was that no one wanted the inhospitable lands of the Bedouin. It was the nomads who were always trying to get out of the desert, not the townsmen who were trying to get in.

It was not until the seventh century A.D., under the early leaders of Islam, that the dam broke and the Bedouin overran Syria, Iraq, Persia and North Africa. Bedouin garrisons were established all over the new Arab Empire, situated usually away from cities and their enervating influence in the hope of perpetuating a warrior caste of pure Arabian blood. The experiment failed. The cities of Basra, Kairouan and Shiraz now stand where these encampments stood.

After two centuries of glory the Arab Empire began to succumb to the disintegrative forces which had always been present within it. Arab civilization continued to develop with scarcely abated brilliance till the end of the twelfth century, but the Crusades and the Mongol invasions took a heavy toll of the weakened empire and in the early decades of the sixteenth century the Arab Empire finally collapsed before the rising power of the Ottoman Turks. Ottoman rule extended into Arabia where the Sherifs of Mecca, descendants of the Prophet and guardians of the Holy Places, recognized the suzerainty of the Sultan. Even the remote and inhospitable Yemen was an Ottoman pashalik from 1537 to 1635. In spite of what Niebuhr, d'Arvieux and the admirers of the high-spirited Bedouin believed, Turkish dominion over the desert was not entirely nominal, even in the nineteenth century when the Ottoman Empire was so obviously in a state of decay. The Bedouin, so long as they did no harm and confined themselves to the desert, were left alone, but when they misbehaved themselves within the confines of civilization they were hauled before the pasha and punished like anybody else. For the rest, it was simply a matter of divide and rule. The Turks saved themselves much administrative trouble and expense by setting the Bedouin against each other, diverting potentially rebellious energies into internecine feuds. During the Ottoman period their freedom was of a type not much more edifying than that of the inhabitants of remote country districts in Britain, where the public houses stay open after hours in flagrant but not very dangerous contravention of the licensing laws. Nevertheless, the Bedouin retained their pride of race and considered themselves vastly superior to those who tilled the soil and paid their taxes. It was this pride of race, discounted by early travellers as either unworthy of comment or unsuitable to ones of their station in life, which so captivated European intellectuals of the Enlightenment and gave plausibility to claims of invincible Bedouin valour.

By 1810 most narratives of travel in the Levant contained a set piece on the Bedouin in which they were described as independent, faithful and hospitable. A situation had arisen in which the traveller who wished to produce a saleable narrative for a public familiar with Gibbon had to include such a piece. The problem was that this could not always be squared with a desire to bear truthful witness to what had been seen. Passages of sub-Gibbonian rhetoric appeared side by side with accounts of the direst treachery. The learned traveller Edward Clarke narrowly escaped death at the hands of a Bedouin guide who had deliberately led him astray, but he quoted d'Arvieux to the bitter end, apparently oblivious of any inconsistency.[26] Whether he believed the evidence of his own eyes or those of d'Arvieux is impossible to say; he did at least permit a doubt to enter his mind as to whether the faithless guide was really a Bedouin. Human minds have room for all kinds of inconsistency and strive for integration of experience and expectation in highly ingenious ways. Lord Valentia decided that he would never have had such irritating experiences at the hands of the pure-blooded Arab tribes described by Niebuhr; not being thoroughbreds, his Arabs could not after all have been expected to display good manners.[27] Eyles Irwin, an East India Company official who travelled up the Red Sea coast of Arabia in the 1770s, produced two accounts of the Bedouin, a factual one and a fictional one. His travel narrative of 1780 was a long recitation of Bedouin treachery, in which we find the following stanzas, part of an 'Ode to the Desert' written during his desert journey:

> O! while thy secrets I explore,
> And traverse all thy regions o'er,
> The patient camel I bestride –
> May no ill hap his steps betide!
>
> But chief, whence lies our daily track,
> O! turn the roving Arab back;

Who, tyger like infests the way;
And makes the traveller his prey.[28]

He tried to be fair to the Bedouin and granted them a certain amiability and a capacity for devotion to their parents and offspring, but the irritations of the journey were far more vividly rendered. In 1802 his comic opera, *The Bedouins*, was performed in Dublin. In it the domestic felicities of Bedouin life were affectingly displayed. It might be supposed that his opinions simply changed with the fashion in the decades between 1780 and 1800, but it would probably be more accurate and more charitable to suggest that his memory was operating selectively. He remembered a chance encounter with a friendly sheikh, a welcome appearance by helpful Bedouin when his guide had lost his way, a pretty girl at a well, and these pleasant recollections assumed a new significance in the light of what had come to be received opinion on the subject.

Once lodged in the public mind, the idea that Bedouin were faithful and hospitable was one which also proved remarkably tenacious. The gentle ridicule of Kinglake and the scorn of Gifford Palgrave were helpless in the face of an idée fixe. Why were these qualities persistently attributed to the Bedouin even though they were frequently belied by the experience of travellers? They obviously possessed, and still possess, a very powerful appeal: people want to believe, against all reason, in the existence of noble beings who are ever faithful, ever hospitable, always accepting, never rejecting. It seems we have a need to be loved unconditionally, and though we recognize that in real life this need can never be fulfilled most of us harbour a faint recollection of a time when it was fulfilled – in the lost paradise of infancy when the mother's breast was freely offered and her tender care consistently experienced. It is in this period of earliest infancy, according to the psychoanalyst Erik Erikson, that we develop a feeling of 'basic trust', a confidence that our needs will be provided for, that we will not be let down. If all goes well in that dangerous period of life we build up a preponderance of basic trust over basic mistrust which helps us to cope with the frustrations which are an inevitable part of every stage of life. This important infantile achievement, no matter how successfully accomplished, leaves a disturbing psychic residue which Erikson describes as 'a sense of inner division and universal nostalgia for a paradise forfeited'. We have an inarticulate sense of loss which some of us try to allay by surrendering once more to the care of a loving parent, God.[29] The warmth of our response to people said to possess the virtues of faithfulness and hospitality might also have something to do with unconscious nostalgia for the lost infantile paradise. Perhaps it is significant that these qualities are often attributed to the inhabitants of a Golden Age long ago, that is, to the historical equivalent of earliest infancy, or else to primitive, 'unspoiled' peoples. James Bruce, the explorer of the Nile, remarked with his customary dogmatism: 'Hospitality is the virtue of Barbarians, who are hospitable in the ratio that they are barbarous . . .', and his remark, for which no explanation is offered, suggests the impossibility in civilized society of being welcomed without reserve, just as in adult life it is impossible to be unconditionally loved.[30]

It was left to Jean Louis Burckhardt to put the finishing touches to the image of the Bedouin as proud, free, hospitable and distinctive. He said little that had not been said before about the Arab character, but he said it well and his opinions were accompanied by a mass of unprecedented detail about life in the Arabian peninsula. He was the first European to produce a detailed eyewitness account of Mecca and Medina and his books were widely read.

Like Niebuhr, Burckhardt was predisposed by personal experience and upbringing to admire a free people. Although his books were written in English and he travelled under the auspices of the African Association, he was of Swiss nationality. He was born in Basle in 1784 into an old Swiss family whose members had celebrated their own festival, 'Burckhardt Day', since the Middle Ages. His father, a political liberal and Anglophile, had known Gibbon at Lausanne, and was also an acquaintance of Goethe and an admirer of Rousseau. He built a farmhouse near Basle so that he and his family might enjoy the natural life. The young Jean Louis was brought up in an atmosphere which combined great pride of family with an enlightened optimism about the future of the human race. The idyll was abruptly shattered by the French Revolution, which the elder Burckhardt loathed. He was forced to go into exile after the formation of the Helvetic Directory. His son Georg, Louis's elder brother, suffered prolonged imprisonment and a long period in a French lunatic asylum. Louis went to Leipzig University and afterwards to England where he hoped to find a

3 Jean Louis Burckhardt

position in the army or the civil service. The job was slow to materialize and he was reduced to living on bread and cheese, but he conceived a devotion to England which was only matched by his loathing of Republican France. England seemed a miraculous haven after the turbulence of Europe, a proud country where the right of free speech was not merely discussed but practised. He wrote to his parents in 1807: 'One can in our time breathe freely only in this country.'[31] When he went to Arabia he was to encounter another free people – the Bedouin.

In 1809 he was engaged by the African Association of London for the dangerous assignment of exploring the interior of West Africa from the north, travelling west from Cairo with a returning pilgrim caravan. His journey to the Arabian peninsula was one of several long digressions from his proposed route and in the end he never reached West Africa. He became fascinated by the Arab East and stayed there till his death from dysentery in 1817. His *Travels in Arabia* and *Notes on the Bedouins and Wahabys* were published posthumously in 1829 and 1830 respectively.

He travelled as a Moslem, and so successful was he in this that the suspicion has arisen that his assumption of Islam was more than mere disguise. Perhaps in the end he simply became the character he had initially adopted for convenience's sake, 'Sheikh Ibrahim', a poor scholar of Cairo and Aleppo. His poverty was real enough, the result of the meagre funds allowed him by the African Association, but there also seems to have been an Orwellian desire to plumb the depths of society, some unexplained but perhaps expiatory impulse to sink to the very bottom. He was often reduced to pennilessness and consequently suffered all the miseries and indignities of mendicancy. His account of the treatment he received from the slave traders with whom he travelled in the Sudan makes painful reading.

His journey to Mecca involved the greatest danger. Notes had to be taken in secret and this was not easy in a crowded pilgrim caravan, among people whose notions of privacy were virtually non-existent. He took notes while pretending to sleep, and even while squatting down in the Arab fashion to urinate. Discovered in this awkward position by his guide one day, he managed to persuade him that he was writing down prayers. At one point he was examined by the Cadi of Mecca in his knowledge of the Koran. He passed the examination with flying colours and was invited to join the Cadi in his evening prayers. This remarkable achievement illustrates vividly the contrast between European and Moslem society at the beginning of the nineteenth century. Europeans like Burckhardt could be more learned in Eastern literature and religion than the Orientals themselves. They cultivated the habit of scientific observation at a time when Moslem society had become stagnant and inward-looking.

Though often ill in Mecca Burckhardt saw and made detailed notes on the Kaaba, the inmost sanctuary of Islam, and attended all the rituals connected with the pilgrimage. He was moved by the simple devotion of the poor pilgrims, as this description of the scene in the Kaaba at the end of the pilgrimage shows.

Disease and mortality, which succeed to the fatigues endured on the journey, or are caused by the light covering of the ihram, the unhealthy lodgings at Mekka, the bad fare, and sometimes absolute want, fill the mosque with dead bodies, carried thither to receive the Imam's prayer, or with sick persons, many of whom, when their dissolution approaches, are brought to the colonnades, that they may either be cured by a sight of the Kaaba, or at least have the satisfaction of expiring within the sacred enclosure. Poor hadjys, worn out with disease and hunger, are seen dragging their emaciated bodies along the columns; and when no longer able to stretch forth their hand to ask the passenger for charity, they place a bowl to receive alms near the mat on which they lay themselves. When they feel their last moments approaching, they cover themselves with their tattered garments; and often a whole day passes before it is discovered that they are dead. For a month subsequent to the conclusion of the Hadj, I found, almost every morning, corpses of pilgrims lying in the mosque; myself and a Greek hadjy, whom accident had brought to the spot, once closed the eyes of a poor Mogrebyn pilgrim, who had crawled into the neighbourhood of the Kaaba, to breathe his last, as the Moslems say, 'in the arms of his prophet and of the guardian angels.' He intimated by signs that we should sprinkle Zemzem water over him; and while we were doing so, he expired: half an hour afterwards he was buried. There are several persons in the service of the mosque employed to wash carefully the spot on which those who expire in the mosque have lain, and to bury all the poor and friendless strangers who die at Mekka.[32]

There must have been times when he wondered if he too would be one of those poor and friendless strangers consigned for burial to the servants of the mosque.

Ill as he was with fever and dysentery he felt happy and at home in the holy city, writing later that he 'never enjoyed such perfect ease as at Mekka'. He found the Meccans amiable, intelligent and hospitable, closer in manner and spirit to his beloved Bedouin than any other Arab townsmen. From the Grand Sherif down they displayed a pride in their city and their race which the former citizen of the Swiss republic found admirable. But his real affection was reserved for the Bedouin, the 'true Bedouin' who lived by a code of honour, were subject to no other race, and spoke the purest Arabic. He exulted as no previous writer had done in their independence and patriotism, the pride 'without which a people cannot expect to sustain its rank among nations'. Among the Bedouin patriotism was universal and it was 'not inferior to any which ennobled the history of Grecian or Helvetian republics'.[33]

From Burckhardt's confident delineation of the character of the true Bedouin one would suppose that he knew them well; but as with Niebuhr this was not the case. Burckhardt's *Notes on the Bedouins and Wahabys* consisted for the most part of material acquired by painstaking questioning of Bedouin whom he met in the bazaars of Damascus and Aleppo. His contact with them in the desert at the period when he was compiling his *Notes* was brief and often unsatisfactory. More than once he was abandoned by Bedouin who had agreed to guide him through the desert – an act quite contrary to received notions of Bedouin honour – and was forced to try to reconcile his experience with his expectations as best he could. He did this by deciding that treacherous Bedouin were not 'true' Bedouin. Eventually he was forced to the conclusion that the only true Bedouin of Syria were the Anaza, the great tribal federation whose pasturing grounds lie between the Euphrates and the eastern part of Syria.[34] But he hardly knew the Anaza at all. His contact with them was confined to a few overnight stays in their encampments on his journey to Palmyra from Aleppo in 1810. This was a journey which began inauspiciously with his abandonment by an Anaza sheikh, met in Aleppo, who had agreed to take him to Palmyra and then on to stay with his tribe in the Hauran for a couple of months. He eventually managed to make a couple of brief tours of the Hauran under his own steam; but he never lived with the Anaza as he had hoped to do. A similar project with regard to the Bedouin of the Hejaz in Arabia also came to nothing because he was too ill to venture away from the cities of Mecca and Medina. Except for the time spent on the road going from one town to another, when he was usually with other pilgrims who went in terror of the Bedouin, his time in Arabia was spent in towns. His information on the Arabian Bedouin was acquired in the coffee shops of Mecca. In Medina he learned little.

The desert was in turmoil because of the campaigns of Mohammed Ali Pasha against the rebellious Wahhabi sect and Bedouin rarely came into town. At no time did he study and observe the Bedouin under conditions which a modern anthropological field worker would regard as satisfactory. He never lived with them, and though the large quantity of information he gathered on Bedouin customs was very valuable, his ideas of 'true' Bedouin morality reflected his own assumptions as an avid reader of Gibbon, Niebuhr and d'Arvieux, and the undoubtedly idealized picture of desert life he received from Bedouin met in the town.

Modern anthropologists are trained to distinguish between the value system of a community as expressed in what its members tell about it and the value system which can be deduced from behaviour which the anthropologist is able to observe. The former is an ideal, an expression of aspiration, and has an interest and value of its own. It influences behaviour but rarely determines it completely. This fundamental distinction, which seems simple and obvious to any social scientist trained in the last fifty years, was not always obvious to Burckhardt, intelligent as he was. He lived at a time when the scientific observation of human society was in its exuberant infancy and his work, though often careful and precise, reflected that immaturity.

The Bedouin he most frequently encountered were those who lived near the cities or the pilgrim road. He readily admitted that their conduct was often deplorable but he blamed this on their contact with foreign manners, 'by which no nation has ever benefited'.[35] Bedouin virtues could not easily withstand contact with Turks, Egyptians and the like – those categories of humanity conveniently labelled Levantine. Like many educated men of his day Burckhardt believed that every nation was endowed with a collective identity which distinguished it from other nations and which would characterize it forever so long as it avoided demoralizing contact with the manners of others. This collective identity was in the nature of a sacred trust. It was the duty of a nation to preserve it. He believed that the true Bedouin of the remotest desert, especially of Nejd in central Arabia, which he believed to be a sanctuary where Bedouin manners retained 'all their original purity', had kept their national characteristics over millennia, giving them a special claim on the admiration of Europe.[36] He seems to have supposed, like Niebuhr and with as little evidence, that the remoter Bedouin of the peninsula, the ones, so to speak, over the next sand dune, were paragons of bravery, patriotism and honour. He believed it because he wanted to believe it. As a Swiss patriot, a man of honour, and an educated man receptive to the nationalist theories of the day, it was important to him to believe that such people existed. The true Bedouin were a mirage which danced tantalizingly before his eyes, and those of many travellers after him.

Burckhardt's books were well received in England and he rapidly came to be regarded as the standard authority on things Arabian. His description of the Meccan aristocracy, the far-ranging Sherifian family who claimed descent from the Prophet, seems to have been of particular interest to English readers. According to Burckhardt the Sherifs were straightforward, manly and frank, and completely free from any otiose Turkish ceremoniousness. The *Edinburgh Review*, extending a rare compliment, was moved to remark that they were 'in short, a race of gentlemen, as compared with the general stamp of even Oriental grandees . . .'[37] Burckhardt attributed the pleasing manners of the Sherifs to the fact that their early years were spent with the Bedouin in the desert. It was the custom for the Sherifs of Mecca to send all their male children, eight days after birth, to live with a Bedouin family for eight to ten years, the intention being to build character. 'By this means, [the boy] becomes familiar with all the perils and vicissitudes of a Bedouin life; his body is inured to fatigue and privation; and he acquires a knowledge of the pure language of the Bedouins, and an influence among them that becomes afterwards of much importance to him.'[38] This must have seemed familiar to Englishmen who had received their classical education and made some useful contacts under the Spartan conditions of their public school.

The concept of a gentleman in England at this time did indeed bear a remarkable resemblance to the Bedouin manners Burckhardt described. Frankness, naturalness and self-assurance were highly regarded; the elaborate manners of the courtier were not.[39] By the 1820s English travellers had already begun to remark occasionally on the good manners of the Bedouin they encountered. William Heude, in 1817, was impressed by the 'unassuming courtesy' and 'intuitive politeness' of the nomad hosts who attended to his every need but were never 'meanly obsequious'.[40] In 1826 the *Westminster Review* published an article entitled 'Arabs and Persians' in which an Englishwoman resident on the Persian Gulf compared the fawning manners of the Persians with the dignified naturalness of the Arabs. Of the Imam of Muscat she wrote that he was 'the only Asiatic I ever saw, who gave me the idea of what is conveyed by the English term gentleman'. She went on revealingly to observe that though 'all ranks and conditions' seemed to associate together on a footing of perfect equality, 'yet good order and subordination seem as well established as if they were guarded by all the etiquette which is elsewhere thought necessary for their preservation'.[41]

It was with the realization that the Arabs, unlike other Orientals, were gentlemen that literate Englishmen began to feel a sense of affinity with them. They perhaps also responded to them as a free people like themselves, but this was not explicitly stated by an English writer for another forty years. Gifford Palgrave, a rather untypical Englishman in many ways, was the first to suggest that the Arabs and the English had this, as well as other things, in common. His observations were received by reviewers with a complacency which suggests that they were not entirely unexpected. By 1860 the stereotype of the noble Arab was sufficiently well established for the suggestion of affinity to be mildly flattering.

When, as a result of the First World War, the English acquired some imperial responsibilities in Arab lands, the perception of a common gentlemanliness contributed a distinctive flavour to their relations with the Arabs. It was partly responsible for the confidence with which they adopted a policy of indirect rule; they felt they could rely on a native aristocracy with whom they felt so much at ease to co-operate with them once it had been established that it was in their interests to do so. It also contributed to a sense of guilt which developed about 'broken pledges' to the Arabs. A number of Anglo-Arab agreements, of varying degrees of formality, arose during the course of the First World War. They were negotiated primarily on a basis of mutual self-interest, but there were those on both sides who persuaded themselves that they were 'gentlemen's agreements' of a rather comprehensive sort which would be honoured in spirit no matter what. The inevitable modifications aroused in certain English breasts an uncomfortable feeling of guilt, which Arab leaders were astute enough to exploit. It was then the Englishman's turn to be upbraided for not living up to his honourable reputation.

2

'Oh! that the Desert were my dwelling-place . . .'

Before 1800 the presence of a European traveller in the Middle East could usually be explained satisfactorily as the result of curiosity, commerce or pure chance. Carsten Niebuhr's great adventure had begun when Professor Kastner of the Academy of Sciences at Gottingen had walked into his room and said, 'Would you like to travel to Arabia?'

'Why not,' replied Niebuhr, 'if someone defrayed the expense?'[1]

If the travellers of the eighteenth century had any intimate personal motives for their journeys, they were not revealed to the public. It was not yet fashionable to have a well-advertised secret sorrow, nor was a narrative of travel considered the proper vehicle for a man's more private responses to his experiences. Burckhardt could write in a letter to his parents: 'Then the sun rises in indescribable majesty over the sand-sea . . . and whose heart could be so without feeling that he would not praise his creator . . .', but such effusions did not find their way into his published works.[2]

Chateaubriand was the first to attempt a subjective Middle East travelogue. In the preface to his *Itinéraire de Paris à Jérusalem*, which was published in 1811, he begged his readers not to expect a conventionally informative travel book, for 'I went in quest of images and nothing more.'[3] But information was what he relentlessly gave, in the form of huge undigested extracts from previous writers. Interspersed with these were accounts of the author's raptures on finding himself in various famous or holy spots. One thing which emerged clearly from the overall confusion of the narrative was that the author found himself by far the most interesting part of the landscape. This was a novel literary convention, of which Lamartine's *Voyage en Orient* was to be a more developed expression.

Chateaubriand naturally recorded his impressions of the Bedouin, and they are of interest as those of a writer closely associated with the notion of the noble savage. He began with a detailed description of their facial characteristics, of which we recognize immediately the high, arched brow, the aquiline nose and the liquid eyes. 'Nothing about them would proclaim the savage,' he concluded, 'if their mouths were always shut.'[4] They were distinguished from the American Indians chiefly by 'a certain degree of delicacy in their manners' which proclaimed them to be, not true primitives like the Indians, but the decrepit remnants of a great civilization.[5] They were human ruins, thus affording Chateaubriand a melancholy pleasure. He considered them in no sense his equal, and though he took care to comport himself towards them in a gentlemanly manner it was because this was demanded by his honour as a Frenchman, not because of any instinct of reciprocity. When he realized as he embarked for Tunis at Alexandria that he had forgotten to send a Bedouin host a promised gift of Egyptian rice, he resolved that, 'As soon as our communication with the Levant is restored, Abou Gosh shall certainly receive his Damietta rice; he shall see, that though the memory of a Frenchman may fail him, yet he never fails to keep his word.'[6] Did Abou Gosh ever receive his rice? One wonders. And if he did, was he a soul won for France?

Chateaubriand's view of the Bedouin as decadent was an unusual one, but it does show how they evoked a more complex response than the conventional noble savage. American Indians and South Sea Islanders existed, so to speak, in vacuo, but the Arabs had a past, historical and biblical, of which every literate traveller was aware. They could also, in the more tolerant atmosphere which prevailed by the end of the eighteenth century, be credited with contributions to the religious life of mankind. They were 'natives of that east, which is the cradle of all the arts, all the sciences, and all religions'.[7]

It was of course with Byron's publication of *Childe Harold* in the years between 1812 and 1818 that the East became established as a setting for the Romantic experience.

> Oh! that the Desert were my dwelling-place,
> With one fair Spirit for my minister,
> That I might all forget the human race,
> And, hating no one, love but only her!

33

Ye elements! – in whose ennobling stir
I feel myself exalted – Can ye not
Accord me such a being? Do I err
In deeming such inhabit many a spot?
Though with them to converse can rarely be our lot.

There is a pleasure in the pathless woods,
There is a rapture on the lonely shore,
There is society, where none intrudes,
By the deep Sea, and music in its roar:
I love not Man the less, but Nature more,
From these our interviews, in which I steal
From all I may be, or have been before,
To mingle with the Universe, and feel
What I can ne'er express, yet cannot all conceal.[8]

Rarely has Romantic egoism been better expressed than in these famous verses. The tiny figure of the poet in the vast and lonely landscape is not at all diminished by that landscape: it is enhanced by it. The poet is firmly at the centre of things, extracting from his communion with Nature, not a feeling of humility, but an ecstatically heightened sense of self. As a perfect setting for this sort of experience the desert suddenly acquired its literary cachet. The novelty of this can scarcely be exaggerated. From now on travellers would actually go out of their way to make sure they passed through the desert, rather than the reverse.

Once in the desert, the Romantic traveller abandoned himself to reverie. No doubt travellers had whiled away the lonely hours with fantasies and memories from time immemorial, but not until the early decades of the nineteenth century did these acquire the dignity of print. It was the influence of Byron, with his insistence that 'there is society where none intrudes', which was above all responsible for this, but other poets suggested through their use of metaphor that the desert was associated with a dream-like state, when thoughts come into the mind unbidden.

I went into the deserts of dim sleep –
That world which, like an unknown wilderness,
Bounds this with its recesses wide and deep –

wrote Shelley.[9] For Leigh Hunt the Nile flowed

through old hushed Egypt and its sands,
Like some grave mighty thought threading a dream . . .[10]

34

Daydreaming became an acceptable, even central, part of the desert experience. Instead of chasing such thoughts away, the traveller indulged them, followed where they led, and at the end of his meditations sometimes made a surprising discovery about himself. The process is similar to that employed in psychoanalysis. Free of all external distractions, the patient is encouraged to follow each train of thought wherever it leads, to embark on a journey into the unconscious mind with its vast repository of memories, some significant, some mere mental bric-a-brac. The analyst is there to help him when he encounters difficulties, when a memory is too painful or too obviously incomplete. The desert traveller is on his own, alone with his unconscious, and must manage as best he can. The self-knowledge willingly or unwillingly acquired during these long meandering meditations is what gives the most interesting writing on the desert in the last century or so its tantalizingly self-revelatory character. Few writers have attempted any coherent formulation of this new knowledge of themselves (and perhaps even fewer have been willing to give it conscious recognition), but it often happens that a writer's most intimate concerns seem to be precipitated out into his account of a desert journey.

Richard Burton, a man much maligned as a writer but capable of fine passages, described very well the desert experience of being immersed in a private world.

The Desert . . . is pre-eminently the Land of Fancy, of Reverie; never ending, ever renewing itself in the presence of the Indefinite and the Solitude, which are the characteristics of this open world. The least accident, the smallest shift of scenery, gives rise to the longest trains of thought, in which the past, the present, and the future seem to blend.[11]

He also put his finger on something which for nineteenth-century travellers was one of the most striking characteristics of the desert – its familiarity. When he was consoling his old age with his work of translating the *Arabian Nights* he would find himself being borne away from his dull surroundings to

the land of my predilection, Arabia, a region so familiar to my mind that even at first sight, it seemed a reminiscence of some by-gone metempsychic life in the distant Past. Again I stood under the diaphanous skies, in air glorious as aether, whose every breath raises men's spirits like sparkling wine. Once more I saw the evening star hanging like a solitaire from the pure front of the western firmament; and the after-glow transfiguring and transforming, as by magic, the homely and rugged features of the scene into a faery-land lit with a light which never shines on other soils or seas. Then would appear the woollen tents, low and black, of the true Badawin, mere dots in the boundless waste of lion-tawny clays and gazelle-brown gravels, and the camp-fire dotting like a glow-worm the village centre.[12]

No other part of the world produced this sort of response in a traveller, this eerie thrill of recognition.

The reason is to be found in two books which occupied a prominent place in the reading of every literate nineteenth-century child – the Bible and the *Arabian Nights*. The desert and its inhabitants were not strange to the adult traveller; on the contrary, they were familiar to him from earliest childhood. Niebuhr was only one of many writers to point this out, and it would be tedious to try to list them. Here were the illustrations in the family Bible come to life, and like an old picture book they could powerfully evoke memories of childhood. The emotions aroused by contemplation of these scenes were more than mere pleasures of the historical imagination, of seeming to go back centuries in time; they were those of a return to the mysterious yet familiar world of childhood. This is what gives the moment of recognition its eerie quality, as though some fragment of a lost world, a lost self, has come back to life.

The *Arabian Nights*, which by the end of the eighteenth century had assumed its status as a children's classic, had an even more potent influence on some minds than the Bible. Many an unhappy boy away at school must have lost himself, like Thackeray's Dobbin and no doubt Thackeray himself, in that spellbinding book. Children happy and unhappy grew up with the tales as part of the furniture of their imagination. As adults the word 'Arabia' possessed for some of them a special resonance which defied any merely geographical definition. It was associated with intensely felt but obscurely remembered experiences. Tennyson expressed this perfectly in his poem, *Recollections of the Arabian Nights*, written in 1830 when he was twenty-one.

> When the breeze of a joyful dawn blew free
> In the silken sail of infancy,
> The tide of time flow'd back with me,
> The forward-flowing tide of time;
> And many a sheeny summer-morn,
> Adown the Tigris I was borne,
> By Bagdat's shrines of fretted gold,
> High-walled gardens green and old;

True Mussulman was I and sworn,
For it was in the golden prime
Of good Haroun Alraschid . . .

Far off, and where the lemon grove
In closest coverture unsprung,
The living airs of middle night
Died round the bulbul as he sung;
Not he: but something which possess'd
The darkness of the world, delight,
Life, anguish, death, immortal love,
Ceasing not, mingled, unrepress'd,
Apart from place, withholding time,
But flattering the golden prime
Of good Haroun Alraschid.

It is not very surprising that a land whose name could evoke such haunting echoes of the unconscious mind – 'the darkness of the world, delight, life, anguish, death, immortal love' – should receive more than its fair share of attention from travellers and should produce a travel literature remarkable for its psychological interest. 'Arabia' was a country of the mind more real than any place on a map, and drew like a magnet those whose journeys were undertaken in search of themselves. Their attitudes towards the Bedouin were fashioned as much by their own preoccupations, given full rein in the silent spaces of the desert, as by their actual encounters with them. What they had to say about them was almost always interesting – but as much for what it tells us about themselves as about their subjects.

Travellers of this type will claim a large share of our attention (the most famous writers on Arabia all fall into this category) but it should not be forgotten that there were a host of others whose views have to be taken into account in any assessment of what the Arabs meant to the English. For some of these travellers Arabia's aura of romance was merely that, a pleasant gloss on their experiences and no more. Others were more deeply engaged by the land and the people but did not allow themselves to succumb to the attraction they felt. Alexander Kinglake is the prototype of such travellers. Still others were quite immune to the fascination exercised by the Arabs over more imaginative travellers. Captain George Sadlier, a man entirely unimaginative and untainted by literature in any form, chased Ibrahim Pasha across Arabia in 1819 in an attempt to offer him official British congratulations on his success against the Wahhabis, and left a diary which is a sad record of Bedouin perfidy. 'I have only to repeat,' he wrote, 'that the procrastination, duplicity, falsity, deception, and fraudulence of the Bedouin cannot be described by one to an European in language which would present to his mind the real character of these hordes of robbers.'[13] Sadlier took the Bedouin as he found them, and the unromantic result is probably one reason why his account of his difficult and impressive journey was not published in book form until 1866, and then only because Palgrave's journey had revived public interest in Arabia.

One who definitely was not immune to the Arabs was Lady Hester Stanhope, the strange, talented and ambitious woman who provides us with the first extraordinary example of an English person identifying with the Arabs as 'her own people'.[14] She was a unique transitional figure, an eighteenth-century eccentric who lived to become the object of a Romantic cult. European travellers in the Lebanon in the 1830s made a point of visiting her in her mountain fastness and recording in their books the harangues, ranging from the mystical to the malicious, to which they willingly subjected themselves.[15] Rumours reached England of her vast influence over the tribes and her alleged possession of a Bedouin lover. It was of her that Kinglake wrote: 'I can hardly tell why it should be, but there is a longing for the East, very commonly felt by proud people when goaded by sorrow.'[16]

This was not quite accurate in Lady Hester's case – sorrow she had known, and it had driven her from her native land; but her progress eastward had been erratic, and it was only after she got there that she realized its supreme appropriateness for one of her temperament and antecedents.

She was the daughter of Lord Stanhope, an eccentric peer whose Jacobin enthusiasms led him to efface the family arms from his carriage and send his daughter to tend turkeys on the common. Far from eradicating her pride in her aristocratic birth, this treatment seems only to have accentuated it, and in 1800 she escaped from her progressive home, first to her grandmother's house at Burton Pynsent, and then to that of her uncle, William Pitt. From 1803 to 1806 she enjoyed, as Pitt's hostess, her period of greatest glory. Her outrageous wit and vivacity procured for her a notable social success; but not, alas, a suitable husband. When Pitt died in 1806 her prospects of a brilliant future in political circles faded abruptly. Her affectionate friendship with Sir John Moore also came to nought when he was killed at Corunna in 1808. She retired to Wales, but finding Wales too small a stage for the exercise of her histrionic gifts, she left on the first leg of a journey which was to lead in 1814 to the village of Joun on Mount Lebanon. Here she remained till her death in 1839, fortified in her proud isolation by the belief that a great destiny in the East was prophesied for her.

Her wretched death, old, poor, and deserted by her multitude of servants, stands in melancholy contrast to her triumphal progress through the Levant in the years between 1811 and 1814. With the help of a plentiful supply of gold, her masterful personality had been imposed on notables from Cairo to Damascus, finding its most satisfying expression in her visit to Palmyra in 1813. The story of this enterprise has often been told, but absurd as it is, it is worth telling again. The response to it in London pre-figured that given to Lawrence of Arabia a hundred years later. It was, even then, the stuff of which imperial dreams were made.

Lady Hester's triumph was the product of long and careful planning from her base at Damascus, where she applied herself to cultivating the most influential citizens. She entertained splendidly ('about twenty-five Arabs dined with me, and were all enchanted') and was clearly regarded with curiosity and some awe by the Damascenes; it was not simply her money which opened doors for her. Her entry into Damascus in 1812 must have been the talk of the town. She rode into the city at the head of a splendid cavalcade, wearing the costume of a Turkish nobleman. Thereafter she adopted Bedouin dress (male) as the most comfortable, and striking, costume.

Her departure from Hama for Palmyra accompanied by a Bedouin bodyguard was watched by thousands of spectators who lined the road for a mile out of the town. A corps of Janissaries provided by the Pasha had to clear the way. Three days out into the desert she paused for a day to receive the homage of the local sheikhs, who were sent on their way with suitable presents. The tedium of the long desert journey was relieved by the Bedouin escort who performed sham fights for the entertainment of Lady Hester and her friends. As the party approached Palmyra the Palmyrenes, who no doubt had had word of the visitor's generosity, came running out to welcome her. Another sham fight followed, this time between the Bedouin and the Palmyrenes, each side competing fiercely, sometimes with deplorable realism, for the favour of the English princess.

The entry into Palmyra was accomplished with great pomp. Beautiful young girls took the place of statues on the empty pedestals of the triumphal way, remaining immobile till Lady Hester had passed and then leaping nimbly down to join in the singing and dancing in her praise. At the triumphal arch she was crowned with a circlet of flowers while the Palmyrenes sang and danced for all they were worth.

The journey back to Hama was equally spectacular, a stately progress through the encampments of Bedouin sheikhs all eager to enjoy the favour of the strange Englishwoman whose supply of gold appeared to be inexhaustible. 'The finest mutton,' wrote Dr Meryon, her faithful physician, 'was never wanting.' Mission accomplished, she reported home:

Without joking, I have been crowned Queen of the Desert under the triumphal arch at Palmyra . . . If I please I can now go to Mecca *alone*; I have nothing to fear. I shall soon have as many names as Apollo. I am the sun, the star, the pearl, the lion, the light from Heaven . . . I am quite wild about these people; and all Syria is in astonishment at my courage and success. To have spent a month with some thousand of Bedouin Arabs is no common thing.[17]

This was as good as presiding over the banquets of Mr Pitt. It was, however, the high-water-mark of her career in the East: the prophecy that she would become the Queen of Jerusalem was never fulfilled.

As she grew old and bitter she became disgusted by what she regarded as Britain's decline from its natural pre-eminence in the world and transferred her allegiance to the Arabs instead. The English were no longer the 'hardy, honest, bold people' they once were; these qualities she now found in the

wild Arabs, who will traverse burning sands barefooted, to receive the last breath of some kind relation or friend, who teach their children at the earliest period resignation and fortitude, and who always keep alive a spirit of emulation amongst them! They are the boldest people in the world, yet are imbued with a tenderness quite poetic, and their kindness extends to all the brute creation by which they are surrounded.

She also admired the 'grace and agility (without capers), which is peculiar to them alone'.[18] Her admiration was, however, distinctly *de haut en bas*. They were persons worthy to be the loyal subjects of the niece of Mr Pitt. Deprived of her rightful position in English society, she had transferred her patriotic feelings and her habit of authority elsewhere.

She invented a theory that the ancient Scottish and Irish families were of Arab descent, and compiled a list of names which she believed to be of Arab origin; for example, Gower came from 'Gaoor' (infidel) and O'Brien from 'Obeyan'. When Kinglake visited her in her old age he found her given up to vague and mystical speculations about 'race'. It is unlikely that these would have been of much interest to William Pitt, but they almost certainly received the sympathetic attention of a more exotic flower of English politics, Benjamin Disraeli. His Eastern novel, *Tancred*, was published in 1847. By then the Prophetess of Mount Lebanon was at the height of her posthumous fame.

Disraeli spent a year in the Levant from 1830 to 1831. His letters home were remarkable only for their author's love of the gorgeous and gave little hint of the racial theories which later bore fruit in *Tancred*, a strange book which the ordinary English public generally failed to appreciate. The plot was confused and improbable, involving complicated amorous and mystical experiences. Briefly, Tancred, Lord Montacute, goes to the East to find himself. Before his departure he is instructed in the mysteries of race by Sidonia, a wise Jewish banker, who informs him that 'All is race; there is no other truth', and furthermore: 'The decay of a race is an inevitable necessity, unless it lives in deserts and never mixes its blood.'[19] Thus forewarned, the reader awaits the entry of the noble Arab and in due course he materializes, in the extraordinary form of the sheikh of a tribe of Jewish Bedouins. Tancred's natural surprise on finding that the tribe speaks Hebrew and follows the Mosaic law is dismissed by his companion with the unforgettable remark: 'The Arabs are only Jews upon horseback.'[20] These Arabs are in fact Rechabites, the descendants of an Old Testament sect who refused to drink wine or live in houses. There is virtually no evidence that the real Rechabites survived the Babylonian exile, but travellers in the East occasionally claimed to have found them, and they suited Disraeli's literary purposes.

When Sheikh Hassan of the Rechabites says to Tancred: 'Let men doubt of unicorns: but of one thing there can be no doubt, that

God never spoke except to an Arab', the reader begins to wonder what Disraeli meant by an Arab; the words 'Arab' and 'Jew' are used by him virtually interchangeably. It turns out that what he means is a member of the Semitic race, and what he is talking about is a special racial sensitivity to the word of God. Christianity, Islam and Judaism, the three great revealed religions, have all been transmitted to the world through the medium of the Semites. This was an idea which was taken up by, among others, Ernest Renan and T. E. Lawrence.[21] For Disraeli this neat synthesis served the purpose of providing him with a legitimate and glorious ancestry – not a mere Christianized English Jew, but a Semite who could claim racial affinity with Christ, and furthermore with the conquerors who had swept out of the deserts of Arabia in the seventh century.[22]

Disraeli's imperial imagination was captivated by the Arabs. He was not interested in desert democracy, or in any of the Arabs' alleged political virtues except pride of race. The combination of this with their unique religious abilities comes to mean, in Tancred's excited brain, the possibility of revitalizing the West via an Arab revival in the East – directed, of course, by Great Britain. There is a remarkable passage in which the Emir Fakredeen exhorts Tancred to persuade Queen Victoria to transfer the seat of her empire from London to Delhi. From there the British could support an Arab campaign against Persia and Afghanistan. The Arabs would then acknowledge Queen Victoria as their suzerain and give her the Levantine coast for good measure.[23] This was the sort of glorious but subsidiary role that imaginative British imperialists had in mind for the Arabs in the First World War.

Disraeli was not alone in his interest in the Arab conquests. Voltaire had already recognized the Arabs as a master race, 'un peuple supérieur' whose genius had been mobilized for action by the Prophet, and by the 1830s the English, with their increasing involvement in the East, were showing an interest in the Arabs' imperial past.[24] During the nineteenth century comparisons of the British Empire with the Roman Empire became rather fashionable, though Victorian optimism often demanded that the comparison not be taken too far; because of its securer moral foundation the British Empire would prove to be more enduring. A similar line was taken towards the Arab Empire. Like that of Rome it was safely in the past and could be admired and moralized upon. Its instability was a favourite theme and the belief that the Arab temper is 'more adapted to rapid conquest than stable settlement' rapidly became conventional.[25] Nevertheless, there was a qualified recognition of the Arabs as an imperial race, and this provided further grounds for a feeling of affinity.

Carlyle, with a characteristic combination of racism and religiosity, admired the Arab Empire as an expression of the spiritual greatness of the Arab race. Before Mohammed, the Arabs, 'a people of great qualities', held together by the *'inward*, indissoluble bond of a common blood and language', had been unknown to the world: through the genius of Mohammed they had become great. His passionate sincerity, which Carlyle was the first English writer to affirm unequivocally, appealed to the 'wild Arab men', who patched up their differences and swept out of the desert on a wave of conquest. They were, even before Mohammed, an 'earnest, truthful kind of men . . . of Jewish kindred', who combined with the earnestness of the Jews 'something graceful, brilliant, which is not Jewish'. They also shared with the Jews the quality of religiosity, which Carlyle agreed with Disraeli in attributing to some inborn racial characteristic. Neither of them gave serious consideration to the possibility that the religious genius of the Arabs owed something to their desert environment. Carlyle observed that 'You are all alone there, left alone with the Universe', but he made nothing of it.[26]

Most Victorian writers on the desert assumed that the Bedouin possessed an instinctive godliness. Disraeli and Carlyle attributed it to a sort of religious gene, an inherited racial ability to commune directly with God, but to other writers less exclusively preoccupied with race it seemed natural that the desert, with its capacity to inspire meditation, should produce a religious experience, in particular an awesome perception of the One God. (The great popular appeal of this idea was demonstrated by the success of Robert Hichens's novel, *The Garden of Allah*, which was the bestseller of 1904.) It is undeniable that some people experience in the desert peculiar psychological states to which they attribute a religious significance; others experience nothing but desolation. There seems to be a complex interaction between the desert, the temperament of the traveller, and the labels which his culture supplies for making sense of his experience. Laurent d'Arvieux, who in the seventeenth-century manner associated religious belief with theological inquiry, found the Bedouin not particularly religious, and thought this the natural consequence of their 'Roving Campaign–way of Life', which did not leave them time to think about such things.[27] But in the nineteenth century, an era of swooning religiosity as well as scientific doubt, the convention arose among the more mystically inclined that desert travel was conducive to religious belief. By some mysterious ecumenical process of projection it was further assumed that the inhabitants of the desert, that is, the Bedouin, were naturally monotheistic. The evidence for a natural monotheism on the part of the Bedouin is not very strong. Before Mohammed they worshipped a host of spirits occupying stones, trees and particular places, and serious scholars have always been sceptical about the completeness of their conversion to Islam. Learned and unsentimental travellers like Burton and Palgrave knew this and said so in their books, but their assertions made little impact on the magazine-reading public.[28]

A good deal of projection is apparent in Carlyle's account of Mohammed and the Arabs. His description of the Arabs as 'a people of wild strong feelings, and of iron restraint over these', earnest and truthful, sounds remarkably like Carlyle himself. And Mohammed, that 'spontaneous, passionate, yet just, true-meaning man! Full of wild faculty, fire and light . . . working out his life-task in the depths of the Desert there' – who is he but the young Carlyle transposed from the lowlands of Scotland to the Arabian desert? We recognize Carlyle, too, in the passage where he praises Mohammed for his freedom from cant: 'He is a rough self-helping son of the wilderness; does not pretend to be what he is not. There is no ostentatious pride in him; but neither does he go much upon humility . . . Not a meanly-mouthed man! A candid ferocity, if the case call for it, is in him; he does not mince matters!'[29] It was no coincidence that Carlyle was referred to by Lady Ashburton as 'her Prophet', and himself thought of the writer as one who 'wanders like a wild Ishmaelite, in a world of which he is the spiritual light, either the guidance or the misguidance!'.[30]

The writings of Disraeli and Carlyle, with their exalted and mystical tone, had many imitators, but they also had their detractors. A whole school of Middle East travel writing grew up in which Romantic rhetoric was subtly or unsubtly mocked. These works were written in a minor key and their authors never completely freed themselves from the influence of the writers they sought to deride, but they are important because they expressed an ambivalence in English attitudes towards the East. Some way had to be found to reconcile the appeal of the exotic East with English common sense, to bridge the gap between the increasingly lofty tone of popular writing on the subject and the more prosaic responses of the ordinary traveller. It was Alexander Kinglake who found the answer. He invented and perfected a type of travel narrative which expressed the feelings of those Englishmen who felt the charm of the East but tried hard to resist it.

Kinglake's *Eothen* is one of the best travel books ever written. For all its apparent casualness it is as finished a thing in its way as *Arabia Deserta* and took as long to write. No other narrative of Middle Eastern travel quite possesses its charm. (This includes Doughty, but then Doughty did not mean to charm.) *Eothen* is one of those books which, though not at all immature in themselves, possess a great appeal for young people. This is because it is, among other things, an account of the successful conclusion to an unusually prolonged adolescence.

When Kinglake set out for the East in 1834 he was twenty-five years old and feeling constricted by the lawyer's office to which his conventional education had led him.[31] Later on, when he came to write up his experiences, he saw his journey as a deliberate attempt to assuage the restlessness he was feeling and put it to a constructive use, but this was perhaps a retrospective view reflecting the happy outcome of the enterprise rather than an accurate statement of his feelings at the time. 'I travelled,' he wrote, 'with the simplicity proper to my station, as one of the industrious class, who was not flying from his country because of *ennui*, but was strengthening his will, and tempering the metal of his nature, for that life of toil and conflict in which he is now engaged.'[32] The ironic presentation of his middle-classness and the dissocation from Childe Harold are both typical of Kinglake. That he was capable of feelings that were far more Byronic is shown by a passage which he wrote about 1840 for use in *Eothen*.

If a man, and an Englishman . . . there comes to him a time for loathing the wearisome ways of society – a time for not liking tamed people – a time for not dancing quadrilles – not sitting in pews – . . . . a time in short for scoffing and railing – for speaking lightly of . . . all our most cherished institutions. It is from nineteen, to two or three and twenty perhaps, that this war of the man against men is like to be waged most sullenly.[33]

At the age of thirty-one Kinglake could recall his earlier feelings vividly, but he could also see them for what they had turned out to be – the manifestation of a transient phase of rebellion against the place in society which had been marked out for him. The mature Kinglake felt that he had successfully integrated society's demands on him and his own demands on himself. In its final published form, when Kinglake was thirty-six, the passage above was considerably modified. It became more ironic and amusing, conveying very well the author's affectionate detachment from his younger self.

Eothen is an account of a psychosocial moratorium, in Erikson's phrase, which was granted to a young man who had not managed to reconcile himself to the identity which the circumstances of his life had compelled him to assume. Kinglake used this moratorium, this respite from normal daily life, to think about his past and his future.

If you are wise [he told his readers] you will not look upon the long period of time . . . occupied in actual movement, as the mere gulf dividing you from the end of your journey, but rather as one of those rare and plastic seasons of your life, from which, perhaps in after-times, you may love to date the moulding of your character – that is, your very identity. Once feel this, and you will soon grow happy and contented in your saddle home. As for me and my comrade . . . in this [Serbian] part of our journey we often forgot Stamboul, forgot all the Ottoman Empire, and only remembered old times. We went back, loitering on the banks of the Thames, . . . Thames the 'old Eton fellow' that wrestled with us in our boyhood till he taught us to be stronger than he. We bullied Keate [his ferocious headmaster at Eton], and scoffed at Larrey Miller, and Okes; we rode along loudly laughing, and talked to the grave Servian forest, as though it were the 'Brocas clump.'[34]

This reliving (and reshaping) of the past was also a feature of the deep reverie into which he was plunged by the desert. He found the desert an ideal setting for introspection and the appearance one day of another English traveller seemed to him an unfortunate intrusion into his private world. His account of this meeting contains elements of parody, but there is no doubt that a real feeling is being conveyed.

As we approached each other, it became with me a question whether we should speak. I thought it likely that the stranger would accost me, and in the event of his doing so, I was quite ready to be as sociable and chatty as I could be according to my nature; but still I could not think of anything particular that I had to say to him . . . I was shy and indolent and I felt no great wish to stop and talk like a morning visitor in the midst of those broad solitudes. The traveller perhaps felt as I did, for, except that we lifted our hands to our caps, and waved our arms in courtesy, we passed each other quite as distantly as if we had passed in Pall Mall.[35]

The inhabitants of the desert remained for Kinglake simply figures in a landscape, albeit interesting ones. No sense of personal destiny was aroused in him by his contact with the Bedouin; his instinct for self-parody saw to that. He went out of his way to meet them – his mother had been a girlhood friend of Lady Hester Stanhope, and the 'Queen of the Desert' and her exploits among the Bedouin had loomed large in his childhood imagination – but in the event his contact with them was disappointing. He found 'the low black tents which I had so long lusted to see' inhabited in crowded and noisy squalor by poor and wretched creatures who begged piteously for tobacco. He observed, with a delicate irony: 'I concluded, from the abject manner of these people, that they could not possibly be thorough-bred Bedouins . . .' He had better luck with another group, almost every one of whom showed 'the suffering of one fallen from a high estate', and who walked along in his simple blanket 'as though he were wearing the purple'.[36] The poverty of the Bedouin did not move Kinglake to any rhapsodies on the spiritual liberty which arises from a want of earthly possessions; he was too much of a bourgeois for that, only too well aware that he could not afford, socially or financially, the striking of histrionic attitudes. His book was a gracious and conscious compliment to the charm of those attitudes and at the same time a statement of his own rejection of them. We understand that he feels a genuine but not very serious regret that the Bedouin failed to come up to expectations, and we also understand that he was probably not very surprised that they did not. He felt the fascination of the desert but successfully resisted it, gently jeering at the romantic notions of himself and others. This elegant version of the supposedly English virtue of common sense was Kinglake's special contribution to the art of travel writing. He was a much subtler exponent of it than those who followed him.

The freedom with which Kinglake wrote of his personal reactions, though it has a possible literary ancestor in Sterne's *Sentimental Journey*, was made possible by the Romantic Movement.

Though he mocked the excesses of Romanticism he was a creature of it, finding society where none intrudes and feeling no embarrassment in informing his readers of the fact. The influence of Romanticism can also be seen in the wild exultation in his own self-sufficiency which was another aspect of his response to the desert. Outdistancing his guides one day he found himself alone 'in this African desert, and I *myself, and no other, had charge of my life. I liked the office well . . .'* Reaching the Red Sea by himself he exulted in the strength and intelligence which had brought him safely across the waste.[37]

This feeling of mastery over the elements was to be expressed more crudely by Kinglake's friend and imitator, Eliot Warburton, in his book *The Crescent and the Cross*, subtitled *The Romance and Realities of Eastern Travel*. 'Onward!' the exuberant Warburton cries, 'over the wide, deep, dashing sea, that owns thee for its master, to the boundless desert that soon shall be thy slave.'[38] The traveller has become a conqueror by virtue of his very presence.

In this unrestrained egoism we detect the genuine imperial note. Warburton's boundless energy must find virgin soil for its expression; he must leave England 'as men leave a crowded room, to breathe awhile freely in the open East'.[39] Just what is 'open' about the East is not made very clear. Apart from the desert, in which he spent the minimum amount of time required to get from one tourist attraction to another, the places Warburton visited seem to have been rather crowded. Cairo and Damascus can only be regarded as 'open' if their inhabitants are considered virtually to be non-persons. This is what they were to Warburton. They were scarcely more real to him than illustrations in a picture book; time and again in his descriptions of them he uses terms such as 'picturesque', '*tableau vivant*', 'the masquerading-looking population', 'that strange and richly varied panorama', 'the curious and vivid drama of oriental life', and so on. He concludes his description of the Frank quarter of Alexandria with: '. . . and here and there a Frank with long moustaches is lounging about, contemplating those unconscious tableaux which seem to have been got up for his amusement'.[40] Precisely. Surrounded by such as these Warburton and his like could feel the sense of mastery they were perhaps denied at home, where the feelings and wishes of others had to be taken into account.

When these charming and amusing picture-book characters

turned out to be importunate human beings Warburton's irritation was intense. Where, he asked, was the hunter Ishmael to be found? Alas, he was a 'swindling, camel-jobbing Sheikh, who will try to cheat you on Mount Sinai'.[41] Such were the 'Realities', as opposed to the 'Romance', of Eastern travel. Lacking Kinglake's more delicate sense of irony, and lacking also his inhibitions about bullying natives, Warburton tended to respond to these importunities with a well-aimed kick.

His peremptoriness probably owed something to his exaggerated notion of English prestige in the East. He regarded himself not as a mere tourist but as the representative of a nation whose name was synonymous with honour and 'from which the East is now expecting great things'.[42] He believed, as did not a few other writers of the period, that 'the East' was longing for the English to come and arrange its affairs. This curious notion was a feature of the growth of English political interest in the area. 'The Englishman domineers as a free man and a Briton, which is different,' wrote Lady Lucie Duff Gordon in her best-selling *Letters from Egypt*, 'and that is the reason why the Arabs wish for English rule, and would dread that of Eastern Christians.'[43] Richard Burton, while believing that the Egyptians longed for European rule (preferably French), never harboured the illusion, so dear to lesser spirits, that Orientals admired the Englishman's moral superiority. He knew the East too well for that, and in any case believed that the race went to the strong, not the saintly.[44]

The chapter Warburton devoted to the Bedouin was a remarkable example of the imperturbability with which all the existing clichés on the subject could be recited by a writer whose experience ought to have taught him differently. His ever-ready sarcasm seemed to desert him when he came to write his set piece on the Bedouin. In this case he seemed to want to hang on to his preconceived notions, though whether because there was a market for them or because of a genuine reluctance to part with them will never be known. Whatever the reason, his account of the Arabs of the desert was little more than a catalogue of such well-known qualities as their independence, chivalry (which he erroneously believed the crusaders to have associated with the Bedouin), hospitality, endurance, and so on. Most of these qualities the Arab shared with his horse. Warburton admired purity of blood in both men and animals, which led him to suppose that it was in the remotest regions, such as Nejd, that the finest specimens of both were to be found.[45] His contempt for the Egyptian fellahin was based partly on his belief that they were not of 'pure Arab race', and partly on his virtuous horror of their 'sensuality', which rendered them fit only for slavery.[46]

Kinglake had pulled off the difficult feat of conveying a consistent freshness of response while exploiting to the full the literary associations of his subject. Warburton attempted the same thing and failed. It is clear from the quotations with which his account is generously interlarded that he carried with him on his journey a formidable amount of literary baggage. When he described Orientals it was with implicit reference to their prototypes in the *Arabian Nights*, the Bible or the works of poets such as Byron, Moore, Lord Lindsay and Bulwer Lytton. The result was an insistent knowingness quite different from the charming worldliness of *Eothen*. Warburton's perceptions were coarse, his responses stale: his book was literary in the worst sense. Unfortunately, it was only the first of many similar efforts on the part of writers inspired by the success of Kinglake. They laboured to convey the 'enchantment' of the East but usually managed only to be tedious or facetious. In 1849 the journalist Bayle St John was reduced to describing his Bedouin guide as 'a very picturesque old object', but worse was to come; in 1852 readers of the *United Services Magazine* were treated to the depressing spectacle of a British military man in 'a paradise of enjoyment' because he was able to peruse his copy of the *Arabian Nights* while actually sitting in a Bedouin camp.[47]

The convention that the inhabitants of the Middle East existed primarily as illustrations for a deluxe edition of the *Arabian Nights* implied a reluctance to see them as having any will of their own or any legitimate vision of their future. The 'unchanging East' came to be regarded as a spectacle; one for which, it was increasingly assumed, the English were entitled to both a front seat and a presence behind the scenes. It was a spectacle which came inevitably to an end when the actors decided, in Gerald de Gaury's phrase, that they were 'in no mind to be gilded and kept in a cage for the diversion of Europeans'.[48] But in 1850 it looked as though it would go on forever.

Another friend of Kinglake's who took himself off to the East was Thackeray. He went in search of copy for a profitable book; *Eothen*

4 'Punch in the East': Thackeray descending the Great Pyramid

51

had appeared the previous year and met with immediate success. His resulting production, *Notes of a Journey from Cornhill to Grand Cairo*, was well received at the time but has deservedly fallen into oblivion.

The book's one and only joke was that the East really did resemble the *Arabian Nights*. Thackeray's advice to those who had loved the *Arabian Nights* in their youth was to

book themselves on board one of the Peninsular and Orient vessels, and try one *dip* into Constantinople or Smyrna. Walk into the bazaar, and the East is unveiled to you; how often and often have you tried to fancy this, lying out on a summer holiday at school! It is wonderful, too, how *like* it is; you may imagine that you have been in the place before, you seem to know it so well![49]

The mysterious and plangent familiarity of the East is comfortably reduced to a joke. After a day or two of delight the traveller will see that the place has its ridiculous side; nowadays 'dark Hassan sits in his divan and drinks champagne, and Selim has a French watch, and Zuleika perhaps takes Morrison's pills . . .'[50] With the publication of *Cornhill to Grand Cairo* the mysterious East arrived within the cosy purview of contributors to *Punch*. We recognize the very English technique of reducing foreigners to insignificance by laughing at them, especially at their attempts to imitate our inimitable ways, and by laughing at ourselves for supposing we could ever take them seriously. Not even the Bedouin escaped Thackeray's determined humorousness. When he assures us that in the desert, 'a British lion with an umbrella is no match for an Arab with his infernal long gun' we do not fail to see that the joke is on the Bedouin as much as it is on Thackeray.[51]

It would have been astonishing of course if Thackeray had presented us with a eulogy of the Arabs. His temperament did not run to eulogy, and besides, the 'gentlemanly' Bedouin probably reminded him more of the predatory Regency bucks he so despised than the Dobbin-like character who was his own idea of a true gentleman. Pride of birth, contempt for practical ways of earning a living, a sense of 'honour' which applied only to one's equals – these were not qualities of which Thackeray could approve, though his notorious ambivalence towards Becky Sharp and his development of the character of Rawdon Crawley show that he was not totally immune to their charm. Aristocratic vices, with their colour and panache, sometimes possessed for him a more vivid appeal than middle-class virtues. There is a passage in *Vanity Fair* in which Becky is compared, with unmistakable if reluctant affection, to a Bedouin.

As the most hardened Arab that ever careered across the desert on the hump of a dromedary, likes to repose sometimes under the date-trees by the water, or to come into the cities, walk into the bazaars, refresh himself in the baths, and say his prayers in the mosque, before he goes out again marauding, – so Jos's tents and pillau were pleasant to this little Ishmaelite.[52]

The truth was that Thackeray liked to have his cake and eat it. 'It is all vanity to be sure: but who will not own to liking a little of it?'[53] This summarizes very well his attitude to the East, and it was one which many Englishmen were to find appealing; it meant they need not take the place too seriously. Their English common sense prevented them from succumbing to the pretensions of the Arabs or their own sneaking fondness for the exotic. It was a fundamentally unsympathetic attitude, and also very largely a middle-class attitude, which flourished in the pages of such family journals as Dickens's *All the Year Round*. In future the Bedouin would receive serious attention mostly from aristocrats – and those who wished they were aristocrats.

PART TWO

3

Richard Burton

(1821–1890)

A wider soul than the world was wide,
Whose praise made love of him one with pride,
 What part has death or time in him,
Who rode life's lists as a god might ride?

Swinburne, *On the Death of Richard Burton*

SIR RICHARD BURTON is in danger of becoming an Eminent
Victorian. In a period of growing English nostalgia for an imperial
past he has begun to acquire a certain aura of respectability. Here is
a man, it is implied, whose confidence in his own superiority was
entirely justified. He was brave, immensely learned in the ways of
native peoples, lacking entirely in prudishness; what he lacked in
compassion for the poor in spirit he made up for with boundless
energy, a quality which once more commands respect. He seems a
fit representative of a more heroic age.

This was not the way he looked to most of his contemporaries.
To them he was a man who could always be counted on to go too
far, and this robbed him of much of the public esteem to which his
achievements entitled him. It is possible to go too far and get away
with it, but Burton was unlucky in this respect. General Gordon
was a man whose behaviour was often extreme, but on one occasion this tendency of his seems to have fitted in with the plans of
politicians and the mood of the British public, and so he was
awarded a martyr's crown while Burton was lucky to get a knight-
hood. Gordon was no more a typical Victorian than Burton was,
but both men lived at a time when a growing national mood of
expansion provided violent and gifted eccentrics with a wider
arena for their activities and a chance of public support.

Burton's Arabism began rather inauspiciously at Oxford with his
choice of Arabic as a subject in which he could excel without

57

5   Richard Burton

having to endure conventional competition. Perhaps the emotional load which his study of the language was originally made to bear explains something of his lifelong devotion to it.

The crisis which resulted in his initiation into Arabic studies had roots going far back into the past, as far back as the year he was born. In that year, 1821, his father, Colonel Joseph Burton of the 36th Regiment, decided to leave England for good.[1] His military career had been cut short in 1820 by his refusal to testify against Queen Caroline in her trial for adultery. Put on half-pay, he was so demoralized by the unhappy result of his honourable action that he made no attempt to retrieve his career and moved to the continent instead. The family wandered from one English colony to another, sometimes staying for only a few months at a time. As the years went by Joseph Burton became less and less equal to the task of bringing up his two wild and gifted sons. He seems to have developed into a remote and carping figure, regularly beating his sons for their transgressions but completely unable to control them. Apart from a brief and miserable spell at an English preparatory school, Richard and his brother Edward received no systematic education. They treated with contempt their succession of governesses and the tutor provided by their father, and went out in search of amusement and instruction in the cities of France and Italy. The result in Richard's case was unorthodox but impressive. He acquired an extraordinary proficiency in European languages and dialects, a competent knowledge of European art and architecture, considerable skill as a fencer, and a precocious familiarity with the brothels of Naples. He was also completely Europeanized and quite unfit for the career his weak and impercipient father had marked out for him. After taking a degree at Oxford he was to enter the church.

In spite of his failure to provide them with the necessary equipment Joseph Burton was ambitious for his sons to succeed in English life. He refused Richard's entreaties to be sent to the University of Toulouse and dispatched him, under protest, to Oxford. Within an hour of his arrival he made a spectacular gaffe: an undergraduate laughed at his splendid moustache and Burton challenged him to a duel. This un-English gesture was naturally greeted with amazement and no duel ensued, but it was the beginning of Burton's fearsome reputation among his compatriots.

It is not difficult to reconstruct his feelings on arriving at Oxford.

He combined a bitter resentment of his father's insistence on sending him to England with a conviction of his own superiority, which he rapidly discovered the dons and many of the under-graduates did not share. In his fury at being unappreciated and misunderstood he assumed what Erikson calls a negative identity.[2] It was as though he said: 'There are things you don't like about me – here they are with interest.' He went out of his way to provoke those in authority and succeeded very well. It is impossible to miss the element of vindictiveness in this; he was getting his own back on his father, as well as on the dons and those undergraduates who regarded him as a freak.

Nowhere is this more apparent than in his conduct at his fellow-ship examination. His father insisted that he try for a fellowship; he failed the examination because he chose to pronounce Greek and Latin in the continental manner rather than in the anachro-nistic English fashion practised at Oxford. The examiners neither understood nor appreciated his tactless display of erudition and the fellowship went to a more conventional candidate. Burton was dimly aware of his perversity. 'The devil,' he wrote, 'entered into me and made me speak Greek Romaically by accent, and not by quantity, even as they did and still do at Athens.'

His failure to get the fellowship made him furious and mis-erable. Failure, he discovered, was a heavy price to pay for the satisfaction of a half-conscious impulse to revenge himself upon his father. He decided not even to try for a First and turned instead to the study of Arabic. This was a subject in which there were then no classes for undergraduates at Oxford, and he had to go out and find himself a tutor. He was on his own and free to shine. Away from the world of fellowships and examinations there was no temptation to indulge in self-destructive impulses. He wanted very badly to succeed at Arabic and worked at it with the methodi-calness and intensity which were characteristic of him. For his father, though, a budding competence in Arabic was no substitute for a fellowship, and he ignored his son's pleas for permission to leave Oxford and go into the army. This was too much for Burton. He embarked on a series of escapades designed to get him rusticated from the university. Unfortunately for him, he went too far and got himself expelled. He made his exit, hoot-ing on a tin trumpet, in a tandem driven over the best flower beds.

His academic boats being irretrievably burnt, the only course left for him was the army. His father capitulated and purchased a commission for him in Bombay. Here he immediately began to learn Hindustani. His remarkable talent for languages could not remain unused – it possessed something like a life of its own – but a knowledge of Hindustani was also a path to promotion, and the study of Oriental languages perhaps was one of the few intellectual pursuits to which were still attached some shreds of self-esteem. Whatever the reason, he plunged into Hindustani and having mastered it began to study other Indian languages and dialects. His technique for learning a language, which when perfected enabled him to learn a new one in two months, is worth passing on.

I got a simple grammar and vocabulary, marked out the forms and words which I knew were absolutely necessary, and learnt them by heart by carrying them in my pocket and looking over them at spare moments during the day. I never worked for more than a quarter of an hour at a time, for after that the brain lost its freshness. After learning some three hundred words, easily done in a week, I stumbled through some easy book-work (one of the Gospels is the most come-atable), and underlined every word that I wished to recollect, in order to read over my pencillings at least once a day. Having finished my volume, I then carefully worked up the grammar minutiae, and then I chose some other book whose subject most interested me. The neck of the language was now broken, and progress was rapid. If I came across a new sound like the Arabic *Ghayn*, I trained my tongue to it by repeating it so many thousand times a day. When I read, I invariably read out loud, so that the ear might aid memory. I was delighted with the most difficult characters, Chinese and Cuneiform, because I felt that they impressed themselves more strongly upon the eye than the eternal Roman letters . . . whenever I conversed with anybody in a language that I was learning, I took the trouble to repeat their words inaudibly after them, and so to learn the trick of pronunciation and emphasis.[3]

In 1844 his linguistic accomplishments and familiarity with native life landed him a job as an intelligence officer under Napier in Sind. Disguised as Mirza Abdullah of Bushire, a half-Arab, half-Persian merchant, he was able to procure for Napier much useful information, and his knowledge of India, its people and its languages, widened and deepened. His experiences resulted in two books, *Scinde; or the Unhappy Valley* (1851) and *Sindh, and the Races that Inhabit the Valley of the Indus* (1851), in which he expressed for the first time in print his admiration for martial races, in this case the Afghans and Baluchis, and his contempt for Negroes. He believed that 'the dark complexion of the Sindhi' betokened his 'arrested development'.[4]

These books were written after Burton's career in India had come ignominiously to an end. The instrument of his downfall was a report he wrote at Napier's request on homosexuality in Sind. In his pursuit of information he visited homosexual brothels in disguise and then wrote up what he saw in detail. Napier read the report, put it in his secret file where it remained for two years, and destroyed the brothels. After Napier left India, Burton was left without a patron, and one of his enemies, of whom no doubt there were many, took the report out of the secret file and sent it to the Government Office in Bombay along with two innocent articles Burton wished to clear for publication. His career in India was ruined. He left India, his health and his pride seriously damaged, in May 1849. In the next two years he wrote *Goa and the Blue Mountains* and *Falconry in the Valley of the Indus* as well as the two books on Sind.

These first books, like all his others, are remarkable for their wealth of detail. The physical features of the landscape, the appearance and habits of the people, all are copiously and precisely described. For anyone interested in what he is writing about this attention to detail is one of Burton's greatest charms as a writer, and it is what made his best books valuable works of reference for many years after his death. But his learning is not lightly worn. Footnote relentlessly follows footnote as though their sheer accumulation will establish once and for all the author's truthfulness, ability and integrity. It is as though he was trying to beat the academics at their own game.

Fame, of course, was the spur, and though his learning was curious he was determined that its presentation should be impeccable. In 1856, just before he left on his search for the source of the Nile, he wrote the following poem:

> I wore thine image, Fame,
> Within a heart well fit to be thy shrine;
> Others a thousand boons may gain –
>   One wish was mine:
>
> The hope to gain one smile,
> To dwell one moment cradled on thy breast,
> Then close my eyes, bid life farewell,
>   And take my rest!

And now I see a glorious hand
Beckon me out of dark despair,
Hear a glorious voice command,
    'Up, bravely dare!

'And if to leave a deeper trace
On earth to thee Time, Fate, deny,
Drown vain regrets, and have the grace
    Silent to die.'

She pointed to a grisly land,
Where all breathes death – earth, sea, and air;
Her glorious accents sound once more,
    'Go meet me there.'

Mine ear will hear no other sound,
No other thought my heart will know.
Is this a sin? 'O, pardon, Lord!
    Thou mad'st me so!'[5]

Though in spite of many disappointments he never had the grace silent to die, and though one smile from the goddess was never enough, the poem seems an honest statement of Burton's motive for churning out book after book and taking on any adventure that offered a chance of recognition and appreciation. He was also driven – the word should be taken literally – by a voracious curiosity whose origin is completely obscure; but the strenuous efforts he made to publicize his knowledge, and to defend it when it was controversial, were the result of his longing for fame.

This longing was almost certainly due in large part to the damage suffered to his self-esteem at Oxford. He had arrived there with an unthinking consciousness of superiority and had left with a sickening knowledge of failure, which had been exacerbated by the Indian débâcle. His bravura exit from Oxford, designed to show his contempt for the institution which had extruded him as a foreign body, was only an attempt to hide his misery and shame. When he got to London he was unable to tell his relatives the true reason for his unexpected arrival: he announced that he had been given a vacation for taking a double First.

His appetite for fame was insatiable, yet he often seemed to throw away a chance to reap the reward of his achievements. After his pilgrimage to Mecca, instead of going straight to London and the accolades which awaited him, he stayed in Cairo for two months; and when he was offered his great opportunity to make good, as consul to Damascus, he did not go immediately to his post but went to the battlefields of Paraguay to take notes for a book. What held him back? Perhaps there was a reluctance to appear too eager for acclaim (and therefore vulnerable) and perhaps there was a fear that the success which he so desired might crumble like Dead Sea fruit when he plucked it from the tree. 'Whilst failure,' he once wrote, 'inspirits a man, attainment reads the sad prosy lesson that all our glories "are shadows, not substantial things". Truly said the sayer, "disappointment is the salt of life" – a salutary bitter which strengths the mind for fresh exertion, and gives a double value to the prize.'[6] No success could ever have been a splendid enough confirmation for him and perhaps he knew it.

As the years went by and success proved more and more elusive, Burton tried to persuade himself that he was indifferent to it. He adopted the stern creed, too bracing for most of us and taxing even for Burton, that self-cultivation ('with due regard to others') was the 'sole and sufficient object of human life'.

> Do what thy manhood bids thee do,
>   From none but self expect applause;
> He noblest lives and noblest dies
>   Who makes and keeps his self-made laws.[7]

Part of him never ceased to hope for applause, though by the time he wrote these lines he had ceased to expect it. When his racy translation of the *Arabian Nights* brought him a commercial success in his old age he could not help commenting bitterly: I have struggled for forty-seven years, distinguishing myself honourably in every way that I possibly could. I never had a compliment, nor a "thank you," nor a single farthing. I translate a doubtful book in my old age, and I immediately make sixteen thousand guineas. Now that I know the tastes of England, we need never be without money.'[8]

India was Burton's first taste of empire. He went out there at the age of twenty-one, hungry for glory, and in no doubt at all about the rightness of the British presence there. He believed that a nation's greatness should be expressed imperially, and this remained his attitude to the end of his life. 'The English of a former generation,' he wrote in 1856 in an energetic defence of the British Empire,

were celebrated for gaining ground in both hemispheres: their broad lands were not won by a peace policy, which, however, in this our day has on two distinct occasions well nigh lost for them 'the gem of the British Empire' – India. The philanthropist and the political economist may fondly hope, by outcry against 'territorial aggrandizement', by advocating a compact frontier, by abandoning colonies and by cultivating 'equilibrium', to retain our rank among the great nations of the world. Never! The facts of history prove nothing more conclusively than this: a race either progresses or retrogrades, either increases or diminishes: the children of Time, like their sire, cannot stand still.[9]

This notion of an inexorable racial dynamic was rather too explicit for most Victorian Englishmen, who tended to discuss their imperialism more pragmatically. It comes as no surprise to discover Burton's fascination with Disraeli and his admiration for German nationalism, which he hoped would inspire England 'to rival our Continental cousins in the course of progress, and in the mighty struggle for national life and prosperity'.[10] He conceived imperialism simply in terms of being top nation: this suited his truculent nature.

For such a fervent imperialist Burton's attitude towards the English in the East was remarkably tepid. He always disliked English colonies, from Bombay to Aden and Zanzibar, except for the few choice spirits who shared his interests. In India he preferred the society of natives to that of his complacent and incurious compatriots, who seemed to him then weak vessels for his imperial enthusiasm. Later he realized his mistake.

I am convinced [he wrote in his *Pilgrimage to Al-Madinah & Meccah*] that the natives of India cannot respect a European who mixes with them familiarly, or especially who imitates their customs, manners, and dress. The tight pantaloons, the authoritative voice, the pococurante manner, and the broken Hindustani impose upon them – have a weight which learning and honesty, which wit and courage, have not.

He went on to suggest that Indian officials should be chosen for posts in Oriental courts, because they possessed the necessary tone of command.[11]

His pride in his Englishness and passionate concern with England's glory could not reduce the distance which his continental upbringing and unusual temperament had put between him and his countrymen. Time and again, beginning at Oxford with his unsuccessful attempt to call out the undergraduate who had laughed at his moustache, he was to miscalculate the likely English response to his behaviour. His habit of lashing out in print at unfavourable critics might have raised fewer eyebrows in France than it did in England; and his expulsion from Oxford was ensured when he spiritedly defended his delinquency instead of taking his punishment like a man.

He came to identify himself less with England itself, Shakespeare's sceptr'd isle, than with Greater Britain, the Empire. He could never have professed a patriotism like Wilfrid Blunt's, founded on love of the ancestral soil; Burton's patriotism had to express itself imperially, because only in the imperial enterprise was there a place for misfits like him. When he was doing intelligence work for Napier in Sind the marginal nature of his relationship to English society and talent for disguise meant he could assume more easily than most whatever exotic role was required. He was a natural spy. Had it not been for his craving for fame, espionage might well have been his métier, for a spy can assume an alien nationality while remaining secure in the belief that it is all for the greater glory of his country. When he went to Mecca disguised as a Moslem his disguise had no patriotic justification, and he was violently criticized for it: even in what should have been his finest hour he managed to fall foul of conventional English sensibilities. In the words of the *Edinburgh Review*:

there is something indescribably revolting to our feelings, in the position of an English officer, even though it be in the pursuit of very interesting and desirable information, crawling among a crowd of unbelievers, around the objects of their wretched superstition; sharing, and perhaps, exaggerating their miserable exhibitions of reverence; . . . and in a word, accommodating himself . . . to every detail of their public and private worship.[12]

Burton reacted with characteristic fury to this insipid carping at the disguise which was an indispensable part of his enterprise. It seemed to him absurd to suggest, as the *Edinburgh* did, that such a disguise was beneath the dignity of an Englishman. He was not English enough to understand the feeling that English prestige was damaged by accommodation to foreign customs; he would never have been able to understand the magnetic charm for English people of those contemptible little clubs immortalized by George Orwell in *Burmese Days*.

Of the three other English travellers discussed in detail in this book, only the devious and equally marginal Palgrave adopted a disguise. Blunt and Doughty disdained it, proclaiming their Englishness with an exaggerated unconcern for the possibly unpleasant consequences. The ultimate affirmation of Englishness was left to Captain Shakespear, the English officer who was seconded to assist Ibn Saud in his tribal wars in 1915. He reportedly lost his life because his refusal to abandon his British topee for an Arab headcloth made him a conspicuous target in battle. It is not difficult to imagine what Richard Burton would have thought of this beau geste.

One might ask why Burton bothered to be patriotic at all. Why did he not abandon England and make his career on the continent? This is a difficult question, but there are one or two possibilities. Expatriate children tend to acquire an abnormal consciousness of their nationality, from other children who fasten on to any distinguishing characteristic and from parents conscious of being in exile. Added to this in Burton's case was probably a pride in England's military prowess, which was bound to appeal to the child's belligerent nature. In the course of his incessant childhood wanderings his Englishness provided one of the few continuous threads of identity. It became a habit, and a source of pride.

Because he was unable to accept the English as they actually were, he had to invent an England as it used to be, otherwise his commitment was meaningless. He regretted the loss of 'those pristine virtues, that tone and temper, which made [England] what she is'.[13] This strikes the authentic reactionary note of the superpatriot, a creature very different from the ordinary placid lover of his native sod.

Burton's aggressive brand of imperialism harmonized with his loathing of democracy. On this subject he held the kind of opinions from which editors of respectable journals take pains to dissociate themselves: he believed that the masses, wherever they were, should be kept severely in their place. He hated republicanism and affected to believe that men had more real freedom under a despotism, where they are not subject to the tyranny of majority opinion.[14] The criticism of democracy is legitimate enough, but the conclusion that tyranny is better simply reflects Burton's instinctive preference for strong government. He admired Mohammed Ali, the despot of Egypt, and despised the Ottoman reforms known as the Tanzimat, preferring 'the old stratocracy'. His authoritarianism was applied impartially at home and abroad: he would have liked the English police to have the kind of powers that would deter 'Fenians, Bradlaugh, Beales, Park-rioters, and treasonable demagogues'; and for all his seeming sympathy with natives he never hesitated to push them around when it suited him. It is difficult to take quite seriously his wife's contention that he was a man 'dearly loved by all Eastern races, by children and servants, and animals', at least with regard to the first and third categories.[15]

Burton at thirty-two, the age at which he set out for Mecca, was a bundle of contradictions – a patriot who despised his compatriots, and an authoritarian who was also a rebel. The conflicting aspects of his character would all find expression in his feeling for the Bedouin Arabs.

The idea of performing the pilgrimage to Mecca, and then going on to explore central and eastern Arabia, had long been in Burton's mind. After he left India he obtained the support of the Royal Geographical Society for this enterprise, but the East India Company, whose employee he still was, refused the necessary three years' leave. He was granted only an additional twelve months to 'pursue his Arabic studies in lands where the language is best learned'.[16] After four years of relative inactivity (by Burton's standards) in Europe, he was eager to set off on this dangerous adventure with its chance of fame and fortune. Only Burckhardt before him had produced a detailed account of Mecca.

He left London on 3 April 1853 disguised as a Persian. On reaching Cairo he discovered that his Persian disguise would render him too conspicuous in Arabia, where Persians were regarded as heretics, and so he became a Pathan doctor. The character, as he conceived it, fitted him like a glove. 'Born in India of Afghan parents, who had settled in the country, educated at Rangoon, and sent out to wander, as men of that race frequently are, from early youth, I was well guarded against the danger of detection by a fellow-countryman.'[17] Substitute France for India, English for Afghan, and Oxford for Rangoon, and you have Burton himself. The disguise was a good one, for the doctor's cosmopolitan background could be used to explain any linguistic slips. Burton, it should be noted, did not attempt to pass as an Arab. Where many fools have rushed in, the great ethnologist, linguist and spy feared to tread.

From Cairo he went to Suez by camel, with an escort of two Bedouin. This was his first encounter with the Bedouin and he did not intend to come off the loser. When one of them moved forward to take the lead his response was instantaneous: 'This is a trial of manliness. There is no time for emotion. Not a moment can be spared, even for a retrospect. I kick my dromedary, who steps out into a jog-trot.' In the blazing heat of midsummer Englishman and Arab raced across the desert until both slackened pace, honour satisfied. Burton was always a snob about his relations with the Bedouin. 'Those travellers,' he wrote, 'who complain of their insolence and extortion may have been either ignorant of their language or offensive to them by assumption of superiority, – in the Desert man meets man, – or physically unfitted to acquire their esteem.' Only a real man, and a gentleman, could hope for their respect.[18]

This first desert journey was an exciting experience for Burton after 'a four years' life of European effeminacy'.[19] He found the desert immensely stimulating to both mind and body, experiencing a sense of great intellectual and physical power. His heart bounded in his breast 'at the thought of matching his puny forces with Nature's might, and of emerging triumphant from the trial'. No civilized society could offer him the kind of affirmation he experienced here. Henceforth he would go to the desert and its inhabitants when he felt the need to 'strengthen' himself. In the desert was 'the type of Liberty, which is Life, whilst the idea of Immensity, of Sublimity, of Infinity, is always present, always the first thought'. Burton, like Byron, was exhilarated rather than chastened by the experience of Immensity.[20]

At Suez he embarked on a pilgrim ship for Yanbu, and his direct friendly contact with Bedouin life virtually ceased. From then on his companions were mostly pilgrims who went in constant fear of Bedouin attack. It is as well to remember this when we observe the confidence with which he expounded on Bedouin character and customs in the *Pilgrimage to Al-Madinah & Meccah*. Much of his information seems to have come from questioning his companions, especially one Sheikh Masud, a Bedouin camel-man hired for the journey from Medina to Mecca. Perhaps it seems presumptuous to suggest that Burton, who can truly be considered one of the great pioneer anthropologists, hardly knew the people on whom he considered himself an authority, but the fact is that at this period of his life he did not know the Bedouin well. Like those of Niebuhr and Burckhardt his opinions were founded less on direct observation than on material he received from Arab informants and on what he had read. Later on, in Syria, he had more opportunity to observe Bedouin life at first hand.

By the time he reached Yanbu Burton was practically lame. While going ashore at Marsa Mahar he had stepped on a sea urchin. He extracted the poisonous spine but the wound became infected and when he arrived at Yanbu he was hardly able to walk. Though he often complained bitterly about minor inconveniences he was undeterred by a catastrophe of this magnitude. He simply bought himself a camel litter like those used by Bedouin women and made the hundred and twenty mile journey to Medina in it. The enclosed litter had the advantage of enabling him to take notes in secrecy. All Burton's major journeys were accomplished under the stress of chronic physical pain. On his expedition to Lake Tanganyika he suffered from severe inflammation of the eyes, paralysis of the legs, and an ulcerated jaw which made it impossible for him to eat solid food.

The pilgrim caravan of which he was a part travelled mostly at night to escape the terrible heat of the desert west of Medina; the days were passed huddled together in a tent for shelter from the sun. Under these conditions Burton saw little of the country, but he was thrown intimately together with his pilgrim companions who come vividly alive in the pages of his book. One night they lost twelve men in an attack by Bedouin. The pilgrimage in those days, and even until fifty years ago, was truly a dangerous enterprise, with Bedouin bandits and epidemic diseases combining to reduce the traveller's chances of returning home to claim the precious title 'Hajji'. The approach to Medina lay across a steep ridge of black basalt and Burton's dromedary stumbled so many times that his litter was in ruins. Towards the end of that long night he noticed that all the pilgrims were hurrying their camels over the rough ground with not a word spoken between them. 'Are there robbers in sight?' he asked. 'No!' replied his companion, 'they are walking with their eyes, they will presently see their homes.' Suddenly in the light of dawn they emerged from a narrow lava defile and saw the holy city below them. The faithful burst into prayers of thanksgiving and Burton confessed that for some minutes his enthusiasm rose as high as theirs. The journey from Yanbu to Medina had taken eight days.

After performing the rituals of pilgrimage at the Prophet's tomb he made a fast march through the Darb al-Sharqi, the desert route to Mecca, accompanied by the Harb Bedouin Masud and his son and nephew. It was a grim journey which included a waterless stretch of three days – an exhilarating experience for Burton who proved himself the equal of any Bedouin in his capacity to endure. He was in his element, as indeed he was throughout the whole journey from beginning to end. His *Pilgrimage to Al-Madinah & Meccah* shows a man well in control of a dangerous situation, self-confident and happy in his ability to respond to any challenge. He jokes around the campfire with his motley companions, sardonically offers a pipe to a puritanical Wahhabi, joyfully lays about him in an affray on board the pilgrim ship, and in short never troubles to make himself inconspicuous. He made many friends on his journey. The flamboyant vitality which often took perverse and self-destructive forms in a European setting opened doors for him in the East. The splendid moustache which had been ridiculed at Oxford elicited an affectionate nickname from old Sheikh Masud – Abu Shawarib, 'Father of Moustachios'.

The crown of his journey was his entrance, dressed in the pilgrim garb of a simple white shawl and loin cloth, into the Beit Allah, the sacred House of God in Mecca. As he approached the Kaaba, the ancient sanctuary which had been a place of pilgrimage long before Mohammed, he was swept up by an intense emotion.

There were no giant fragments of hoar antiquity as in Egypt, no remains of graceful and harmonious beauty as in Greece and Italy, no barbarous gorgeousness as in the buildings of India; yet the view was strange, unique – and how few have looked upon the celebrated shrine! I may truly say that, of all the worshippers who clung weeping to the curtain, or who pressed their beating hearts to the stone, none felt for the moment a deeper emotion than did the Haji from the far-north. It was as if the poetical legends of the Arab spoke truth, and that the waving wings of angels, not the sweet breeze of morning, were agitating and swelling the black covering of the shrine. But, to confess humbling truth, theirs was the high feeling of religious enthusiasm, mine was the ecstasy of gratified pride.[21]

Having performed all the rites of the pilgrimage he returned to Egypt and began work on his book, which was published two years later in 1855. In spite of criticism such as that of the *Edinburgh Review* it went through four editions.

The *Pilgrimage* contains Burton's fullest discussion of Bedouin society. It also contains a summary of the character of the inhabitants of Mecca and Medina, but it was the Bedouin who chiefly fascinated him.

Burton took the convention of Bedouin independence and individualism and used it as the basis for a portrait of what he called the *société léonine*, a society 'in which the fiercest, the strongest, and the craftiest obtains complete mastery over his fellows . . .' Among the Bedouin extreme individualism led, according to Burton, neither to anarchy nor democracy but to a kind of society in which the strongest, and only the strongest, ruled. Anarchy was averted by the leader's sheer force of personality, assisted by the tribesmen's fear of reprisals under the law of the blood feud and by the body of custom administered by the Cadi al-Arab.[22]

Life in this armed camp was not without its niceties; indeed the finest characteristics of Bedouin life were directly traceable to each man's fear of his neighbour.

The loom and the file do not conserve courtesy and chivalry like the sword and spear; 'man extends his tongue,' to use an Arab phrase, when a cuff and not a stab is to be the consequence of an injurious expression. Even the ruffian becomes polite in California, where his brother-ruffian carries his revolver, and those European nations who were most polished when every gentleman wore a rapier, have become the rudest since Civilisation disarmed them.[23]

The leonine society, based on a healthy respect for cold steel, clearly had Burton's approval. A great swordsman himself, he regarded the sword as a weapon which possessed an almost mystical power. In *The Book of the Sword* (1884) he described it as 'a creator as well as a destroyer', meaning that it had shaped warring individuals into cohesive societies.[24]

Though the Bedouin had to behave himself in camp, in raiding his love of fighting could be indulged without restraint. To die in a raid was to die the death of a hero. Burton was the first writer who explicitly admired the Bedouin's predatory character. He wrote of it with great sympathy.

It is easy to understand this respect for brigands. Whoso revolts against society requires an iron mind in an iron body, and these mankind instinctively admires, however misdirected be their energies. Thus, in all imaginative countries, the brigand is a hero; even the assassin who shoots his victim from behind a hedge appeals to the fancy in Tipperary or on the Abruzzian hills . . . The true Badawi style of plundering, with its numerous niceties of honour and gentlemanly manners, gives the robber a consciousness of moral rectitude.[25]

In Burton's hands the detested bandit became a romantic rebel against society.

The conclusion will be obvious that he found in the 'wild man' (his favourite term for the Bedouin) a reflection of his own nature. He too was a wild man, but one who had the misfortune to live in an effeminate society where strength was not rewarded by power. He persuaded himself that Bedouin society, though crude (he had no desire to live among them permanently), possessed at least the virtue of giving physical and intellectual superiority its just reward. Furthermore, the Bedouin, like himself, were rebels with a sense of honour. 'Honour, not honours' was Burton's motto. If the world would not respect him he would respect himself. He devoted much space to a discussion of Bedouin chivalry.

His choice of the phrase *société léonine* is an interesting one, for there is some evidence of a tendency to identify himself with this predatory beast. Fawn Brodie, Burton's most perceptive biographer, has noted two curious references to lions in his books. The first one is in *First Footsteps in East Africa* (1856). During the course of the journey described in this book Burton's mother died, though he did not learn of it till he reached Aden. His published account of the events of 18 December 1854, the day of his mother's death, contained no explicit reference to her, but it did include, in a discussion of native lion lore, the interesting observation: 'The people have a superstition that the king of beasts will not attack a single traveller, because such a person, they say, slew the mother of all the lions . . .' Brodie interprets this as perhaps an involuntary expression of unconscious guilt over his mother's death. If it is true that the 'single traveller' somehow refers to Burton himself, it is also true that he implicitly identifies himself as the offspring of 'the mother of lions'.[26]

The second interesting reference to lions is in Burton's strange article on the Jew, which he wrote in 1871 at one of the lowest points in his career, immediately after his recall from the Damascus consulate. Instead of making his usual vigorous effort to defend himself, this time against probably unjustified charges of anti-

Semitic behaviour among other things, he shut himself up in the British Museum and wrote an anti-Semitic tract, though not an ordinary one. He found in the Jews many virtues which he also possessed himself – boldness, passion, persistence, intellectualism – and also one virtue which he seemed not to possess: a vigorous instinct for survival when persecuted, a natural buoyancy. But for all his admiration of, and apparent identification with, the Jews (in *The Highlands of Brazil* (1869) he had written that if he had a choice of race he would choose to be Jewish), he was willing to accept the charge of ritual murder against them. He reproduced without further evidence the traditional list of ritual murders, and concluded from it that even the modern, civilized Jew was a 'sleeping lion', ready when provoked to awake and do murder. Mrs Brodie's interpretation of Burton's article seems absolutely correct:

Stripped to its essentials Burton's argument was as follows: The Jew is persecuted, therefore he becomes capable of murder, and has in the past murdered, therefore it is right to persecute him. So too Burton – so often called 'a lion' by his wife – seems to have felt unconsciously about himself: I am persecuted; I am capable even of murder; therefore it is right to persecute me. So one begins to have some intimation of the guilt that immobilized him, and to understand why he made no attempt to defend himself before the Foreign Office until he was goaded to do so by his wife.

The ageing lion's instinct to defend himself had for once deserted him, and he had retired to lick his wounds.[27]

Lions appear to have been often in Burton's mind. He had a marked fondness for metaphors involving them: the desert wind caressed him 'like a lion with flaming breath'; the 'lion-tawny clays' of the Arabian desert enchanted him; some tame Bedouin at Tyre who had formerly been 'noted wreckers' were now 'lions with their fangs and claws drawn'.[28] Perhaps this fascination with the animal had something to do with childhood pride in the prowess of the 'British lion'. For Burton the man, the lion was undoubtedly an appropriate symbol of Britain's imperial power.

His extreme concern for the glory of the British Empire goes some way to explain the repressive measures he advocated against those very Bedouin he found so appealing. This is his prescription for ruling the Hejaz.

By a proper use of the blood feud; by vigorously supporting the weaker against the stronger classes; by regularly defeating every Badawi who earns a name for himself; and, above all, by the exercise of unsparing, unflinching justice, the few thousands of half-naked bandits, who now make the land a fighting field, would soon sink into utter insignificance.[29]

It was of course *British* rule that he envisaged in Arabia. He looked forward to the day when 'the tide of events [would force] us to occupy the mother-city of Al-Islam'. A British presence in Arabia seemed to Burton to be the natural desire of the true Englishman 'who would everywhere see his nation "second to none"'.[30] He accordingly made many helpful suggestions, in the *Pilgrimage* and in later books, on how to handle the Bedouin. Should the British ever 'find it necessary to raise regiments of these men, nothing would be easier. Pay them regularly, arm them well, work them hard, and treat them with even-handed justice – there is nothing else to do.' Treated thus they would make 'excellent light infantry' and even manual workers.[31] So much for the proud Bedouin, accustomed to do battle mounted on his dromedary and contemptuous of all physical labour save tending his flocks.

Considerations of national prestige can only partially explain the violent contradictions in Burton's attitude towards the Bedouin. Few imperialists have been as ruthless as he was in advocating their subjection to the iron rule of law and order. The conflicting elements of his attitude originated in a conflict within himself, in the struggle between his lawless instinct for power and self-assertion and his knowledge that his instinct must be kept in check if it were not to ruin him utterly. He knew that to succeed in English life certain conventions, which he was not inclined by training or by temperament to accept, must be observed. In his journal he recorded his regret that he had not been 'brought up in a particular groove . . . the preparatory school, then Eton and Oxford' but instead had roamed about Europe 'under governesses and tutors, to learn fencing, languages, and become wild, and to belong to nowhere in particular as to parish or county'.[32] His authoritarianism towards others was in part an extension of (sometimes a substitute for) his attempt to control himself. He was obsessed with the need for repression of people's lawless instincts. And if he could be one of the instruments of repression, then this also served his desire for power. To some extent this desire was satisfied by his identification with the British Empire. It gave him a national identity which was also a certificate of superiority. It made legitimate his urge to dominate and he was therefore prepared to defend what he conceived to be its interests to the best of his ability. He regarded his explorations not only as quests for knowledge and fame but as pathfinding ventures for the Empire. They also served his need for self-assertion; when the chains of civilized convention became too hard to bear he went off to assert himself in Central Africa, the Arabian desert, or the wilds of Brazil, always coming back with a book which he hoped would be the key to recognition and acceptance.

Burton indulged his passion for dominance in many ways, including the practice of hypnosis, but he was not entirely a monster of egotism. By all accounts he was devoted to his sisters and brother, and he was capable of giving generous recognition to an equal. He paid Burckhardt the very highest compliment when, instead of giving his own description of the Beit Allah at Mecca, he reprinted Burckhardt's description in its entirety. He permitted himself one criticism of Burckhardt, that in his writings on the Bedouin he had not produced 'a precise physical portrait of race'.[33] Nothing of course could have been further from Burckhardt's mind: he was not afflicted with the nineteenth-century obsession with race; rather he accepted the eighteenth-century notion of the 'nation' as a group of individuals united by the social contract.

Burton, however, was obsessed with 'blood' and its phenotypical expression in facial features, cranial formation, and so on. He was fascinated by the 'new science' of ethnology and the new theory, invented by the Austrian biologists, Gall and Spurzheim, that cranial bumps could be used to elucidate character. His racial portrait of the Bedouin began with the following learned observations:

The temperament of the Hijazi [Bedouin] is not unfrequently the pure nervous, as the height of the forehead and the fine texture of the hair prove. Sometimes the bilious, and rarely the sanguine, elements predominate; the lymphatic I never saw. He has large nervous centres, and well-formed spine and brain, a conformation favourable to longevity.

In the course of the next five pages he treated the reader to observations on the bent eyebrows betokening thoughtfulness, the thick lips 'denoting rudeness and want of taste', and the small but perfectly proportioned penis which distinguished the Arab from the inferior Negro.[34]

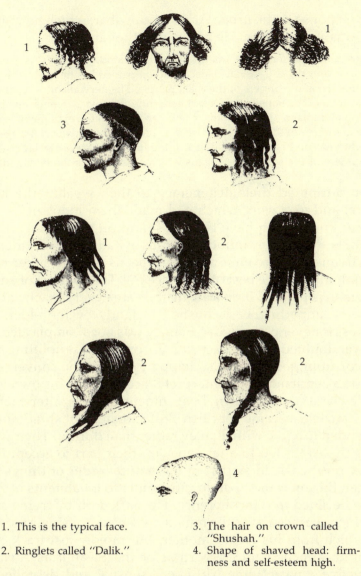

1. This is the typical face.

2. Ringlets called "Dalik."

3. The hair on crown called "Shushah."

4. Shape of shaved head: firmness and self-esteem high.

6   A phrenological exercise from Burton's *Personal Narrative of a Pilgrimage to Al-Madinah & Meccah*

Unfortunately, it was not always possible to find a satisfying correspondence between character and physique. The corrupt inhabitants of Medina displayed very similar physical characteristics to the 'true Arab type, that is to say, the Badawi of ancient and noble family'; Burton was constrained to find them coarser.[35]

His response to the urban Arabs of Zanzibar, which he visited in 1856, was very similar. He noted that though

the extremities preserve the fineness of Arab blood, the body is weak and effeminate; and the degenerate aspect is accompanied by the no less degraded mind, morals, and manners of the coast-people. The nervous or nervoso-bilious temperament of the Sons of the Desert here runs into two extremes: many Arabs are bilious-lymphatic, like Banyans; a few, lapsing into the extreme of leanness, are fair specimens of the 'Living Skeleton' . . . And as the Zanzibari Arab is mostly of burgher race in his own land [Oman], the forehead rarely displays that high development of the perceptive organs which characterizes the Bedawin.[36]

Burton attributed their degeneracy to their wealth, the humid climate, and to slavery which had made them indolent.

Other Englishmen have been less hard on the Zanzibaris than Burton. H. M. Stanley found the Arabs of Zanzibar, 'whether from more frequent intercourse with Europeans or from other causes . . . undoubtedly the best of their race . . . The conduct of an Arab gentleman is perfect. Indelicate matters are never broached before strangers; impertinence is hushed instantly by the elders, and rudeness is never permitted.'[37] Stanley was not a complicated man; he never doubted that contact with Europeans was uplifting rather than corrupting. He was also happy to accept the convention of 'the Arab gentleman' and interpret it according to his own lower-middle-class standards. In 1890, nineteen years after Stanley's visit, Zanzibar became a British Protectorate. British administrators tended to agree with Stanley rather than Burton. Their partiality for the Arabs led to a tendency on their part to accept Negro slavery on the island as part of the natural order of things.[38]

When Burton came to discuss the mulatto inhabitants of Zanzibar he declined into incoherence. He started off by trying to sort out which characteristics the mulatto received from his Arab father and which from his Negro mother, but rapidly lost track of this idea and launched into a portrait of the Swahili as cowardly, destructive, quarrelsome, drunken, sensual and degraded. He was ready to grant their 'careless merriment and . . . abundance of animal spirits; strong attachments and devoted family affection', but the concession of these points does little to mitigate his obvious loathing. In *The Lake Regions of Central Africa* (1860) he similarly deplored the 'unusual development of cunning and deceitfulness, which . . . results from the grafting of the semi-civilised Semite upon the Hamite'.[39]

But consistency was not Burton's strong point. In 1864 he found some good words to say for the Arab–Negro cross, reserving his full contempt for the Anglo Saxon–Negro cross, the sight of which goaded him to fury. He found it difficult to believe that a man of the calibre of Toussaint L'Ouverture, the hero of the Haitian Revolution, could have been a pure ('ignoble') Negro; he 'might be of Hausa, or other Semiticised blood; and this would be confounding Norman with Saxon'. Those Negroes who possessed the precious drop of Semitic blood were designated 'noble'. The one hope for Africa, Burton wrote, was the spread of Islam and the infusion of Semitic blood into the Negro, who in his pure state was incapable of improvement 'individually and *en masse*'.[40] The one point on which Burton was completely consistent was the inferiority of the Negro. He jeered at the Anti-Slavery Committee's emblem of the kneeling Negro, 'who, properly speaking, should have been on all-fours', and was eager to accept craniometric evidence of the Negro's inferiority.[41]

He was of course influenced by the racial theorizing of his time. Before he went to Mecca he had read James Cowles Prichard's *The Natural History of Man*, and he thought highly enough of it to take it with him on his expedition to Tanganyika. *The Natural History of Man*, published in 1843, was one of the most influential of the early textbooks of ethnology. Prichard's earlier and less popular book, *Researches into the Physical History of Mankind* (1813), was also undoubtedly read by Burton.

Drawing on travel books, especially Chateaubriand, and on the *Description de l'Égypte* produced by the scholars Napoleon took on his Egyptian expedition, Prichard had produced a remarkably favourable portrait of the (linguistically defined) 'Syro-Arabian or Semitic Race'. He was especially taken with the physical perfection of the Arab skull, using as his authority Baron Larrey, a surgeon who had been with Napoleon in Egypt. The almost perfectly spherical skull 'with a remarkable elevation of the upper part', the numerous convolutions of the brain, the dense texture of the brain and nervous system, all tended to show that the Arabs' intellectual capacity was '*without doubt*, superior to the faculties of those nations who inhabit the northern regions of the globe, meaning the Europeans'. It seemed, furthermore, that the Arabs' physical perfection extended to other areas of the body. According to Baron Larrey, whom Prichard quoted extensively, 'the heart and arterial system display the most remarkable regularity and a very perfect development; . . . the external senses of the Arabs are exquisitely acute and remarkably perfect: their sight is most extensive in its range; they hear at very great distances; and can, through a very extensive region, perceive the most subtle odour'. 'Upon the whole,' Baron Larrey concluded with pre-Darwinian logic, 'I am convinced that the cradle of the human family is to be found in the country of this race.'[42]

Prichard's treatment of the Arab was in marked contrast to his treatment of the Egyptian, whose kinship with the Negro he was concerned to prove. The Arabs typified restless, expansionist energy and the Egyptians voluptuous repose, and it went without saying which was to be preferred. The Egyptians, as represented by the modern Copt, were conceived as being an entirely different race from the Arabs. They were descended from the ancient Egyptians whose culture the Victorians regarded with fascinated horror. The descendants of people who worshipped snakes and crocodiles, even if nominally Christian, were not to be compared with the naturally monotheistic Arabs.

This prejudice against Egyptians continued for many years; many an Englishman in Egypt prided himself on being able to distinguish between the Egyptian and the 'true Arab'. There was much ignorance and confusion as to the racial ancestry of the Egyptian fellah, but it was usually felt that his Arab blood, if any, did not offset his general lack of charm. E. W. Lane, the great Victorian authority on the modern Egyptians, believed that the fellahin, while descended more from Bedouin than from ancient Egyptians, preserved mostly the worst traits of their desert ancestors. Lord Cromer, perhaps the greatest proconsul of them all, seems to have been one of the few literate British officials who did not waste time on these futile distinctions. It made no difference to him at all whether the Egyptians were 'true Arabs' or not; his natural affinity was with those members of the Ottoman upper class who preserved some remnants of the demeanour of an imperial race.[43]

Burton shared Prichard's belief that the Egyptians were not Arabs, arguing that the 'most superficial glance at the Egyptian Fellah, and at any given Arab from El-Hejaz will supply the measure of the ethnic difference'.[44] His ethnological distinctions tended to be made mostly on the basis of appearance. Too sophisticated a scholar to make language the major criterion of race, he nevertheless allowed his faith in appearance to lead him into superficial and contradictory judgements. Appearance is determined by genetic factors, that is by 'blood', and this is why he placed such reliance on it in making racial distinctions. He was unwilling to entertain the possibility that genetic inheritance might be too complex for the kind of classifying he indulged in.

His fascination with race almost certainly originated in his own marginality, which made him extremely receptive to racial theorists like Prichard and Disraeli. English by race though scarcely by upbringing, 'blood' was of the utmost importance to him as a criterion of nationality. It was his only claim to Englishness. He also had pretensions to aristocracy (yet another of his many claims to superiority) which reinforced his respect for blood. He rejoiced in his dubiously authenticated left-handed descent from Louis XIV, asserting that he would 'rather be the bastard of a King, than the son of an honest man'.[45]

He was not, so far as his position can be coherently determined, an inflexible purist about race. He was prepared to admit that the Tawarah Bedouin, though of 'impure race', were good enough fellows, and he had moments when he perceived some benefits to miscegenation; but he was a tireless classifier, and he reserved his unstinted admiration for such exemplars of racial purity as the Anaza Bedouin and the inhabitants of Nejd, who displayed 'those signs of "blood" which distinguish even the lower animals, the horse and the camel, the greyhound and the goat of Arabia'.[46]

Only once did Burton hold a position of responsibility in the Arab world. This was his disastrous consulship in Damascus. He attempted as usual to carry things with too high a hand and made powerful enemies who did not hesitate to seize their opportunity to unseat him when it inevitably came. In 1871 he was recalled to London, where he occupied himself for the next few months in revising for publication his old manuscript on Zanzibar, which had reappeared after being lost for many years, and in writing his article on the Jews. His diplomatic career was ruined. Eventually he accepted the sinecure post of consul at Trieste, though he still hoped that some day his reputation would be rehabilitated and he would get the coveted embassy to Morocco. This hope was finally dashed in 1886 when his application for the post was rejected. 'We don't want to annex Morocco, and we know that you two would be Emperor and Empress in about six months', a friend in the cabinet explained.[47]

Burton spent the last eighteen years of his life, from 1872 to 1890, as consul at Trieste. His days of serious exploration, though not of travel, were over, and he occupied himself with literature, chiefly that labour of love, his annotated translation of the *Arabian Nights*. In the 'Terminal Essay' which he wrote in 1886 the mature Burton, seasoned by adversity and by years of study and reflection, gave his final assessment of the Arab character, as revealed for eternity in the *Arabian Nights*.

As a child he is devoted to his parents, fond of his comrades and respectful to his 'pastors and masters,' even schoolmasters. As a lad he prepares for manhood with a will and this training occupies him throughout youthtide: he is a gentleman in manners without awkwardness, vulgar astonishment or mauvais-honte. As a man he is high-spirited and energetic, always ready to fight for his Sultan, his country and, especially, his Faith: courteous and affable, rarely failing in temperance of mind and self-respect, self-control and self-command: hospitable to the stranger, attached to his fellow-citizens, submissive to superiors and kindly to inferiors – if such classes exist: Eastern despotisms have arrived nearer the idea of equality and fraternity than any republic yet invented. As a friend he proves a model to the Damons and Pythiases: as a lover an exemplar to Don Quijote without the noble old Caballero's touch of eccentricity. As a knight he is the mirror of chivalry, doing battle for the weak and debelling the strong, while ever 'defending the honour of women.' As a husband his patriarchal position causes him to be loved and fondly loved by more than one wife: as a father affection for his children rules his life: he is domestic in the highest degree and he finds few pleasures beyond the bosom of his family. Lastly, his death is simple, pathethic [sic] and edifying as the life which led to it.

. . . [His] sublime conception of the unity and omnipotence of the Deity . . . [underlies] his moderation in prosperity, his fortitude in adversity, his dignity, his perfect self-dominance and, lastly, his lofty quietism which sounds the true heroic ring. This again is softened and tempered by a simple faith in the supremacy of Love over Fear, an unbounded humanity and charity for the poor and helpless; an unconditional forgiveness of the direst injuries ('which is the note of the noble'); a generosity and liberality which at times seem impossible and an enthusiasm for universal benevolence . . . which, exalting kindly deeds done to man above every form of holiness, constitute the root and base of Oriental, nay, of all, courtesy. And the whole is crowned by pure trust and natural confidence in the progress and perfectability of human nature, which he exalts instead of degrading; this he holds to be the foundation-stone of society and indeed the very purpose of its existence . . .

Nor is the shady side of the picture less notable. Our Arab at his worst is a mere barbarian who has not forgotten the savage. He is a model mixture of childishness and astuteness, of simplicity and cunning, concealing levity of mind under solemnity of aspect. His stolid instinctive conservatism grovels before the tyrant rule of routine, despite that turbulent and licentious independence which ever suggests revolt against the ruler: his mental torpidity, founded upon physical indolence, renders immediate action and all manner of exertion distasteful: his conscious weakness shows itself in an overweaning arrogance and intolerance. His crass and self-satisfied ignorance makes him glorify the most ignoble superstitions, while acts of revolting savagery are the natural results of a malignant fanaticism and a furious hatred of every creed beyond the pale of Al-Islam.

It must be confessed that these contrasts make a curious and interesting tout ensemble.[48]

4

Gifford Palgrave

(1826–1888)

I am a part of all that I have met;
Yet all experience is an arch wherethro'
Gleams that untravell'd world, whose margin fades
For ever and for ever when I move.

Tennyson, *Ulysses*

On 30 September 1888 William Gifford Palgrave, the most mysterious of all the English explorers of Arabia, died at Montevideo where he held the post of British Minister. In due course obituaries appeared in the English papers. They were pervaded by a note of unease which was summed up by the *Athenaeum*: 'Certainly those who knew Gifford Palgrave's special qualifications would not have expected that a man with such complete command over Eastern matters would have ended his days as official representative of the British government in South America.'[1] Like Burton, Palgrave was a brilliant failure, but he differed from Burton in that his career began with a blaze of conventional academic glory and in that he left little of lasting value behind.

He sprang from one of those formidable Victorian families which produced more than their fair share of the country's able and intellectual men. His brothers were Francis Turner Palgrave, compiler of the *Golden Treasury* and Professor of Poetry at Oxford, Robert Harry Inglis Palgrave, editor of *The Economist*, and Sir Reginald Palgrave, clerk to the House of Commons and author of a biography of Oliver Cromwell. His father was Sir Francis Palgrave, the distinguished mediaeval historian and founder of the Public Record Office. Gifford Palgrave was considered by some to be the most abundantly gifted of this able and successful family, but instead of proceeding along the expected smooth, well-travelled

84

7 William Gifford Palgrave

path his career lurched along with dramatic twists and turns, and when he finally entered the public service at the age of forty it was only to fill a succession of minor diplomatic posts.

He must have been a disappointment to his father. Sir Francis Palgrave was one of the optimistic Victorians – pious, industrious, a believer in progress, self-help, and the vitality of the English social system. The great strength of English national life, he wrote in *The Rise and Progress of the English Commonwealth* (1832), lay in the aristocracy's willingness to recruit new members on the basis of 'desert and industry . . . thus increasing the energy of the State without endangering its stability . . . This is true equality; for it is the only equality which is conformable to human nature, and acceptable to mankind. Where it exists, as in England, it imparts contentment to each individual, and vigour to the Commonwealth.'[2] Sir Francis himself was an example of this felicitous process; he was knighted in the year *The Rise and Progress of the English Commonwealth* was published.

Sir Francis's rise was the result of talent allied to ambition. Born Francis Cohen, the son of Meyer Cohen, a wealthy member of the Stock Exchange, he displayed remarkable intellectual precocity as a child. At the age of eight he translated *The Battle of Frogs and Mice* from Latin into French and his proud father published the translation, 'par M. Françqis Cohen de Kentish Town, âgé de huit ans'.[3] He had a protected childhood in a cultivated home, but it came abruptly to an end when Meyer Cohen lost his money in a slump at the beginning of the nineteenth century. At sixteen Francis Cohen became an articled clerk and was chronically short of money till his marriage to Elizabeth Turner in 1823. The marriage was preceded by his conversion to Christianity and adoption of the name Palgrave, his fiancée's mother's maiden name. At the time of his marriage he was intending to become a barrister, a profession from which Jews were barred; a handsome marriage settlement, a place granted by Blue Mantle on the Palgrave pedigree, and a church wedding, cannot have been inopportune. For the rest of his life Sir Francis was piety itself. He took his family to church on Sundays and weekdays and was a personal friend of Newman, though he never made the mistake of following him into the Roman Catholic Church, which would have incurred a disability almost as bad as being Jewish.

Gifford Palgrave was his second son. In 1838 he was sent to Charterhouse where he distinguished himself by winning the gold medal for classical verse and becoming captain of the school. He seems to have been happy at school, accepting the frequent beatings as part of the natural order of things. In Arabia he was to find Wahhabi justice mild compared with that administered at Charterhouse.[4] His career at school was crowned with an open scholarship to Oxford and he matriculated at Trinity, Newman's old college, in 1844. After only two and a half years he took a First in Classics and a Second in Mathematics. At this point his career should have taken off, but it did not. Instead of going on to seek further academic distinction he went out to India as a cadet in the 8th Bombay Native Infantry.

His decision to join the army is only one of many mysteries in the life of Gifford Palgrave. It was not entirely out of character: he was an excellent athlete and lover of horseflesh, and also enthusiastic about Britain's recent victories over the Sikhs. But it was certainly unexpected. A news item on Palgrave which appeared in *The Times* on 16 July 1865 suggests the reason for his leaving Oxford, but provides no enlightenment on his decision to join the army. It contains the information that Palgrave, being 'what was thought in those days an ultra-Tractarian', had refused ordination into the Church of England and gone to India instead.

At the time of Palgrave's residence there Trinity was very much under the influence of the Tractarian movement. In 1842 Newman had resigned in the wake of the furore created by his 90th 'Tract for the Times', and in 1845 he was converted to Roman Catholicism. Many Trinity men, in an exodus which scandalized the country, followed him into the Church of Rome. Palgrave, with his High Church background and family connection with Newman, could hardly have escaped being profoundly influenced by these events. If he was indeed an ultra-Tractarian he must have been presented with a cruel dilemma when he considered his academic future, for the holding of the fellowship to which he might now aspire was contingent at that time upon eventual ordination into the Church of England. Evidently he felt unable to go through with ordination; but he was unable to make a commitment to Rome either. That did not come until two years later, when he was received into a house of the Jesuit Order in Southern India.

His two years in the Indian Army are virtually a blank. They appear to have been little more than a prelude to that moment when he knocked on the door of the Jesuit College at Negapatam. They were perhaps a moratorium, a breathing space which Palgrave needed. He removed himself entirely from the scene of his dilemma and plunged into a life of physical activity which was probably quite pleasant to him. It is impossible to know what finally impelled him to enter the Roman Catholic Church. His obituary in the *Proceedings of the Royal Geographical Society* claims that 'an early passion for mission work among the Arab races, aroused by the translation of the old Arabian romance, Antar, now returned upon him with overmastering force'; but a desire to be a missionary does not dictate one's choice of church. Palgrave's commitment to Catholicism, while it lasted, was vehement and narrow. When he eventually went out to Syria as a Jesuit missionary, after an unusually long period of probation which seems to suggest his superiors' anxiety about the fragility of his faith, he became notorious for his hostility to the Protestant missionaries there.[5] One of them, the Rev. G. P. Badger, became his enemy for life.

When Palgrave became a Jesuit he did an extraordinary thing: he changed his name to Cohen. One can only guess at his father's reaction to this, if indeed he was aware of it. There are no indications of strained relations between the two men. Cohen means 'priest' in Hebrew, and so is both a reference to Palgrave's Jewish blood and to his Catholicism. There is no doubt that he was very interested in his Jewish ancestry at this time. While at the Collegio Romano as part of his Jesuit training he apparently wrote to his father about what his brother Reginald referred to as 'the Judaic extraction'. He also wrote to his brother Inglis saying that 'what with so frequent change of abode, companions, language &c. I feel equally at home, or, if you wish, equally a stranger and a sojourner, as all my fathers were'. Again we are confronted with a mystery. Why did he start to dwell on the Jewishness which his father had put so firmly behind him? He may have become disturbed by what would now be called his father's inauthenticity: his books certainly show a tendency to admire those races which kept themselves free from foreign influence, as well as an intermittent desire on his part to civilize them. The contrast between his pious Anglican home and his Jewish ancestry may have acquired a sudden poignancy for him when he put himself beyond the pale by joining the Jesuits. He was known during his years with the Jesuits as Guillaume Cohen, Gulielmus Palgrave, Michael Cohen, Michael X. Cohen, and Michel Sohail, but never as Gifford, his family's name for him. Sohail is a common Jewish name and is also the Persian and Arabic name for Canopus, the star for which throughout his life Palgrave had a special affection.

Whatever the reason for it, the concern with Jewishness which manifested itself at the Collegio Romano never left him. It was a concern with the Jewish race rather than the Jewish religion, which he seems never to have considering adopting. Judaism can have had little to offer his passionate and mystical nature. He was painfully aware of the historical tragedy of the Jews, the ruin of Israel and with it the obliteration of the Jews' claim to true nationhood.[6] Race and nationality, as all his books show, were subjects of overwhelming importance to him, perhaps because, like Burton, his perception of his own national identity was flawed. His case was the opposite of Burton's: Burton was English by race but not by upbringing; Palgrave was English by upbringing but not wholly by race. There was also a religious anomaly in his case. For a Jew, race and religion are ideally one. Palgrave, the son of an apostate Jew and a convert to Catholicism, had moved far away from this simple unity of racial and religious identity. He eventually became intensely preoccupied with it, believing at one period of his life that religion was, and ought to be, little more than a badge of nationality. The theme of much of his later writing was the relationship between race, religion and nationality, and the seeds of the obsession were sown in those early years at the Collegio Romano, in his parallel attachments to Jewishness and Catholicism and his consequent inability to decide satisfactorily who and what he was.

The years in Syria seemed at the time to be good ones, an active and successful demonstration of his commitment to Catholicism. He is said to have made many converts through his Arabic sermons in the native churches. According to Richard Burton, who detested him, he was also active politically, denouncing England from the pulpits of Beirut.[7] This is not unlikely in light of his future involvement with the imperial ambitions of Napoleon III, though how he came to be involved with the French in the first place is yet another mystery. He spent part of his training period in France and was much in the company of French Jesuit missionaries in Syria, but this does not fully explain why one who professed in his published works to be extremely proud of his Englishness should have become so deeply involved with the imperial interests of England's greatest rival.

Using documents in French archives his biographer, Mea Allen, has recently shown the remarkable extent of Palgrave's collaboration with France in the Middle East. His first contact with Napoleon III was the result of the massacres of Syrian Christians which took place during the Druse–Maronite civil war of 1860. Palgrave barely escaped with his life from the fighting at Damascus. It was rumoured at the time that he organized the defence of Zahle against the Druses and averted what would have been an inevitable massacre, but Mea Allen accepts his assertion that he refused to violate his priestly vows by taking up arms. After peace was restored by a French expeditionary force he left Syria for Europe. He gave a report on the situation in Syria to Napoleon III and also went on a lecture tour of Ireland to raise money for a new Syrian mission. He then returned to France and began to make plans for a missionary journey to Nejd in central Arabia, the territory of the fanatical Wahhabi sect of Islam. The great plateau of Nejd was ruled by the Saud family, the original patrons and protectors of the eighteenth-century Islamic iconoclast Mohammed ibn Abd-al-Wahhab. It was now the stronghold of a new, purified form of Islam which aroused considerable interest in the west. For his expedition Palgrave sought the financial support of Napoleon III and the spiritual support of the Pope, both of which he received. Louis-Napoleon exacted a quid pro quo, apparently with Palgrave's enthusiastic assent.

In 1861 [he later had the effrontery to write to Gladstone] I was charged by Napoleon III to visit Egypt, while on my way to Syria &c., and there to confer privately with Halim Pasha [son of the great Mohammed Ali Pasha, the Albanian adventurer who had made himself ruler of Egypt] on the Emperor's project of making him Viceroy of Egypt &c. under French suzerainty. I was of course in possession of the whole plan, which had very wide ramifications, and which had indeed been in the main elaborated between the Emperor and myself.[8]

The mission to Halim was a failure, but on his return to France from Arabia Palgrave wrote a report for the Emperor which is still to be found in the archives of the Affaires Étrangères. In it he set forth a detailed plan for a French-directed invasion of Syria from Egypt, which was to result in the union of Egypt with Syria and the control of France over both.

Palgrave's admiration for Napoleon III, like most of his other enthusiasms, was a transitory phenomenon. He later denounced the 'false glitter of the second empire', 'that colossal imposture' overthrown at Sedan'.[9] But while it lasted his commitment was sincere. He seems at the time to have been attracted by the *mission civilisatrice* of French imperialism and perhaps looked in vain for a similar interest on the part of the English. In his *Narrative of a Year's Journey through Central and Eastern Arabia* (1865) he confessed to a 'desire of bringing the stagnant waters of Eastern life into contact with the quickening stream of European progress'.[10] His nationalism appears to have been allied with a cosmopolitanism, like that of Voltaire, which made it possible to serve the interests of any nation which seemed worthy of devotion. In this he was very different from Burton, who could appreciate other cultures, but for whom it was axiomatic that England's interests came first.

The strange expedition, made possible, as Palgrave coyly informed his readers, 'by the liberality of the Emperor of the French', set out for Arabia in 1862. His superiors did not allow him to go alone; Father Elias, a native Syrian Christian who had studied for years in France and Italy, was chosen as his companion. Unfortunately, Father Elias had to be abandoned because of rheumatism and Palgrave, against the wishes of his superiors, chose a young French layman to replace him. The first attempt to penetrate Wahhabi territory failed, and Palgrave returned to Syria and found a new companion, a Syrian Christian whose ordination was hurried along in time for the journey.

In the Jesuit tradition, Palgrave travelled in native dress and conformed as closely as he could to the customs of the country. He set himself up as a Syrian Christian doctor, but made no show of his Christianity, leaving this for the moment when he felt his preaching could safely and productively begin. The name which he chose for himself was 'Seleem Abou Mahmood-el-'Eys', the Quiet One. All of this was in line with usual Jesuit practice. He had some harsh words, obviously aimed at Richard Burton, to say about Europeans who travelled in the East disguised as Moslems, and claimed that though it was dangerous to be known as a European in Arabia it was not dangerous to be known as a Christian. This was hard for many of his compatriots to credit. There has been a persistent belief that Palgrave travelled as a Moslem: Doughty, who travelled in that part of Arabia in 1876, was convinced of it.[11] There can be no doubt, though, of Palgrave's courage in undertaking the journey. Central Arabia at that time was virtually unknown to Europeans, and the Wahhabis might be expected to deal shortly with a Christian missionary.

He went straight down the middle of the peninsula from Maan to Hail, which meant crossing the terrible Nafud, a strip of waterless desert which proved far worse than anything he had ever imagined. His description of the Nafud was ridiculed by ignorant reviewers, but subsequent travellers proved him correct.

We were now traversing an immense ocean of loose reddish sand, unlimited to the eye, and heaped up in enormous ridges running parallel to each other from north to south, undulation after undulation, each swell two or three hundred feet in average height, with slant sides and rounded crests furrowed in every direction by the capricious gales of the desert. In the depths between the traveller finds himself as it were imprisoned in a suffocating sand-pit, hemmed in by burning walls on every side; while at other times, while labouring up the slope, he overlooks what seems a vast sea of fire, swelling under a heavy monsoon wind, and ruffled by a cross-blast into little red-hot waves. Neither shelter nor rest for eye or limb amid torrents of light and heat poured from above on an answering glare reflected below.[12]

91

At Hail, a fortified town of 20,000 people ruled over by Telal ibn Rashid, he was recognized by an acquaintance from Damascus and had to bluff his way out of danger, not altogether successfully as it turned out. On his way to Riyad, the capital of Nejd and the heartland of Wahhabi Islam, he took care to open the letters of recommendation sent with him by Telal and his uncle Obeid. Telal's letter was harmless, but he found that Uncle Obeid was recommending him to the Nejdi monarch as one skilled in magic, a capital crime in that austere theocracy. He destroyed Obeid's letter, without knowing that he had also sent word independently to Abdullah, the eldest son of the Emir Feisal of Nejd, saying that the Syrian doctor was not to be trusted.

At Riyad, where he stayed for a month practising his medical trade, he became dangerously embroiled in court intrigue. Abdullah watched him closely and thought he saw a way of using him for his own ends. One day he sent for Palgrave and asked him to provide him with a quantity of strychnine. Abdullah was at odds with his father and brother, and Palgrave had no doubt as to the poison's intended use. He refused the request, affecting not to understand why Abdullah should wish to acquire the lethal drug. Twice more he was summoned into the presence and confronted with the same request. On the third occasion he went up to Abdullah, lifted up the edge of his head-dress, and whispered: 'Abdullah, I know well what you want the poison for, and I have no mind to be an accomplice to your crimes, nor to answer before God's judgement-seat for what you will have to answer for. You shall *never* have it.' The murderous Wahhabi went black in the face with rage but the subject was not broached again. It was now obvious that Palgrave should find some way to escape from Riyad, but before he could so do he was summoned, alone and at night, for another audience with Abdullah.

He found the heir-apparent in a gloomy chamber lit only by the flickering of firewood burning on the hearth, surrounded by members of the extreme Wahhabi party. After a long silence Abdullah said: 'I now know perfectly well what you are; you are no doctors, you are Christians, spies, and revolutionists . . . come hither to ruin our religion and state in behalf of those who sent you. The penalty for such as you is death . . . and I am determined to inflict it without delay.'

'Istaghfir Allah,' replied Palgrave – 'Ask pardon of God.'

'Why so?' exclaimed Abdullah.

'Because,' said Palgrave, 'you have just now uttered a sheer absurdity. "Christians", be it so; but "spies," "revolutionists," – as if we were not known by everybody in your town for quiet doctors, neither more nor less! And then to talk about putting me to death! You cannot, and you dare not.'

Abdullah called for coffee and a black slave appeared bearing a single ominous cup which he placed in front of Palgrave. Deciding that in view of Abdullah's anxiety to acquire the strychnine the coffee was unlikely to be poisoned, Palgrave drained the cup and said to the slave: 'Pour me out a second.' The bravura performance had its effect and the meeting petered out. A few days later, while the pious inhabitants of Riyad were at their evening prayers, Palgrave and his Syrian companion slipped out of the town and made their escape into the desert. They struck north-east to Bahrein and then southwards again to Oman where Palgrave took ship for Basra. His adventures were not over yet. Just off Oman the ship was caught in a terrible storm and sank. Palgrave was washed ashore at Muscat, where he immediately came down with typhoid fever. When he was well enough he completed the journey to Basra and eventually, by way of Baghdad, returned to Aleppo.

It was an impressive journey by any standards of exploration, with enough adventure to delight a reader of the *Boy's Own Paper*, but there has always been a reluctance on the part of some Englishmen to believe that it was performed at all. It is possible for even a casual reader of the *Narrative* to catch Palgrave out in some apparent inconsistencies, and these slips were made the most of by those who disliked and distrusted him. When he addressed the Royal Geographical Society on his return from Arabia the Rev. G. P. Badger was ready with a volley of geographical queries and criticisms. He was probably the author of a hostile article which later appeared in the *Quarterly Review*. The author of this article, after accusing Palgrave of untruthfully claiming to be the first to explore Nejd, and drawing attention to what he claimed were other exaggerations and inaccuracies, concluded disingenuously that 'we see no sufficient reason to doubt that the outlines of what he depicts from personal observation are for the most part faithfully drawn'.[13] This sparked off a debate about Palgrave's truthfulness which is still going on among afficionados of Arabian exploration: Mea Allen has recently struck a blow for his veracity. His most savage critic has been St John Philby, who concluded from his own explorations of Arabia after the First World War that Palgrave had never been further than Hail. But Philby, too, seems to have got some of his facts wrong, and to have been carried away by his belief that Palgrave's book was simply an alibi for his espionage activities for Napoleon III.[14] The suspicion of spying, not proved until recently, seems to have been the basis of the animus against Palgrave. The author of the *Quarterly Review* article permitted himself an oblique but cutting reference to it: 'By what special means he hoped to bring the stagnant waters [of Eastern life] into contact with the quickening stream, he probably did not feel at liberty to inform us – at all events, we may safely infer that the quickening stream was not to be supplied by this country.' Palgrave himself did not help matters. In the *Narrative* he could not refrain from dropping hints that his journey had some grave import that he was not at liberty to divulge.[15]

He returned from Arabia in 1863 and was eventually given permission by the Jesuits to go to Paris and London. He was told that he would have peace to write his book at the Collegium Maximum at Maria Laach, near Coblenz. While at Maria Laach he heard that the Vatican was not going to reopen the mission in Upper Egypt, and that it had been decided not to send another mission to Arabia. He had pinned his hopes on another Middle East mission and he was furious at what he considered a waste of his knowledge and talents. Palgrave was not one to labour anonymously in the Lord's vineyard. His superiors observed that he was in spiritual difficulties. Eventually he wrote a letter, now unfortunately lost, to Father Beckx, the general of the order in Rome, giving his reasons for being unable to continue as a Jesuit. He went to Berlin and made a public renunciation of Roman Catholicism. Characteristically, he later denounced in print 'the tawdry finery and pious sensuality of the Catholic system'.[16]

Palgrave was clearly not suited to the discipline of the Jesuit order. His commitment to Jesuitry seems to have been too closely associated with an inspiring vision of himself as a missionary to the Arabs. When this was denied him he could not continue with the order. No doubt this disappointment came on the heels of more purely spiritual difficulties, but it is in character that a blow to his ambition should have been the proximate cause of his break with the order. He was worldly enough to believe that 'Christian humility may condemn, as Mahometan humility has frequently done, the vice of pride; but a philosophical mind will hardly be severe in its censure of what is the root of much real gentleness, of noble exertion, of dignity in misfortune, and of moderation in success.'[17]

Nothing seems to be known of the precise nature of the spiritual difficulties Palgrave found himself in on his return from Arabia. Father Michel Jullien, in *La Nouvelle Mission de la Compagnie de Jésus en Syrie, 1831–1895* (1898), surmised that at some point in his journey Palgrave had been forced to make a public profession of Islam.[18] The most likely occasion for this would have been when he and his companion were accused at Riyad of being 'Christians, spies and revolutionists'. It is true that a forced act of apostasy would have produced an explosion of self-doubt, but there is no evidence for it. Palgrave lost his faith – that much is certain – but how it happened and when is impossible to determine. He made a very curious admission in an article published in 1872 that twice in Nejd he had been 'invested for the nonce with the character and duties of Imam, and as such [had] conducted the customary congregational worship'.[19] How a Jesuit missionary, even allowing for the evasions sanctioned by the order in the penetration of a new mission field, came to be preaching in mosques in the most fanatical part of Arabia, is a question that one would dearly like to answer but which is likely to remain unanswered.

There is a possibility that in Arabia Palgrave's religious beliefs experienced strains quite independent of any Moslem pressure. It appears that he was much influenced in his desire to visit Arabia by Lamartine's *Voyage en Orient*.[20] Certainly he expressed at various times ideas very similar to those of Lamartine, and the fact that he took pains to ridicule Lamartine in the *Narrative* suggests, to those familiar with the successive enthusiasms and denunciations of Palgrave's life, that the *Voyage en Orient* had once meant much to him.

Lamartine's book is an account of a religious crisis. In 1821 he had a vision of the spirituality of all matter, striving to become one with God. After this he began rapidly to doubt the orthodox Catholic opinions he had been brought up with.[21] His journey to the Holy Land was undertaken in search of a conclusive religious revelation. He was in no sense sympathetic to Islam in its present form but he became convinced that at successive moments in history the desert had produced a man who established, for a while, 'the pure worship, undefiled by sacrifices, of one immaterial God'. We are familiar with this idea. For Lamartine it was a confirmation of his heretical views. 'Every succeeding age,' he went on, 'lifts a corner of the veil which hides the great presence of the God of Gods, and discovers him behind, under all those symbols which characterize him – alone, eternal, evident throughout nature, and imprinting his oracles on the conscience.'[22] With the publication of *Voyage en Orient* in 1835 he announced his apostasy from the Catholic Church.

Though Palgrave did not touch at all upon his religious opinions in the *Narrative*, in *Hermann Agha*, the Eastern romance which he published in 1872, he presented sympathetically ideas which were very similar to those of Lamartine. The wise Oriental, Tantawee Beg, who is the spiritual mentor of the story's European hero, declares that he believes not in an autocratic God, but in

an intelligent and all-pervading Life, Thought, Act, under countless modes and forms, working on everywhere to higher existence and enjoyment; and perfecting while it pervades them, the manifestations it assumes, and the matter which it vivifies; not as things separate or distinct from itself, but ultimately One, One only with it in the great All of Being.[23]

This is not a view which has ever been acceptable to the Catholic Church, and the suspicion that it was Palgrave's view seems to be confirmed by his later intense attraction to Shintoism, with its emphasis on the spirituality of natural objects. If he was already under the influence of Lamartine when he set out for Arabia it is possible that in the desert he fancied for a moment that he had lifted a corner of that veil of which Lamartine had written, and which few are permitted to see beyond. Perhaps for him the vast and terrifying wastes of the Nafud were not just a geological phenomenon but an awful confirmation of the existence of an all-pervading God.

Palgrave was also in agreement with Lamartine in his loathing of the Bedouin. For English reviewers this was one of the chief novelties of his book. They noted with astonishment how he had turned the traditional portrait of the Bedouin on its head. Their response showed more clearly than anything else could that the Bedouin's public image had become that of the noble Arab.[24]

There were noble Arabs in Palgrave's book, but they were not Bedouin.

The first chapter of the *Narrative,* entitled 'The Desert and its Inhabitants', was a systematic dismemberment of the Bedouin character. One by one Palgrave proceeded to destroy what he regarded as the prevailing fallacies on the subject. The Bedouin were not faithful to pledges; on the contrary they often led astray travellers entrusted to their protection, in order to plunder them. They were not good Moslems but basically sun-worshippers with blasphemy often on their lips. Their manners were appalling. They were hospitable – that much could be granted them – but they were always on the look-out for what they could get out of the guest, and the meat they served was half-raw. It must also be granted that they were not bloodthirsty, but this could be traced to 'the absence of all those national and religious principles which so often in other countries . . . urge men on to bloodshed. The Bedouin does not fight for his home, he has none; nor for his country, that is anywhere; nor for his honour, he has never heard of it; nor for his religion, he owns and cares for none.' The Bedouin were not as people supposed the most genuine type of the Arab race; they were merely 'a degenerate branch of that tree'. Palgrave conceded that there was evidence in the Bedouin of some fine innate qualities (tact, manliness, shrewdness, generosity) but 'he is at best an ill-educated child, whose natural good qualities have remained undeveloped or half stifled by bad treatment and extreme neglect'.[25]

It may be supposed that Palgrave was merely drawing conclusions from his own experience, and, as this included the discovery of a plot by his Bedouin guides to rob him and leave him to die in the Nafud, he was being more consistent than travellers who had similar unpleasant experiences and then produced the same old clichés. But Palgrave 'knew' the Bedouin no better than Burckhardt did. He based his conclusions largely on his observations of his Sherarat guides, members of a tribe which he himself admitted was the 'most miserable' of all the nomad tribes of Arabia.[26] He made little allowance for the confessed narrowness of his experience. He seems to have had an instinctive aversion, reinforced perhaps by his reading of Lamartine, to the notion of the noble savage; he believed in civilization, commerce, and, at this point in his life, progress. He also had little time for the tribal system of Bedouin life, and for a revealing reason.

97

There has been a tendency [he wrote], I hardly know why, to praise the clannish system, and decorate it with the title of 'patriarchal'. But the patriarchs were not a nation, nor even a people; and when the Jewish race did at last become such, one has only to look over their national history from Judges to Chronicles, to find painful evidence that the ruin of Israel was, humanly speaking, owing for the most part to that very clannish spirit which set 'Manasses against Ephraim and Ephraim aganist Manasses, and these together against Judah.'

To make any progress as a race the Arabs would have to abandon tribalism and find a common identity. At present the appearance of national identity was illusory.

The rods, so long as some strong hand binds them together, may seem to unite and form themselves into a single stem; but no sooner is the blending hand withdrawn, than they start asunder, and resume their former severance. Or, to take another and a not inappropriate metaphor, if the elements mix together awhile, it is only mechanically, never chemically.[27]

This is nationalism of an extreme type. No one possessed of a normal unthinking sense of his own identity thinks it desirable for members of a community to fuse together like chemical elements, but to Palgrave the idea of absorption into a greater whole was of overwhelming importance. To be 'One, One only with it in the great All of Being' was one aspect, the religious aspect, of his lifelong quest; to be absorbed into a national community was the other. He was at different times in his life in the service of Great Britain, France and Germany, though the country to which he was most deeply attracted, unfortunately for him, was Japan. To be a part of a meaningful whole, God or country, was for Palgrave not an obliteration but an affirmation of identity. It was as though his fragile ego could not stand alone and unsupported in what was conceived as a struggle for survival. In the long Dantesque poem, *A Vision of Life*, which he wrote in his last years, he described the emergence of individual personalities from the general mass of existence. The punishment for a misspent life (and in this he included failure to rise above the commonplace) was to return to the undifferentiated flux, to be 'fused into indistinct substance', to be merely material for new identities. For Palgrave loss of identity was hell itself.[28]

The firm sense of national identity which he failed to find in the Bedouin he found in the settled Arabs of Nejd. These, and not the Bedouin with their incorrigible localism and individualism, were the true type of the Arab race. Palgrave claimed that the European public had been misinformed on this point, having derived their idea of Arab character from 'materials collected in Syria, Mesopotamia, Egypt, and 'Irāk, perhaps Tunis, Algiers, and Morocco; or at the best in Djiddah and on the Red Sea coast'. The inhabitants of these countries, despite the fact that they spoke Arabic, were not Arabs. They were

a mixture of Curdes, Turcomans, Syrians, Phoenicians, Armenians, Berbers, Greeks, Turks, Copts, Albanians, Chaldaeans, not to mention the remnants of other and older races, with a little, a very little Arab blood, one in twenty at most, and that little rediluted by local and territorial influences . . . These unlucky and much talked of Bedouins in the Syrian, also miscalled Arabian, desert, are in fact only hybrids, crosses between Turcoman and Curdish tribes, with a small and questionable infusion of Arab blood, and that too none of the best, like a wine-glass of thin claret poured into a tumbler of water. In short, among these races, town or Bedouin, we have no real authentic Arabs. Arabia and Arabs begin south of Syria and Palestine, west of Baṣrah and Zobeyr, east of Kerak and the Red Sea. Draw a line across from the top of the Red Sea to the top of the Persian Gulf; what is below that line is alone Arab: and even then do not reckon the pilgrim route, it is half Turkish; nor Medinah, it is cosmopolitan; nor the sea-coast of Yemen, it is Indo-Abyssinian; least of all Mecca, the common sewer of Mahometans of all kinds, nations, and lands, and where every trace of Arab identity has long since been effaced by promiscuous immorality and the corruption of ages. Mascat and Ḳaṭeef must also stand with Mokha and 'Aden on the list of exceptions.[29]

This extraordinary tour de force of racial classification tells us far more about the nature of Palgrave's obsessions than the nature of the Arab race. He demonstrates a concern with blood more extreme even than that of Burton; Burton had been nothing like as stringent in his definition of the Arab. He also displays a rather paradoxical concern with cultural rather than simply genetic criteria of national identity. Using terminology similar to that employed in *A Vision of Life* to describe the death of the individual personality he implies that the Meccans have lost their Arab identity through sinfulness. This suggests a fundamental confusion in Palgrave's thinking about race, nationality and personal identity. The mark of blood is not indelible as it should be if it is to be worthy of the importance attached to it; on the contrary genetic endowment can be so fully counterbalanced by culture and behaviour as to be reduced to insignificance. This is the paradox whose implications for Palgrave's prolonged crisis of identity were never fully confronted until very late in his life. If right action is what matters, what is the point of being concerned with Jewishness,

Englishness, or any other genetic component of individuality? Universalist Christian ethics can never be logically squared with racism and nationalism, and Palgrave's parallel obsessions were a fertile source of conflict for him throughout most of his life.

The passage quoted above also reveals Palgrave's pride and ambition. It followed from such an exercise that he was one of very few people, perhaps indeed the only European, competent to hold opinions on the subject of Arab character. Having defined away the competition he is left in full possession of the field. He also seems genuinely to have felt that by virtue of having penetrated to the very centre of Arabia he had discovered the 'real' Arab. Almost everything seen by previous travellers, he wrote, was only the outer surface – 'of the interior, whether physical or moral, they have less to tell'.[30] We have already seen in earlier writers the tendency to identify geographical remoteness with moral and physical superiority. Like the psychoanalytic idea that the 'real' self lies deeply concealed in our innermost mental life, this is one of those crocks of gold at the end of the rainbow that seem to be an indispensable adjunct to much human thought.

For many subsequent travellers, to reach Nejd was the sine qua non of successful Arabian travel. The Blunts were lured there by Palgrave's narrative.[31] For some reason the inhabitants of the south, whose authenticity as Arabs Palgrave was also willing to affirm, never quite caught on in the same way. Perhaps Palgrave's own glowing account of the Nejdi was responsible. The inhabitant of Nejd, he wrote, was

patient, cool, slow in preparing his means of action, more tenacious than any bulldog when he has once laid hold, attached to his ancestral uses and native land by a patriotism rare in the East, impatient in the highest degree of foreign rule, sober almost to austerity in his mode of life, averse to the luxury and display of foreign nations, nay, stranger still, to their very vices . . .

What was more, he fully understood 'the important truth that self-restraint is the first condition of being a gentleman'. A Nejdi, Palgrave assured his readers, 'makes it his boast to put up with rudeness and passion, and considers the bearing such with equability and composure to be the test-proof of superiority in character and good-breeding'.[32] The resemblance to our old friend 'the English gentleman' will be instantly apparent, and indeed the best known of all the purple passages in Palgrave's book is the one in which he describes the Arabs, in their finest manifestation, as 'the English of the Oriental world'.

A strong love and a high appreciation of national and personal liberty, a hatred of minute interference and special regulations, a great respect for authority so long as it be decently well exercised, joined with a remarkable freedom from anything like caste-feeling in what concerns ruling families and dynasties; much practical good sense, much love of commercial enterprise, a great readiness to undertake long journeys and voluntary expatriation by land and sea in search of gain and power; patience to endure, and perseverance in the employment of means to ends, courage in war, vigour in peace, and lastly, the marked predominance of a superior race over whomever they come in contact with among their Asiatic or African neighbours, a superiority admitted by these last as a matter of course and an acknowledged right; – all these are features hardly less characteristic of the Englishman than of the Arab; yet that these are features distinctive of the Arab nation, taken, of course, on its more favourable side, will hardly, I think, be denied by any experienced and unprejudiced man.[33]

The Arabs, like the English, were a master race. When most of Palgrave's careful distinctions between Bedouins and townsmen, Nejdis and Syrians, and so on were forgotten by all but connoisseurs of the subject, the notion that Arabs were a superior race (superior at least to other Orientals) somehow remained, though couched usually in less extravagant terms. It says something perhaps about the basic un-Englishness of Palgrave's own temperament that the *Westminster Review*, in discussing the passage, did not quote it, but offered instead a homely paraphrase.[34]

In Arabia Palgrave discovered a ruler who seemed to him to combine all the princely virtues. In this he was the forerunner of the Blunts and St John Philby, who each in their own way developed an extravagant admiration for a particular Arabian prince. The object of his admiration was Telal ibn Rashid, the ruler of Jebel Shammar. He compared favourably in the arts of government with any other ruler, European or Asiatic, that Palgrave had ever known.

Affable towards the common people [the sonorous roll-call of his qualities began], reserved and haughty with the aristocracy, courageous and skilful in war, a lover of commerce and building in time of peace, liberal even to profusion, yet always careful to maintain and augment the state revenue, neither over strict nor yet scandalously lax in religion, secret in his designs, but never known to break a promise once given, or violate a plighted faith, severe in administration, yet averse to bloodshed, he offered the very type of what an Arab prince should be.

He made it his business to subdue the Bedouin in his domain, made the roads safe for travellers, and encouraged merchants to establish themselves at Hail.[35] In his devotion to an orderly urban life and in his qualities of leadership Telal exemplified for Palgrave the most developed type of Arab. The Arabian Bedouin, though of the same stock and possessing a substratum of fine qualities, had, through the harshness of their existence and their extreme isolation from improving influences, degenerated from this ideal.[36]

Palgrave went on to assert that Telal, simply by virtue of being 'an Arab governing Arabs after their own native Arab fashion', possessed a legitimacy as a ruler and a potential for creating happiness which no Ottoman administrator could have. It followed that the chief hope for Asia, 'at least as much of it as lies between Kara-Dagh and 'Aden', was in the 'redintegration of its nationality', or, to put it anachronistically, in self-determination.[37] It is difficult to believe that Palgrave was entirely serious in this suggestion in view of his involvement in a plan for French control of Syria. Perhaps he was simply carried away momentarily by his admiration for Telal. In any case he seems to have been perfectly sincere in his admiration for Telal's instinctive grasp of the arts of government. English reactions to his proposals for national redintegration in Asia were mixed, ranging from an ominous fraternal concern on the part of the *Westminster Review* (which felt that Englishmen would be moved 'to meditate gloomily on those trackless deserts which shut off so mighty a people from the ken and help of their kind') to the indignant response of *Blackwood's*, which demanded to know where the redintegration of nationality, once started, would stop.[38]

Palgrave himself had no doubt that the Arabs, once they had shaken themselves free of the stultifying grip of Islam, of the cultural influence of Turks and Persians (the latter 'essentially and irretrievably rotten'), and of the tribal system, were well equipped to take their place in the modern industrial world. They were 'hardly less adapted "to the railroad, to the steam-ship," or any other nineteenth-century invention or natural research than the natives of Sheffield or Birmingham themselves'.[39] This was, and remains, an unusual opinion on the part of an Englishman.

Palgrave did not remain convinced of the virtue of technology, or the desirability of its adoption by Eastern races. In his disillusioned old age he fulminated against the 'Patriarchs of Steam and Rail' who had interfered with Nature in order to construct a world where Man would reign supreme, and against the inventor of the telegraph who had broken the barriers 'wisely set between nations'.[40]

When Palgrave broke with the Jesuits he had to find some other outlet for his talents. Apparently, continued service with Napoleon III was out of the question; whether because of a change of heart on Palgrave's part, or of a rebuff from the Emperor, is not known. While in Berlin he began, inevitably, to develop an interest in Bismarck. When a senior official in the Prussian government offered him the consulship at Mosul he was delighted by the chance to use his knowledge and accepted. Then another, more tempting opportunity came up. While in London he had offered his services to negotiate for the release of the English captives being held in Ethiopia by the mad King Theodore. When the offer was accepted by the Foreign Office he sent in his resignation as consul at Mosul. He arrived in Egypt en route for Ethiopia and then sat there for a year while contradictory instructions flowed back and forth. Eventually news came that a previous envoy, Hormuzd Rassam, had effected the release of the prisoners – he had in fact joined the others in prison – and Palgrave was recalled. When he arrived back in England he was appointed consul at Soukhoum-Kalé in Anatolia. It was scarcely a glorious position.

While in England he fell in love with Clara Jekyll, the ward of Sir Francis Goldsmid, a distant relation. She eventually married Lord Henley and her disappointed suitor, apparently in love for the first time, consoled himself with writing *Hermann Agha*, a conventional Oriental romance ('One kiss, Zahra!') which is chiefly of interest for the light it seems to shed on its author's religious views. Palgrave's future literary productions were confined mostly to essays on the various countries to which the Foreign Office saw fit to send him.

The list of his postings does not suggest any eagerness on the part of the British government to utilize his well-advertised talents. In 1867, after leaving Soukhoum-Kalé, he became consul at Trebizond; in 1873 he was consul at St Thomas; later in 1873, consul in Manila; in 1878 he was consul-general in Sofia; in 1879 consul-general in Bangkok; and finally, in 1884, British Minister in Uruguay. Perhaps, like his former superiors in the Society of Jesus, his superiors in the Foreign Office were doubtful of his loyalty and stability. The accusations of spying for the French which were bandied about at the time of his return from Arabia cannot have been easily forgotten. Also, Palgrave did himself no good by his tendency to act independently of instructions. He was dismissed from Sofia because Disraeli disapproved of his conduct towards the Austrians; in Bangkok he was rebuked by London for discussing with the King the establishment of a legation and the revision of the treaty of 1874; in Montevideo he infuriated the Foreign Office by selling the British Cemetery to the mayor and moving the bodies to a site outside the city. Like Burton, he was not cut out to be a diplomat. 'Give me Gifford Palgrave,' General Gordon is reported to have said, 'and I will govern the Arabs!'[41] Gordon wanted Palgrave appointed British Minister to Cairo, but the British government did not see its way to awarding him this plum.

The essays Palgrave published during his diplomatic career are collected together in two books, *Essays on Eastern Questions* (1872) and *Ulysses, or Scenes and Studies in Many Lands* (1887). They show his increasing preoccupation with the relationship between religion and nationality. In *Essays on Eastern Questions* he frequently observes that in the East nationality and religion are virtually synonymous. Though he does not always distinguish clearly between nationality and race, his discussion of the phenomenon is interesting and sophisticated, his perceptions being sharpened perhaps by the obsessive nature of his interest in the subject. During his years in the Far East he became convinced that every nation must have its spiritual symbols, in the way St James of Compostella was a spiritual symbol for Spain, for 'the nation that has not these, however abundant in mechanical inventions, and the grosser forms of ungraceful wealth, is a mere association of ignoble aims and deeds, a banded rabble of vulgar enterprise and selfish adventurers, nothing more'. In Canton he found 'a priesthood kept within its proper limits of ceremonial observances and national rites, [not] permitted to arrogate overweening dictation to the minds and souls of men . . .'[42]

The final revelation came during a visit to Japan. His article on Kyoto, which is reprinted in *Ulysses*, is pervaded by a serenity which contrasts strikingly with the knowingness and petulance which spoil much of his earlier writing. In the contemplation of the religious life of Japan Palgrave briefly experienced spiritual rest.

Shintoism seems to have possessed a double appeal for him.

First of all, it postulated 'the correlation, if not the absolute identity, of all natural and external forms, man included, with spiritual or divine powers'. Secondly, and perhaps more importantly, the nature-worship which was Shintoism's fundamental precept was allied with a cult of the sacred Japanese race. The object of veneration was Japan itself, in all its aspects, from the Mikado to the leaves on the trees.

Japanese nationality and Shinto [Palgrave concluded] are in truth one thing – nay, the latter is to all intents the summed-up expression, the concentrated essence of the former, living with its life, decaying with its decay, not to be divided from it but by death, the death of both. Born together, they will perish, if perish they must, together; the death-note, as the birth-note, of Shinto and Japan is one.

The proof of Shinto's moral value was to be found in Japan itself, in

the wonderfully high degree of true civilisation, that is of honour, of courage, of social self-respect, of regard for others, of reverence for authority, age, and learning, of delicate artistic sense and practice, of subordination, of organised government, of courtesy, of cleanliness, of industry, that she has in long ages, guiltless of Europe and all its works, developed for herself and out of herself . . .[43]

Here was the simple unity of race, nationality and religion which Palgrave, with his Jewish ancestry and disastrous experiments with Catholicism, had left far behind. In Japan he beheld it in all its perfection, and found it magnetically attractive. But this was an ideal community of which he could never be a part; by its very nature Shintoism is not a proselytizing religion.

More than half of *A Vision of Life* was written in Japan, and in its exaltation of patriotism it clearly shows the influence of Shintoism on Palgrave's receptive mind. In the first part of the poem he imagines himself joining the true patriots of ages past in the shining city where they live on in eternal splendour. Thus he escapes the horror of extinction, achieves his apotheosis as a patriot, and is rewarded in heaven if not on earth. It is evident that his patriotism has been soured and driven into the realm of fantasy by his failure to make his mark in public life, and though he is still proud of England's imperial power ('O England! O my country! thou whose birth / To Greece, to Rome, a nobler sister gave, / Empress of nations, crown of the whole earth . . .') he is convinced that England herself is in decline. He now sees her industry as a blight on the land, and fears that the triumph of democratic ideas will complete the ruin that technology has begun.[44] His experience of Japan apparently brought home to him the ugliness of Western industrial civilization.

After his transfer to Montevideo the poem takes on a rather more Christian tone as he begins, for reasons unknown to us, to become reconciled to the Catholic Church. He seems to have decided that nationalism did not after all provide the spiritual nourishment he required and in the last year of his life he was again actively practising the Catholic religion. He received the last sacraments and was buried in a Catholic cemetery. Before he died he experienced a mystical union with Christ, which he described in the last cantos of *A Vision of Life*.

> Me too those hands contained, that beauty drew
> Never to sunder more; in him the want
> Summed and complete; the vision sealed and true.[45]

All previous attempts at identification with a greater whole were thus triumphantly superseded and Palgrave the disappointed patriot went to his grave convinced of his final unity with God.

In the full context of Palgrave's sad and puzzling life it becomes apparent that though he is best known for his Arabian journey the Arabs were but a way-station on his long spiritual and emotional Odyssey. Were it not for his hatred of the Moslem religion he might have found in Arabia, in the domain of Telal ibn Rashid, the ideal community of which he dreamed.

In spite of the naturally imperialist bent of his mind Palgrave seems to have considered the possibility that a man like Telal, a paragon of all the Arab virtues, might reasonably be left to get on with the job of governing his own people. He never fully articulated this view, if indeed it was his view, but what he said about the little court of Jebel Shammar contained the germ of the idea, to be developed explicitly by his admirer Wilfrid Blunt, that the 'true Arabs' were somehow an exception to the White Man's Burden.

5

Wilfrid Scawen Blunt

(1840–1922)

I like the hunting of the hare;
New sports I hold in scorn.
I like to be as my fathers were,
In the days ere I was born.

W. S. Blunt, *The Old Squire*

WILFRID BLUNT was the first Englishman to take up a lance for the Arabs. He went beyond admiration to the active pursuit of what he conceived to be their interests. Unlike Palgrave he seems to have had no overwhelming early interest in them; rather, Arabia came into his life when he needed it.

He was born into the aristocracy, the younger son of Francis Scawen Blunt of Crabbet Park, Master of Hounds and squire of four thousand Sussex acres. When Blunt was only two his father died and Crabbet had to be let. He was not to know a permanent home until he inherited Crabbet on the death of his brother in 1872. In 1892 he published a long poem, the sonnet sequence *Esther*, which contains his only published reference to the circumstances of his father's death. It is so bizarre that it might easily be dismissed as fantasy were it not for the indisputably autobiographical context in which it occurs. *Esther* chiefly describes, with a few insignificant distortions of detail, Blunt's youthful affair with the courtesan Catherine Walters, and the reference to his father's death is embedded in an otherwise demonstrably factual narrative of his childhood. It is difficult to avoid the conclusion that the following lines, with their strange combination of vague suggestion and precise detail, are more than the product of a mischievous imagination.

107

8 Wilfrid Blunt as a young man

You know the story of my birth, the name
Which I inherited for good and ill,
The secret of my father's fame and shame,
His tragedy and death on that dark hill.
You know at least what the world knows or knew,
For time has taken half the lookers-on,
As it took him, and leaves his followers few,
And those that loved him scarce or almost none.
To me, his son, there had remained the story,
Told and retold by her who knew it best,
A mystery of love, perhaps of glory,
A heritage to hold and a bequest.
Ah, how it loved him, that sad woman's heart,
What faith was hers and what a martyr's part!

In another stanza he writes of his youth being overshadowed by 'duty of revenge some day for blood', and of being set apart from his fellow men by 'a whole legend of romance sublime, / Perhaps by the dead virtue of a crime'.[1]

The almost certain knowledge that his subject spent his early life under the shadow of a great but obscure tragedy, ambiguously referred to in terms suggestive of high romance and low scandal, puts a psychologically-inclined biographer in a difficult position, especially when, as in the present case, no previous writer has aired such suspicions. Blunt's biographers, and others who have written memoirs of him, have without exception failed to mention the existence of these verses.[2] It would be only too easy to misinterpret them or exaggerate their significance, yet to disregard them might be to throw away the key to a man's life. The feeling of singularity which permeated Blunt's whole existence and which is crucial to any understanding of his behaviour and opinions is evident throughout his published works. It must have had a cause, or causes, and Blunt's assertions that the circumstances of his father's death, and the events consequent upon it, set him apart from his fellow men will be taken at their face value.

When Francis Blunt died his children were left wards in Chancery and Crabbet was entailed on the elder son, Francis. After Crabbet had to be let, the children and their mother moved in with their Wyndham relations at Petworth. Here they were surrounded by the luxurious and worldly atmosphere of one of the greatest of English country houses, but whatever pleasures and security Petworth afforded were not to be enjoyed for long. After only a year they began a wandering life in England and on the continent. In later life Wilfrid Blunt felt this to have been 'a considerable misfortune . . . It almost seems as if the ideal life ought to begin and end under the same roof tree.'[3] In 1847 the two boys were sent off to a private school at Twyford which Blunt remembered fifty-two years later as 'a mere hell upon earth'. It gave him satisfaction to record in his diary for 1 December 1899 that he had received a letter 'from old Roberts who used to cane me . . ., begging piteously for pheasants to eat in his old age'.[4] The boys were removed from Twyford in 1849 after Wilfrid fell seriously ill and the family spent that winter on the continent. In 1851 the boys were expecting to go to Harrow, when their mother announced to them that they would travel to Italy with a tutor instead. On arrival at Boulogne she explained to them that she had entered the Roman Catholic Church at Easter. Edith Finch has recorded that on hearing the news the children, 'filled with unspeakable shame, burst into tears'.

In the years since her husband's death Mrs Blunt had begun moving tentatively towards Catholicism. She was a friend of Archbishop Manning and when he entered the Catholic Church in 1851 she followed him. The children were told nothing of their mother's spiritual difficulties. Rather than face the problem of their religious instruction she left them alone. The result was that they imbibed their religious ideas from a Calvinistic Scottish nurse who damned Papists and regaled them with tales of hell-fire.

By the end of the winter the 'conversion' of the children had been accomplished by the tutor. At Aix-en-Provence they were received into the Catholic Church. Wilfrid's religious feelings were deeply aroused during the period when he was being prepared by the Jesuits for his first communion. He became, so far as this is possible for a child of twelve, a devout Catholic.[5] It was an emotional commitment, not an intellectual one. Later on the intellectual difficulties of Catholicism became too great for him to continue as a practising Catholic, but he retained his emotional need for religion. To the end of his life he had 'a belief in holy places and holy people quite apart from all religious creeds'.[6]

In January 1853 the boys were sent to Stonyhurst but were shortly afterwards removed to Oscott. They were at Oscott when their mother died in June 1853. Though they continued at Oscott the holidays were spent with the Wyndhams, now their guardians, in the secular atmosphere of Petworth. In 1856 Charles Meynell came to teach at Oscott and Wilfrid found in him a mentor who was able to convince him that Catholicism was intellectually as well as emotionally true. At this stage of his life his emotional attachment to the Catholic Church was profound. The Church became a strong and loving parent in the place of his adored but distant mother, now tragically lost, and the father he had hardly known.

> The Church became
> My guardian next and mother deified,
> Who lit within me a more subtle flame
> Of constancy, and clothed me in her mood.
> No sound, no voice within that sanctuary
> Told me of common evil. Unsubdued
> And vast and strange, a thing from which to flee,
> The world lay there without us. We within,
> Fenced in and folded safe in our strong home,
> Knew nothing of the sorrow and the sin.
> 'Tis no small matter to have lived in Rome,
> In the Church's very bosom and abode,
> Cloistered and cradled there, a child of God.[7]

By the time he left Oscott and entered the diplomatic service in 1858 he was possessed of a strong sense of singularity. His parents' deaths and his Catholic upbringing had marked him off from his kind.

> Thus through these griefs I had been set apart,
> As for a double priesthood.[8]

The word 'priesthood' seems to imply a special blessedness, but Blunt recalls that at this time he was experiencing the most painful anxiety.

> I saw Mankind a tribe, my natural foe,
> Whom I must one day battle with; and Woman,
> Ah! Woman was a snare I did not know . . .
> Man, only Man I feared with eyes bent down,
> Man the oppressor, who with pale lips curled,
> Sheds blood in the high places of the world.[9]

He was conscious of himself as someone special, yet this special-ness was full of ambiguity. It gave him both a sense of superiority and a terrible feeling of being an outsider.

His religion eventually became a casualty of his anxiety about being different. 'I began,' he wrote, '. . . to find my religious profession, even among Catholics, in many ways irksome; . . . for in early youth there are few things which a sensitive person feels more keenly than any singularity, whether it is of person or mind, or even of dress.'[10] In the diplomatic service, especially in Germany, he met for the first time people who openly aired their scepticism about the Christian religion; at the British Embassy in Frankfurt Darwin was the talk of the day. Blunt wrote to his confessor in England for permission to read *The Origin of Species*, *Essays and Reviews*, and *Vestiges of Creation*. When permission was refused he read them anyway and his reading deepened the doubts he had begun to feel. Then his sister, to whom he was devoted, became a nun. Now the Church, not mankind, became his enemy. He went to England and persuaded her to postpone her decision for a year. After this his doubts became overwhelming and 'from looking on God as my enemy, I began to disbelieve in his existence altogether'.[11]

By 1863, when he was transferred to the embassy at Paris, he had abandoned the Christian religion. He became the lover of the intelligent and vivacious Catherine Walters, and his passion for her absorbed for a time all his capacity for emotional commitment. Religion was set aside and love enthroned in its place. 'Skittles' was the first of many mistresses; Blunt was an extremely handsome man and kept until old age his ability to attract women. He was associated with the Souls, the group of Edwardian aristocrats who devoted themselves to the pleasures of love and conversation.

He was married in 1869 to Lady Anne Noel, the granddaughter of Lord Byron, and resigned from the diplomatic service. Lady Anne was an unusual woman – prim and scholarly (it was she who made the literal translation of the Moallakat on which Blunt based his English verse rendering) and inclined in later life to be mildly eccentric. She was a capable horsewoman and a reliable but unimaginative companion on the Arabian journeys. For some reason it was her accounts of these journeys which were published. Blunt merely contributed chapters to her rather pedestrian narratives; his own accounts came later, in his published diaries. In 1870 she gave birth to a son who died when he was four days old. Later a daughter, Judith, was born, but Blunt never ceased to regret his lack of a male heir. His poem *Worth Forest* describes how he heard the news of his child's death as he was walking in the forest with the nurse, explaining to her the history of his family, whose name the child was to carry on. The death of his heir was followed two years later by the deaths, within a few months of each other, of his sister and brother. On the death of his brother he inherited the Crabbet estates.

By the time Blunt was thirty-three his parents, his sister, his brother, and his son were all dead. He was also affected deeply by the death of Helen Leutwein, a girl he had fallen in love with while he was with the British Embassy in Athens. She died in his second year there. He himself had been near death more than once. It was hardly surprising that one of the religious issues which tormented him was whether or not there was a life after death. When he first encountered the Bedouin their attitude to the hereafter was one of the things he found most attractive about them. To understand why this was so it is necessary to know something of his prolonged struggle with the Christian doctrine of heaven and hell.

On the one hand Blunt seems to have wanted some assurance of personal immortality, and on the other hand to have been terrified of hell. His Calvinist nurse and Jesuit teachers had made the latter very vivid to him.[12] When he went out into the world and began to experience religious doubts and worldly temptations the fear of damnation was one of the things which made it psychologically impossible for him to drift painlessly away from religion. He had to persuade himself that by succumbing to his doubts he would not incur the penalty of hell. In order to do this he had to prove that hell did not exist, and in order to prove that there was no hell he had first to prove decisively that there was no God. If he merely turned away from God without disproving his existence he would surely be damned. In 1861 he wrote a paper expounding materialism and arguing that there was no need to bring in the existence of a personal God to explain the laws of the universe; they just were. This was a way out of his difficulties, but he seems to have been unable to stick to his brave new materialism and in the next fifteen years his need to believe reasserted itself periodically. Once, during a serious illness in Athens, he was nursed by a Sister of Charity and for a time regained his belief.

In 1876 he made one last attempt to believe, or perhaps to put belief behind him. He wrote to Charles Meynell, his tutor at Oscott, asking him to provide him with intellectual proofs of the Christian religion, specifically of the existence of a personal God and of a future life. The ensuing correspondence was published in 1878 as *Proteus and Amadeus*. Blunt was 'Proteus', and the choice of pseudonym (which he also used for publishing his first book of poems in 1875) seems to express a confused sense of identity. At the age of thirty-six he had not managed to sort out his religious position, and though he had dabbled with considerable natural facility in the arts of poetry, painting, sculpture and architecture, and had tried his hand at diplomacy, he had not yet settled on a career. He felt that a crisis had been reached in his life. 'The fact is,' he wrote to Meynell, 'I am just now at that point in life where, the fever and the fret of youth being mostly spent, I am looking round me for some means of making a composition with my soul's creditors, and resettling the little that is left to me of my intellectual estate.'[13] It is hard to imagine a better description of what is now fashionably known as a mid-life crisis.

To illustrate his position he used an interesting parable.

There was a young man, the son of a great lord, and heir to a great estate, who, tempted of the devil, or his own vanity, and having access to the muniment room in his father's castle, looked one day into the box which held the title deeds and registers of his descent. Of these the young man found that some were missing, others obscure or tampered with, and some again which cast suspicion on his birth. In deep concern, and troubled by this doubt, he goes to the family lawyer, a prudent man, who shakes his head, assures him that his claim will never be disputed, and bids him hold his tongue and enjoy without more ado the property, as soon as it shall be his. But the young man is too unhappy for this, and with the mystery uncleared refuses to take again his place as son and heir. Then, having argued all the case, and become convinced that he is in truth no nobleman's heir, but a gipsy's son, he leaves his home for ever, and his name and titles and his father's roof, and seeks to gain an unhappy living by telling fortunes and stealing fowls.

He goes from bad to worse, and is brought at last to justice. Then, as he sits upon the prison floor, loaded with chains, and with his own bitter thoughts for company, he sees how grievously he has erred, throwing his life away, and bewails his folly. To have been content with ignorance had been better wisdom; but how undo the past, how force back faith to its old channels, and believe again in his lost estate? Then too (may I say it?) in his distress a wise man comes, an expert, a reader of genealogical riddles, a decypherer of manuscripts. The missing papers are restored. The register shewn to be a forgery, and the young man, restored in blood, and proved once more to be the son of a lord, is let out of prison, (for such is the custom of the country), and lives an honest life happy for ever after.

All of which means that I would give everything I possess for a reasonable excuse to abandon reason, or better still, to find a cure for my madness in reason itself, a hair of the dog that bit me.[14]

This tale has a number of peculiarities but the most striking is the use of the metaphor of inheritance to describe faith and its loss. It is not one which would occur to many people, even Catholics accustomed to pious references to the believer as a 'child of God', but it seems to have occurred readily to Blunt, for he used it often. The insistence with which it finds its way into his writings is striking. We have already seen his reference to his 'intellectual estate'. In *The Love Sonnets of Proteus* we find the following lines in a sonnet entitled 'The Pride of Unbelief'.

> Yet, strange rebellion! I, but yesterday,
> Was God's own son in His own likeness bred.
> And thrice strange pride! who thus am cast away
> And go forth lost and disinherited.[15]

And in Sonnet XXI of *Esther*:

> Nature designed me for a life above
> The mere discordant dreams in which I live.
> If I now go a beggar on the Earth
> I was a saint of Heaven by right of birth.[16]

At the end of his life he reverted to the disinheritance metaphor to describe his feelings after writing the paper on materialism in 1861.

I found myself as it were deprived of my soul's birthright, proved to be no lawful heir; no child of God with Heaven for my inheritance and eternal bliss for my reward, but just a common 'by-blow' of Nature, undistinguishable from her humblest offspring the thousand and one forms of the brute beasts that perish – a humiliating and demoralizing thought.[17]

For Blunt this metaphor obviously possessed a compelling force. It enabled him to express the fact that his inability to believe was a blow to his pride. Though it would be wrong to say that his religion meant no more to him than the specialness he felt it conferred, when he lost his faith it seems to have been this specialness which he regretted more than anything else.

When we remember the overwhelming shame with which Blunt and his brother and sister received the news of their mother's conversion it seems strange that he should ever have come to perceive his Catholicism as a source of pride. It had been thrust upon him at a time when he appears to have been already weighed down by a sense of being different from other people. The 'secret' of his father's death, the necessity of letting Crabbet, the family's wandering life, had all deprived him of a normal unselfconscious

115

feeling of belonging. Catholicism at first can only have added to his woes, but his eventual response seems to have been to make the best of it. Whether he liked it or not he was different from other members of his class and he took refuge in a romantic notion that his singularity was not a liability but an asset, marking him off from the common herd.

This solution worked tolerably well so long as he was at school and able to draw strength from a Catholic environment. When he left school the tension between his conviction of being special and his anxiety about his isolation from his kind assumed unmanageable proportions. He was receptive to the articulate doubt of his sophisticated companions and the intellectual foundations of his faith were rapidly eroded. But his emotional attachment to the Church was not easily put aside. By persuading himself that a special distinction was conferred by belief, he had put himself in a position where to abandon belief was to abandon a claim to superiority which was of the utmost emotional importance to him. This was one difficulty. His fear of hell was another. The final difficulty standing in the way of rational unbelief was guilt about betraying an institution which had been father and mother to him after he was left an orphan in the world.

This feeling that the Church was his parent, and no ordinary parent but a spiritual aristocrat imparting distinction to her sons, explains Blunt's use of the disinheritance metaphor, but it does not exhaust its significance. It came so naturally to him because he also had a more worldly feeling of disinheritance. His father had been the squire of four thousand acres but his death had robbed his children of their normal enjoyment of their birthright. They spent their early days, not securely at the apex of the little social pyramid formed by an English landowner, his dependants, his employees and his tenants, but as vagabonds of rather ambiguous status, wandering unpredictably from country to country and from house to house.

When he eventually inherited Crabbet Blunt entered with extraordinary relish into the role of squire. He identified himself passionately with his land and took pride in carrying on what he conceived to be the best traditions of the squirearchy.

> The lags, the gills, the forest ways,
> The hedgerows one and all,

These are the kingdoms of my chase,
And bounded by my wall;

Nor has the world a better thing,
Though one should search it round,
Than thus to live one's own sole king,
Upon one's own sole ground.[18]

He found in his early birthright a more secure foundation for his sense of specialness than in religious belief: the fact that he was squire, unlike the book of Genesis, was not open to dispute. Nevertheless he always displayed a self-consciousness about his position which suggests that the old wounds never completely healed. In his books he never tired of discussing the virtues, rights and duties of the aristocracy, and a number of writers, including himself, have testified to the archaic and patriarchal manner in which he ran his estate. The old gaffers in smocks, the agent with his 'Yes, Squire', 'No, Squire', 'Certainly Squire, O certainly', were all part of the almost ludicrously aristocratic ambience which he created for himself.[19]

When he initiated the correspondence with Meynell in 1876 he was in the process of abandoning Catholicism for squiredom. His unresponsiveness to Meynell's intelligent arguments, which allowed a very wide latitude of belief, suggests that the correspondence was largely a *rite de passage*. Blunt constantly shifted his ground and raised new difficulties until Meynell finally had no choice but to abandon him to the grace of God. Twenty-eight years later, when discussing *Proteus and Amadeus* in a letter to his friend Father Gerard, Blunt admitted that he had always considered 'the psychological proofs of religion' to be a much stronger argument 'that those founded on material nature'.[20]

He continued all his life to feel the psychological attraction of religion and also to be concerned with immortality in one form or another. Though he abandoned his belief in a life beyond the grave he was concerned that his name should live on in an heir or in some 'personal school where my name has authority'.[21] His failure in both these respects hurt him deeply. The thought of total extinction, which he had to accept intellectually in order to eliminate the possibility of damnation, was hard to bear for a man as self-absorbed as Blunt.

117

This long prologue has been necessary to show the state of mind Blunt was in on the eve of his involvement with the Arabs. A year after he concluded the correspondence with Meynell he and his wife set off on the journey to Mesopotamia which resulted in their book, *Bedouin Tribes of the Euphrates*. Blunt contributed a preface, a postscript, and six chapters on various aspects of Bedouin life.

The Blunts had already visited Turkey, Algeria, Egypt and Syria in the years between 1874 and 1876, but this was their first attempt to venture away from the beaten track, and it was also their first real experience of Bedouin life. They were both enchanted by what they saw and Wilfrid had his first intimation of a mission in life, a task which would take him beyond the narrow though delightful world of squiredom into the larger sphere of public life. In *Bedouin Tribes of the Euphrates* his 'first political views in regard to Arabian liberty' can be found.[22]

The journey to Mesopotamia took the Blunts among the Anaza, Ruwalla and Shammar tribes. After the publication of *Bedouin Tribes of the Euphrates* these latter tribes, along with the Anaza who had been praised so warmly by Burckhardt, began to take on a certain cachet as tribes for the connoisseur. It was the Shammar sheik, Faris, with his beautiful manners and ease of bearing, who typified for the Blunts the best the desert had to offer. They had no hesitation in according him the supreme compliment: he was 'that thing we have been looking for, but hardly hoped to get a sight of, a *gentleman* of the desert'.[23]

The Blunts' approach to the Bedouin was an odd mixture of uncertainty and arrogance. They expected to be received with the deference they felt was appropriate to their rank and yet were anxious to earn Bedouin esteem. 'In the Desert man meets man' Richard Burton had said. Would they measure up?

Their first encounter with the Shammar was a momentous event for them and they treated it with suitable solemnity. Lady Anne describes the occasion.

We . . . saw below us a scattered camp of about twenty-five tents, a great number of camels and a few mares, perhaps half a dozen. I got on my mare, so as to arrive with becoming dignity; and Wilfrid . . . put on a sword which he has been keeping for state occasions. Mr.S—[the British consul at Aleppo] had told us what to do, and how to behave among the Bedouins; but we both, I think, felt rather shy at this our first visit, arriving as strangers and unannounced. Nobody came to

9   Faris, sheikh of the Shammar, drawn by Lady Anne Blunt

meet us or seemed to pay the least attention to our party, and we rode on without looking to the right or to the left toward the largest tent we could see. There we dismounted slowly and walked into the tent.

The etiquette of an Arab reception is a rather chilling thing, when experienced for the first time, and we have never before been *en cérémonie* among the Bedouins; for in the French Sahara and the Egyptian desert European travellers are well known, and are treated after European fashion. Here we are probably the first

119

Europeans ever seen. Nobody moved till we had come inside the tent, and Wilfrid had said in a loud voice 'Saláam aleykoum,' to which everybody – for there were perhaps a dozen men sitting there – answered also in a loud voice 'Aleykoum saláam.' Then they rose to their feet and politely made way for us to enter, the principal man bustling about to have a carpet spread and a camel saddle brought for us to lean our elbows on, for such is the custom. We sat down without ceremony, merely making the usual salute of raising the hand to the mouth and head, and looking solemn and unconcerned, for so Mr S— had recommended us to do; but the ice once broken, Hatmoud and his friends seemed willing enough to talk, and anxious to do everything they could to make us comfortable . . . Of course, there is no question of paying for anything here . . .

Hatmoud's tent is a very poor one, and we are disappointed in finding no external signs of greatness among these Shammar, more than in the tents of their lower brethren, Jibúri, Delím, or Aghedáat. Except one carpet and the saddle, there is absolutely no furniture, and the coffee is made in pots no better than Sotámm's among the Jerîfa. The men, however, are better behaved than most of those in whose tents we have been, and have asked no impertinent questions.[24]

The artless snobbery of Lady Anne's narrative ('These Amr are evidently very low Arabs . . .') provides an amusing gloss on the more sophisticated pretensions of her husband. While Wilfrid Blunt was content merely to observe that 'good breeding and good birth are nearly always found together in the desert', his wife was incapable of making any distinction between them; for her, bad manners were incontrovertible evidence that the offender was not *asil*, that is, of noble birth. Lapses from her very high standard of politeness were noted in her diary. In their response to impertinence the Blunts were instinctively united: they assumed an uncompromising haughtiness until their 'position as people of consequence' was recognized.[25] Thus, they believed, they carried all before them; and perhaps they did. Blunt, at any rate, was in his element. He gave 'a deal of good advice' on politics to Faris, who, Lady Anne tells us, took it 'in the best possible spirit', remarking gratifyingly to Wilfrid, 'You are my father . . . and know better than I.' Wilfrid no doubt agreed with Lady Anne that it was 'impossible not to be fond of so charming a character'.[26]

Of the four travellers discussed at length in this book Blunt was the only true Bedouinophile. He never deviated from his initial assessment of their virtues. On this first Arabian journey he conceived a life-long sympathy with them which was based upon two things: his perception of the nature of their religious beliefs and his perception of their form of government, both of which possessed for him an acute emotional appeal.

He was immediately struck by the apparent simplicity of Bedouin religion. 'With the exception of a belief in God, inherited from the earliest times, the Bedouin possess no religious creed whatever; neither have they, it may almost be said, any superstitions. No people in the world take less account of the supernatural than they do, nor trouble themselves so little with metaphysics.' They had no belief in a personal God who dispensed favours and punishments: for them God was simply 'the fate to which all must bow'. Most interesting of all, according to Blunt, they had no belief in a future life. He wrote of this very feelingly.

It is difficult for a European to put himself into the position of one who is content to die thus – who neither believes, nor despairs because he does not believe. The Bedouin knows that he shall die, but he does not fear death. He believes that he shall perish utterly, yet he does not shudder at the grave. He thinks no more of complaining than we do because we have not wings. In his scheme of the universe there has never been room for a heaven or a hell.[27]

The Bedouin appeared to have what Blunt craved but could never possess – a simple unintellectual belief in God, and the ability to face extinction. Of the possibility of hell they were not even aware. Beholding them, he could only 'bow and reason not'.[28]

Though he later became interested in Islam and even toyed with the idea of becoming a Moslem, he never forgot his first exhilarating experience of the uncomplicated religion of the desert. He believed that the Bedouin were not degraded by the simplicity of their belief; on the contrary, they were liberated by it. Their strict ideas of right and wrong were founded not on a craven desire to propitiate an angry god, but on their own sure instincts, and on respect for traditional opinion.[29] The affection which Blunt later developed for the poetry of the 'Days of Ignorance', that is, of the time before Mohammed, was based on his belief that it was the finest expression of the Bedouin spirit. It was 'frankly, inspiritingly, stupendously hedonistic'. The virtues it exalted were the manly and aristocratic ones of courage, generosity, lavish hospitality, and the protection of the weak. Unconcerned by any fear of what lay beyond the grave, the heroes of the ancient odes lived life to the full, enjoying equally the love of women and the pursuit of honour.[30] In his own life Blunt tried hard and often to live by such a creed of enlightened hedonism.

As for the Bedouin political system, Blunt was enchanted by it at first sight. He was not to see it in its full glory until he visited the fabled land of Nejd in 1878, but what he saw of it in Mesopotamia, among the Shammar, Anaza and Ruwalla tribes, convinced him of its value.

The first thing that impressed him about Bedouin society was its complete freedom from bureaucracy. The Bedouin was subject to no interference from tax-gatherers or policemen and to Blunt this represented an ideal state of affairs. In Turkey he had already observed that the peasants of the loosely administered Ottoman dominions were freer than those of 'magistrate-ridden England'.[31] He had a squireish contempt for the growing bureaucratization of English life and was ready to admire a people whose way of life was so simple and patriarchal that bureaucracy was unknown. For the sake of protection the Bedouin yielded a little of his independence to the tribe, but even so, his position was rather 'that of a member of a political club than of a subject or citizen'. He could at any time withdraw from the authority of the tribe if its decisions did not suit him, though while he was with the tribe he had to abide by its rules.[32]

Though Blunt perversely labelled the Bedouin political system a democracy, the system he described was in fact a primitive form of aristocracy. The sheikh, whose powers were indeed limited by the exercise of public opinion and the right of secession, was almost always, Blunt recorded, a man of noble birth, and his breeding and position entitled him to 'the kind of familiar deference paid by well-brought-up people to their fathers'. The Bedouin, in fact, as he discovered with delight, were great respecters of persons. The sheikhs, he observed, possessed the true aristocratic demeanour. They accepted easily the respect which was their due, but indulged in no vulgar display of power and magnificence and were courteous towards their inferiors.[33] This was a type of behaviour Blunt admired wherever he found it. In the 1880s he was present at a tenants' ball given by Gladstone's friend Mrs Howard at Naworth Castle. It was 'unlike other tenants' balls in that there was absolutely no *gêne* between host and guests . . . The life of this house is like that of a Bedouin camp.'[34]

Blunt's description of the functions of a Bedouin sheikh emphasizes the onerous nature of the position:

The sheykh has many duties, and few advantages. On him falls the trouble of deciding small cases of dispute, quarrels between wife and husband, disputes as to ownership in a camel or sheep. He has to transact the political business of the tribe, to sign the letters that are sometimes written by the public scribe, who is often a townsman, to receive strangers, and, above all, to keep open house at all hours for his people. He it is who is called in to stop quarrels, by the authority of his presence, and to rebuke disturbers of the peace.[35]

That Blunt regarded these things as duties rather than privileges shows that his conception of government was one of *noblesse oblige*. Those possessing the qualities for governing, 'which seem to be hereditary everywhere', should exercise them, he believed, because of a duty to do so, not because of any vulgar desire for power. The spectacle of a struggle for power always disturbed him profoundly. Power was something to be accepted with grace and sobriety by those who were born to it.

At the time of his return from Mesopotamia in 1878 Blunt had not yet come to see the Arabs as a cause, or himself as having any personal involvement with them. He admired them, but his political activity on their behalf was confined to expressing to Lord Salisbury his opinion that the proposed Euphrates Valley Railway would be a 'danger to Arabian liberty'.[36]

In the autumn of that year he and his wife set out for Nejd, which they knew from Palgrave and their reading of pre-Islamic poetry was the home of the true Arab. The resulting book was significantly entitled *A Pilgrimage to Nejd, the Cradle of the Arab Race*. Lady Anne again wrote the narrative while Blunt contributed a preface and a final chapter on the political system.

He set out in an appropriate frame of mind for what turned out to be an experience of almost religious intensity.

To us, [he wrote] imbued as we were with the fancies of the Desert, Nejd had long assumed the romantic colouring of a holy land; and when it was decided that we were to visit Jebel Shammar, the metropolis of Bedouin life, our expedition presented itself as an almost pious undertaking; so that it is hardly an exaggeration . . . to speak of it as a pilgrimage.[37]

The pious expectations were justified and he discovered in Nejd a 'sacred land' which possessed all the charms of Mesopotamia and more besides.[38] The inhabitants of Nejd were remote from the curse of Ottoman administration and this had enabled them to develop the Bedouin form of government, which Blunt labelled 'shepherd rule', to a level of perfection unknown elsewhere.

Blunt argued that shepherd rule developed naturally from a

desert terrain. Towns could exist only at oases, and as the nomadic tribes controlled the roads between the towns the townsmen had to put themselves under the protection of a Bedouin sheikh in order to carry on trade with each other. When the sheikh became rich and powerful he built a castle near one of the towns for a summer residence. Aided by the prestige of his pure Bedouin blood, the sheikh eventually became the ruler of the town and took the title of Emir. Such was the origin of the power of the great Mohammed ibn Rashid, Emir of Nejd, whom Blunt extravagantly admired. This great personage received the Blunts 'with all possible honour. Our quality of English people was a sufficient passport for us in his eyes . . .'[39]

The advantages of shepherd rule were obvious to Blunt. Under the benevolent despotism of a Bedouin prince it was possible to have 'a community living as our idealists have dreamed, . . . without compulsion of any kind, whose only law [is] public opinion, and whose only order a principle of honour'. There was no need for any elaborate machinery of constitutional rights, for the prince could not transgress the unwritten law of Arabia.[40]

His experience of Nejd convinced Blunt that in order to develop the full limits of their potential the Arabs must be free of Ottoman domination. He determined to do what he could to this end. He had found his career.[41]

In championing the Arab cause Blunt was striking a blow for the principle of aristocracy. Nejd had seemed to him to be a unique repository of the traditional virtues, an example to the world of a society ruled with a light but confident hand by a rural aristocracy whose claim to legitimacy was based on birth and not on wealth. By publicizing the existence of such a society and the desirability of preserving its independence he was affirming in a vivid public manner the virtues of aristocracy – and the legitimacy of his own social position.

Blunt's personal insecurity, the result of family upheavals over which he had had no control, coincided with a historical crisis for the English aristocracy. During the latter half of the nineteenth century there was a gradual curtailment of the power and privileges of the landed gentry. By 1880, the year in which Blunt began his public career with the publication of his article 'Recent Events in Arabia', county police forces had been established and competitive examinations for the civil service had been introduced. In the next decade the Ground Game Act of 1881, the Agricultural Holdings Act of 1883, and the establishment of County Councils in 1888 made further inroads into the authority of the squire. With his heightened sensitivity to the subject, Blunt was quick to perceive the significance of these developments. His response was to make the defence and promotion of aristocratic principles the theme of his public career. From his base at Crabbet, a little world where aristocratic principles reigned supreme, and from the small estate at Sheikh Obeid near Cairo which he purchased in 1881, he made his forays into the world of high politics; and to these havens he returned in periods of frustration and distress. At Sheikh Obeid he wore Bedouin dress and played the patriarch to his heart's content. 'Altogether there must be at least a hundred Arabs under the paternal rule of our Sheykh', wrote Frederic Harrison after a visit in 1895.[42] He also took to wearing Bedouin dress on his English estate, and nothing could better illustrate his identification of the Bedouin sheikh with the English squire.

The world he created for himself was a world of the past, a reminiscence of the golden age of the squirearchy. He even remodelled his house to complete the illusion. At a time when the Gothic revival was carrying all before it in English architecture he turned Crabbet into an early-eighteenth-century country house. The conversion was accomplished with a truly aristocratic disregard for convenience. Often there were no doors from room to room, only out onto the lawn, and the only way to get upstairs was by a little stairway belonging to the old house.

It was characteristic of Blunt to refuse to be fussed by minor details. He was interested in the grand design, whether it was for the remodelling of a house or the regeneration of a race. His plan for the Arabs was conceived on the boldest lines: he himself would go to Arabia and lead a movement for the restoration of the caliphate from Constantinople to Mecca.[43] It was a dazzlingly egotistical and impractical scheme which could only have been conceived by a man afflicted with a pathological sense of his own singularity. He confided to his diary: 'People have been called great who have sacrificed themselves for smaller objects, but in this I feel the satisfaction of knowing it to be a really worthy cause.'[44] The venture was abandoned because of the natural reluctance of the Foreign Office to support it and Blunt had to content himself for the time being with contacting religious leaders in Cairo and Jedda and with writing 'The Future of Islam'.

In this series of articles he tried to show that it was desirable for the caliphate to return to Mecca, preferably in the person of the Sherif of Mecca, a potentate who possessed many agreeable Bedouin characteristics and who was descended from the Prophet himself. This was a strategy for Arab regeneration which clearly appealed to Blunt's strong sense of legitimacy. He went on to suggest, in the article entitled 'England's Interest in Islam', that, after the inevitable and perhaps imminent collapse of the Ottoman Empire, the caliphate 'must be taken under Britsh protection, and publicly guaranteed its political existence, undisturbed by further aggression from Europe'.[45] The Arabian peninsula would be the temporal domain of an Arabian caliph as the Vatican state was the temporal domain of a European pope. Under an Arabian caliphate the Arab genius would flower again and Islam would renew itself. According to Blunt's reading of history the English were distinguished from other Europeans by their tradition of tolerance towards Islam: Moslems, recognizing this, naturally looked to England as their adviser and protector. It was in England's interest, as the ruler of the huge Moslem population of India, to respond to what Blunt believed to be Moslem hopes.

No one in authority took his argument seriously; it was an idea whose time had not yet come. Thirty-five years later, when the British were casting around for ways to defeat the Turks in the First World War, a small group of officials hit on the idea of striking a bargain with the Sherif of Mecca. In return for his sponsorship of an Arab revolt against the Turks they would support his claim to the caliphate and offer a guarantee of Arab independence after the war. The resulting entanglement with the Sherifians originated with men who for the most part cared nothing for Wilfrid Blunt; but the Cairo settlement of 1921, in which thrones were handed out to the more able members of the Sherif's family, owed much to the influence exercised over Churchill by Blunt's most devoted, perhaps only, disciple: T. E. Lawrence. For Lawrence, Blunt was one of his 'Master Arabians' – the other being Doughty. The master returned the admiration: Lawrence's copy of Blunt's poems is inscribed 'to T. E. Lawrence in admiration of his courage and honesty in public life and much else, from Wilfrid Scawen Blunt, July 28th, 1922'.[46] By 1922, the year of his death, Blunt was a forgotten man. He had the ambiguous experience of seeing his political ideas become reality without being able to take credit for them.

At first he pinned his hopes for Arab regeneration on the British government. The anti-imperialism for which he was to become notorious had not yet developed and he still retained some faith in England's ability and willingness to do good in the world. When he visited Egypt in 1880 he found the Anglo-French Condominium a great improvement on the Khedive Ismail and thought Syria would benefit from a similar arrangement.[47] But he was already beginning to have doubts about England's ability to fulfil what he regarded as her political mission. On his first visit to India in 1879 he was shocked, characteristically, by the way the Indian peasant was taxed to pay for the Anglo-Indian bureaucracy, and he regarded General Burrows's defeat by the Afghans in the following year as an inglorious performance reflecting national decay. He wrote in his diary at the time:

We fail because we are no longer honest, no longer just, no longer gentlemen. Our Government is a mob, not a body endowed with sense and supported by the sense of the nation. It was only by immense industry, immense sense, and immense honour that we gained our position in the world, and now that these are gone we find our natural level. For a hundred years we did good in the world; for a hundred we shall have done evil, and then the world will hear of us no more.[48]

The last sentence is often quoted as proof of Blunt's prophetic abilities. He liked to think of himself as a prophet – prophecy is a kind of immortality – but the statement is more interesting for what it shows about the roots of his anti-imperialism. Even in his bitterest moments he never became an isolationist in the true sense. He always looked back with regret to the time when the English possessed sufficient moral fibre to pursue a career of international knight-errantry. In the most famous of his many letters to *The Times*, on 24 December 1900, he mourned the passing of

England – high-minded England, with her traditional love of liberty, who never feared to speak her mind to princes and to peoples when they abused their strength – who helped the cause of many nationalities in all this century's earlier days, who focussed what was noblest in public indignation in the cause of the Spanish colonies, of Poland, of Hungary, and of Italy . . .[49]

When England was a nation which met Blunt's rather stringent and very aristocratic criteria of moral worthiness she had a right, indeed a duty, to interfere in other people's affairs: *noblesse oblige*.

When she lost her claim to moral worth no good could come of such interference.

In his disillusioned old age he came to regard European rule of primitive peoples as inevitably evil, but in 1880 he was ready to apply the same strict criteria of moral worth in deciding which races were worthy of independence and which were fit only for servitude.

The Arabic-speaking Copt of the Nile, and the Canaanite of Syria, are Arab only in language, and are without the political instincts inherent in the pure race; the bastard Iraki has been for centuries a slave. These may never be worthy of their independence, or capable of a self-government of which they have lost the traditions; but they are not real Arabians, and should not be confounded with them.[50]

Virtue was a condition of liberty, and liberty could legitimately be given or taken away by those nations whose political pedigree entitled them to act as arbiters of the international scene. It was a vision of the world order which was squirearchy writ large.

The great irony of Blunt's career was that when he finally saw political action it was on behalf of a man who was very far from being a 'real Arabian'. On looking around for a way in which he could redeem the Arab race he attempted unsuccessfully to offer his services to the Algerian leader, Abu Yemama, and to trace the whereabouts of the mysterious Jemal-ed-Din al-Afghani in America. It was the Egyptian Nationalist Movement of 1881 which gave him a completely unexpected opportunity to influence events. After the army's revolt against the corrupt and despotic rule of the Khedive Tewfik, Blunt's prophetic eye alighted on Ahmed Arabi, the fellah leader of the revolt.

Arabi, whom Blunt described as a 'typical fellah, tall, heavy-limbed, and somewhat slow in his movements', was as different as it is possible to imagine from the high-bred Nejdi sheikhs who had captivated him in 1879.[51] But after his first meeting with him Blunt was able to persuade himself that this might be the man to realize his dreams. Arabi spoke with dignity of his opposition to the Turkish rulers of Egypt and his desire to make secure the position of the Assembly of Notables which would maintain the rights of the people. Just as important to Blunt was what he did not say: 'Here was no nonsense about railroads and canals and tramways as nostrums that could redeem the East, but words that went to the root of things and fixed the responsibility of good government on the shoulders which alone could bear it.'[52] After this meeting Blunt drafted a manifesto for the National Party and sent it, with Arabi's approval, to Gladstone. He also sent a copy to *The Times*.

For a brief time it looked as though the constitutionalist position in Egypt might be consolidated without bloodshed, but French nervousness about 'pan-Islamism' initiated a rapid series of events which, via the Anglo-French Joint Note and the bombardment of Alexandria, led in September 1882 to the defeat of Arabi by Lord Wolseley's forces at Tel-el-Kebir.

Blunt's plans had gone badly awry. Within the short space of a year he had been moved by events from a simple vision of Arab renaissance under the aegis of the British government to an entanglement with an idealistic Egyptian fellah who was now the prisoner of an English general. Arabi's failure as a military leader was a bitter pill for his English supporter to swallow. Referring to the accusation that Arabi was a physical coward, Blunt wrote that it was 'difficult to avoid the conclusion that there was some truth in this. Arabi was too pure and unadulterated a fellah to have any of the strong fighting instincts which are found in some races but are conspicuously absent in his own. His courage was of another kind . . .'[53] He had proved to be too weak a vessel for enthusiasm such as Blunt's. To his credit, Blunt did not abandon Arabi: his sense of honour and the extent of his public commitment did not permit it. He put a great deal of energy and a large sum of his own money into Arabi's defence and succeeded in saving him from execution. He and his associates were exiled to Ceylon.

As it became obvious that the British had no intention of leaving Egypt once they had got in, Blunt's remaining faith in his country evaporated. He never forgave the British government for betraying his high hopes and squashing the man whom he regarded as his protégé. From then on he dedicated himself to the fight against British imperialism. It was the only political career left to him. He became a thorn in the flesh of Sir Evelyn Baring (later Lord Cromer), the British Agent in Egypt, and took pains to publicize examples of British misrule. His weapons were his pen and the charm which ensured that no matter what his political eccentricities might be he would continue to be invited to most of the best houses. What he heard in confidence on a social occasion he was not above repeating in print if it suited his purposes, but he never paid a significant social price for his indiscretions. The English governing class was capable of tolerating, and therefore largely neutralizing, a renegade like Blunt.

After the Arabi débâcle he turned his attention to India, which he visited in 1883–4. What he saw there convinced him that though the English had once been a power for good in rousing India from intellectual and spiritual torpor, they could do good no longer. In the series of articles, 'Ideas about India', which he contributed to quality of the Anglo-Indian group. Open competition for the civil believed to be the deterioration of the quality of British rule. Firstly, the British government's India policy was no longer formulated for the benefit of the Indians, but for the benefit of Manchester capitalists, a class of people Blunt naturally abhorred. Secondly, there had been a change for the worse in the social, and therefore moral, quality of the Anglo-Indian group. Open competition for the civil service had led to the arrival in India of

another class of official . . . who is distinctly of a lower social grade, and who in so far exercises less authority over his trading fellow-countrymen, and, the natives say, is less kind and considerate towards themselves. A young fellow, say the son of an Ulster farmer, is pitchforked by a successful examination into high authority in Bengal. He has no traditions of birth or breeding for the social position he is called to occupy, and is far more likely to hobnob with the commercial English of his district than to adapt himself to the ceremonial of politeness so necessary in Oriental intercourse.

In the good old days of Blunt's imagination the Company officials had been 'imbued with traditions of rule which, though far from liberal, were yet on the whole honourable to those who held them, and not antagonistic to native sympathies'; and they had known how to mingle with the better elements of Indian society. The new officials, hampered by their lack of breeding, had also to contend with the bureaucratic red tape which was slowly strangling whatever initiative they possessed.[54]

For Blunt everything was beginning to interconnect: the ruin of his class, the ruin of his country, the ruin of India. He therefore advocated the eventual return of the government of India to a native aristocracy revitalized, he believed, by the better effects of British rule. After his visit to the court of the Nizam of Hyderabad he reflected on 'how much there was that was good in the past in the harmonious relations of governors and governed, in the personal connection of princes and peoples, in the tolerance which gave to each caste and creed its recognized position in the social family'.[55]

His next attack on the British imperialism took the form of standing for Parliament as a Home Ruler. Failing in his attempt to get into Parliament, he went over to Ireland to exhort the peasantry to resist their English landlords. He immediately took to Ireland, which seemed to him a land of happy peasants and saintly priests. 'If I pitied them,' he wrote, 'it was not for the poverty of their dwellings, for the broken thatch and the gaps in their walls letting in the rain, but for the English laws which were driving them from these happy homes . . .'[56] Eventually he was arrested for holding an illegal political meeting at Woodford, County Galway, and spent two months in Kilmainham and Galway jails. In prison he had certain privileges which he apparently considered his due as a political prisoner and a gentleman. His cell was swept out every morning by another prisoner, and he was allowed to keep his own overcoat, shoes and travelling rug, and to sit cross-legged on the floor rather than perched on a stool, 'a privilege which enabled me to imagine myself once more in the East, perhaps in my own tent detained by stress of weather'. He read the Old Testament, following 'the Beni Israel in their desert wanderings, Amos and Elisha in their Arabian sojournings, and Moses in his passage of the Red Sea. Every step between the Nile and the Euphrates was familiar ground, and it was there that I regained the freedom of my soul.'[57]

After his spell in prison Blunt's active political life was over, though he continued to write articles and pamphlets and correspond with Egyptian and Indian nationalists. He spent the winters at Sheikh Obeid, lording it over the Bedouins in a manner reminiscent of a District Officer gone native.

In 1897 he visited the Senussi oasis of Siwah with the intention of making a profession of Islam, but he was attacked and robbed by the Siwahis. He was released, irony of ironies, after he announced that he was an Englishman. After this he washed his hands of Islam and eventually he persuaded himself that the Siwahis could not have been 'real Arabs' but were 'probably descended from the criminals formerly sent here in Roman and later times . . .'[58] This was his last desert journey.

His declining years were marred by domestic quarrels which have been recorded, perhaps with more passion than accuracy, by his daughter Judith.[59] But he continued to be active in London society till 1912, hearing much political gossip which he recorded in his diary, and writing poems and plays. Occasionally he took to wandering about the south of England with a tent, as though reliving the desert journeys of the past. In 1912 he retired to Newbuildings Place, but illness and a sense of failure spoiled his enjoyment of the lovely old house. Even his stud of Arab horses had not been the success he had hoped.

In the latter part of his life, when he could do little but fulminate from afar, his ideas about England's decline developed into a full-blown theory of racial decay. He arrived at this theory, whose chief element was anti-Semitism, by several overlapping stages. First he saw that the aristocracy was being dislodged from its traditional role as the governing class by bureaucratic laws and by the rise to power of crude middle-class capitalists interested, Blunt believed, only in profits. Then he saw that these same capitalists were responsible for deflecting England from her high political mission in the world to an unworthy policy of economic imperialism: 'The White Man's Burden, Lord, is the burden of his cash.'[60] Eventually he was able to connect up bureaucratic inroads into the power of the gentry with the capitalism that kept India poor so that Manchester would flourish. In 1904 he wrote an article describing how his attempts to build a cheap sanitary iron cottage for one of his tenants has been thwarted by the by-laws which prohibited the use of anything but bricks and mortar. It was clear to Blunt that these by-laws had been framed simply to serve the interests of the builders who dominated the local council. He concluded his article with the observation that those tradesmen who were able through the newfangled councils to exercise their unnatural sway over rural affairs were only doing the same thing as those other tradesmen who pushed their imperial interests in Parliament.[61]

At some point he began to focus on the Jews as the source of all evil. He had already decided that it was the pursuit of money which was dishonouring his country, and he came to believe that the concern with money stemmed particularly from the increased political influence of Jews, which was so great that it amounted to a racial change in the governing class. Was it not Disraeli, 'our first Jew Minister', who tricked the Sultan into ceding Cyprus, and who bought the Suez Canal shares? And was it not 'due to the pressure put on Gladstone's government by the Rothschilds and the Goschens that Egypt was occupied'? And was not Lord Cromer a

10 'A fire yet flickering over the ashes of an old fury' – Blunt in old age

member of the financial family of Baring, 'of Dutch, it is generally said of Jewish, origin'? By 1913 it was obvious to Blunt that the ignoble policies of the Asquith administration were due to the presence of Jews in the cabinet. In language worthy of Hitler he denounced 'the alien gang of Jew financiers which has captured the House of Commons'.[62]

Blunt had always disclaimed any tendency to racism and never tired of proclaiming in print the vulgarity of Social Darwinism, which he described as 'a pseudo-scientific doctrine of the fundamental inequalities of the human kind which, true as a statement of fact, has been exaggerated and made political use of to excuse white selfishness and white exclusiveness, and to reinforce the white man's pretension of rightful domination over the non-white world at large'.[63] He was repelled by Social Darwinism's ethic of struggle and disrespect for traditional hierarchies. Much more to his taste was the aristocratic version of racism expounded by his friend Gobineau. He possessed Gobineau's own private copy of *Sur l'inégalité des races humaines*, and one can see how he would be attracted by the idea of a transnational 'Aryan' aristocracy which is tragically drained of its vital energy in imparting civilization to lesser breeds. But he did not get his loathing of Jews from Gobineau. Gobineau was not anti-Semitic in the conventional sense; he merely believed in a general way in the desirability of racial purity.[64] Blunt's anti-Semitism sprang from a source within himself, perhaps from his bitterness at being so little able to influence the course of events.[65] The Jews who were prominent in public life provided him with a convenient target for the malice which arose from powerlessness.

In his last years, immured in Sussex because of his failing health, he occupied himself in reflection on his varied and turbulent life. He prepared his diaries for publication, wrote poetry, and received visits from his many friends. Among them was T. E. Lawrence, who left a vivid picture of him sitting in his great chair, robed as a Bedouin sheikh, 'a fire yet flickering over the ashes of an old fury'.[66] He acknowledged to himself, in a poem written at the end of his life, that power had once meant a great deal to him.

> I had ambition once. Like Solomon
> I asked for wisdom, deeming wisdom fair,
> And with much pains a little knowledge won
> Of Nature's cruelty and Man's despair,

And mostly learned how vain such learnings were.
Then in my grief I turned to happiness,
And woman's love awhile was all my care,
And I achieved some sorrow and some bliss.

Till love rebelled. Then the mad lust of power
Became my dream, to rule my fellow-men;
And I too lorded it my little hour,
And wrought for weal or woe with sword and pen,
And wounded many, some, alas, my friends.
Now I ask silence. My ambition ends.[67]

He died at Newbuildings Place in 1922, having manifestly failed in his mission to make the world safe for aristocracy. He was buried, as he had wished, in the woods near the house, without religious rites.

6

Charles M. Doughty

(1843–1926)

A new voice hailed me of an old friend when, first returned from the Peninsula, I paced again in that long street of Damascus which is called Straight; and suddenly taking me wondering by the hand 'Tell me (said he), since thou art here again in the peace and assurance of Ullah, and whilst we walk, as in the former years, toward the new blossoming orchards, full of the sweet spring as the garden of God, what moved thee, or how couldst thou take such journeys into the fanatic Arabia?'

. . . the sun made me an Arab, but never warped me to Orientalism.

C. M. Doughty, *Arabia Deserta*

BURTON, BLUNT AND PALGRAVE were all men to whom the problem of identity presented itself with unusual urgency. For Doughty it was never consciously an issue. Very early in life he seems to have formed a conception of himself which was virtually impervious to change. The basic components of his identity, active devotion to his country and the profession of the Christian religion, remained always the same, though the peculiar and wilful manner of their public expression suggests that this remarkable consistency was not achieved without strain.

The known facts of Doughty's life are few, just enough to demonstrate his singlemindedness without explaining it. He was born in 1843 at Theberton Hall in Suffolk, of landed background on both sides.[1] His father and his maternal grandfather were both clergymen. His mother's family was distinguished for its tradition of public service. In the past two hundred years it had produced six admirals, three general officers, a bishop, a judge, and a colonial governor. His mother died a few months after he was born and his father died when he was six. He went to live with an uncle, Frederick Goodwin Doughty of Martlesham Hall, and the following year he was sent to school, first at Laleham, then at Elstree,

11   Charles M. Doughty

then at Portsmouth to prepare for the navy in the tradition of his mother's family. His schooldays were not particularly happy. He was big for his age, and though shy had the reputation of being a formidable fighter when provoked: already he seems to have been distinguished by his exceptional seriousness. In 1856 he failed his navy medical because of 'a slight impediment of speech'. The disappointment was a grave one, for he had been committed to the navy as his patriotic vocation. 'My object in life since, as a private person,' he wrote to Edward Garnett in 1922, 'has been to serve my country so far as my opportunities might enable me.'

After a few years of private tuition Doughty matriculated in 1861 at Cambridge as an undergraduate of Caius College. He read geology, a subject to which he had devoted himself since his rejection by the navy. In 1862 he read a paper to the British Association on flint implements from Hoxne. In 1863, the year in which

137

Charles Lyell published *The Antiquity of Man*, Doughty joined several other Caius College men in a migration to Downing. The object of the move was to be able to study geology away from the pious scrutiny of the Caius College dons. Later that year Doughty went to Norway to study the Joestedal-Brae glaciers and the resulting paper was read to the British Association in 1864; but any thoughts of making geological research his career had to be abandoned when he only took a Second in the Natural Science Tripos in 1865. One of his examiners said many years later that he had been deprived of a First by his 'dishevelled mind. If you asked him for a collar he upset his whole wardrobe at your feet.'

After leaving Cambridge he turned to the study of early English literature, for already the idea was forming in his mind of writing an epic poem in which he would describe the origins of the English race.[2] His longing to serve his country, which rejection by the navy seems not to have quenched but intensified, was finding a means of expression. The next ten years were spent in devoted preparation for this great work. From 1865 to 1870 he studied English Literature in London and at the Bodleian Library. He then continued his studies on the continent, an interest in Erasmus and Joseph Scaliger taking him first to Holland. His study of Dutch, along with the Danish he had picked up in 1863–4, gave him 'a philological feeling in English'. From Holland he went to Louvain and then he moved south through France into Italy and Sicily. In October 1872 he was in Algeria on his way to Spain. After a winter in Spain he spent most of the next year in Greece. Then he turned away from Europe and entered the lands of the Bible, Egypt and Syria. Apart from a visit to Vienna in 1875 the years between 1874 and 1878 were spent in the East.

He did not go to the East originally with any intention of penetrating the Arabian peninsula. When he did go there he seems not to have been much conscious of following in anyone's footsteps. The writings of previous travellers were known to him only from Albrecht Zehme's *Arabien und die Araber seit hundert Jahren*.[3] Still less was he influenced by childhood recollections of the *Arabian Nights*: his austere taste found them sadly wanting. The Arabian images in Doughty's mind were those of the Bible.[4]

The proximate cause of his Arabian journey was his desire to see and describe the carved monuments of Madain Salih which no European scholar had visited. But he made it clear in the preface to the second edition of *Arabia Deserta* that the desire to visit Arabia was a logical extension of his interest in 'the Story of the Earth, Her manifold living creatures, the human generations and Her ancient rocks'. The tendency of Doughty's thought was often towards origins: the origin of his own race, of the human race, and of the earth itself were all questions which he sought with great seriousness to answer. It was perhaps inevitable that he should find his feet turning towards Arabia, a land which he eventually came to associate with the beginnings of things – of Christianity, perhaps of mankind itself.[5]

On 10 November 1876 Doughty set out from Damascus with the great pilgrim caravan. He carried with him no letters of introduction from important personages – these had been denied him by an indifferent British consul – but only his scientific instruments, some medicines, his pistol, and his books. Among the latter was a seventeenth-century edition of his beloved *Canterbury Tales*. Though he was dressed as a Syrian he made no bones about proclaiming himself to be a Christian and an Englishman. Unlike Palgrave he was not content merely to let the Arabs draw their own conclusions as to his religion. The resulting dangers and humiliations, of which there were many, were all painfully, and painstakingly, described in *Arabia Deserta*.

After visiting Madain Salih and copying the inscriptions his original purpose in coming to Arabia was fulfilled, but he did not go home. Instead he struck out into the high desert to live with the nomads. The journey which began with his departure from the hajj fortress near Madain Salih ended a year and a half later when he reached Jedda, exhausted by hardship and hunger, on 2 August 1878. He had journeyed through the most desolate land on earth, with no protection but the force of his own character and the unpredictable humanity of the Bedouin. His motives for undertaking further and further journeys into the peninsula were never clearly explained.

His guide and host during the first part of his wanderings was Zeyd, a sheikh of the Fukara Bedouin whose grazing circuit encompassed the country near Madain Salih. He was a typical nomad, gaunt and hollow-faced, his eyes those of a man who looked out 'from the lawless land of famine, where his most nourishment was to drink coffee from the morning, and tobacco; and where the chiefest Beduin virtue is *es-subbor*, a courageous forbearing and abiding of hunger'.[6] There would be many days ahead when Doughty himself would be called upon to display this dismal virtue; the nomads had little enough for themselves and sometimes they shared it grudgingly or not at all. Riding away from the pilgrim road on that first day of his long journey, Doughty and his guide entered a waste of gravel and sand punctuated by bare sandstone crags. 'This, said Zeyd, showing me the wild earth with his swarthy hand, is the land of the Beduw.' Doughty felt himself watched for signs of irresolution: he betrayed none, and so his life with the Bedouin began.

It cannot be said of Doughty that he never really knew the Bedouin. He lived with them in conditions of the greatest intimacy for many months, sharing their coffee-fires and joking gravely with their women. He often went where he was not wanted but he was not easily pushed out. He counted on the Bedouin tradition of hospitality to see him through; more than once he had to throw himself on their mercy, saying 'dakhilak', the formula for invoking the guest's sacred right of protection. He was abandoned by faithless guides in the desert, he was taunted by children and frequently laid hands on, but he never compromised his identity as a Christian English gentleman. He submitted to many indignities, with nothing more than verbal protest. When Richard Burton read *Arabia Deserta* he was revolted by the author's forbearance: this was not his idea of the behaviour of an English gentleman.[7]

In the course of his wanderings Doughty visited Hail and met its emir, Mohammed ibn Rashid, the leading figure in the Arabian politics of the day. Doughty deplored his bloody history but found him a competent and intelligent ruler, bringing much-needed order to the unruly tribes and villages of central Arabia. The emir treated him kindly, but Doughty's shameless visibility, a proclaimed Christian wandering openly around the town, began to irritate him in the end and he gave orders that the stranger should be removed from Hail. Under protest, and not before extracting a letter of safe conduct from the emir, Doughty left Hail with three guides who abandoned him at the first opportunity at a camp of Huteimi Bedouin. From there he found someone to take him to Khaybar. And so he went on, alternately taken in and abandoned, welcomed and ejected, until he reached Jedda and the hospitality of the English consulate.

From Jedda he took ship for Bombay on the first leg of the

journey home. He broke his journey at Aden to rest, but on arrival in Bombay he was still so feeble that he was admitted to the European Hospital. When he first attempted to enter the hospital, wearing a long beard and Arab dress, he was turned away, most galling of ironies for a man who had risked his life rather than disguise his nationality, with the announcement 'Only Europeans are admitted!' After explaining who he was he was admitted to the hospital to begin his long convalescence.

For the next six years, as he gradually regained his strength, he was absorbed in writing *Arabia Deserta*. It was not the great patriotic work for which he had been preparing himself, but it had a patriotic purpose. In a letter to his biographer, D. G. Hogarth, in 1913, Doughty wrote: 'The *Arabia Deserta* volumes had necessarily a personal tone. A principal cause of writing them was besides the interest of the Semitic life in tents, my dislike of the Victorian English; and I wished to show, and thought I might be able to show, that there was something else.' He intended to rescue the English language from the pit into which he believed it had fallen. The 600,000 words which he eventually produced were a strange amalgam of archaisms, Arabisms, dialect, and eccentric punctuation. The book was not easy to read, nor was it meant to be. 'The book is not milk for babes,' its author wrote: 'it might be likened to a mirror, wherein is set forth faithfully some parcel of the soil of Arabia smelling of *sámn* and camels.'[8] Four publishers in succession perceived that it would sink like a stone. One publisher offered to consider it if the author would allow it to be rewritten by a competent literary man. After much argument from Doughty, who would not allow a single comma to be changed, it was published by Cambridge University Press in 1888. It had a small *succès d'estime*.

After *Arabia Deserta* Doughty turned at last to his patriotic epic, digressing only to produce *Under Arms*, a short volume of poetry published by the Army and Navy Stores, in which he urged British soldiers on to glory in the Boer War. The epic finally appeared in 1906–7, in six thick volumes. Its title was *The Dawn in Britain*. Like *Arabia Deserta*, there was probably not a word in it whose claims had not been gravely weighed against those of others before being committed to writing. In 1908 *Adam Cast Forth*, an Arabian version of the Adam and Eve legend, appeared. His next long poem, *The Cliffs*, published in 1909, was written to warn his countrymen of

141

the imminent danger of German invasion. His warning passed unheeded, and his next poem, *The Clouds* (1912), painted a gruesome picture of an England devastated by war. When war actually came in 1914 he was occupied with larger themes. *The Titans*, an epic treatment of the uses and abuses of technology, appeared in 1916, and *Mansoul (or the Riddle of the World)*, a long eclectic meditation on the meaning of the universe, was published in 1920. A revised edition came out in 1923 and Doughty was working on yet further revisions when he died in 1926.

No work of Doughty's was conceived on less than a heroic scale: he nothing common wrote or mean. The last forty years of his life were spent, completely cut off from the world, in the disciplined production of what he believed to be great poetry. As his contact with life decreased he drifted away from the Chaucerian realism of the portraits in *Arabia Deserta* to the production of magnificent abstractions derived impartially from early English literature and the *Morning Post*. The villainous Kaiser and joyfully dying English soldiers of *Mansoul* are figures straight out of its editorial page.[9] T. E. Lawrence and his 'imperishable enterprise' in the service of his country inevitably appealed to him, but he was no less characteristically shocked to learn from the unexpurgated 'Oxford' edition of *Seven Pillars of Wisdom* along what curious by-ways of the mind his hero's reflections ran.[10]

Discussion of Doughty as an Arabist falls logically into two parts: his experiences in Arabia and the peculiar way in which he wrote them up. It will be seen, I think, that they are not unrelated.

His experiences were determined by his uncompromising profession of Christianity, and this brings us immediately to a mystery; for Doughty was not a Christian in any conventional sense. His hatred of Islam, which he described as 'the dreadful-faced harpy of their religion', was worthy of the most vituperative mediaeval bigot, but it was not allied to any orthodox belief in the religion of his fathers. Christianity, he believed, was distinguished from other religions by its consecration of human brotherhood, but as with other religions, 'the verity of the things alleged cannot be made manifest on this side the gate of death'. Each man could only 'stand to his hope, and depart to the Gulf of Eternity in the common faith'; if it was truth he was seeking he must look for it in 'the indestructible temple-building of science'. Doughty's objection to Islam was that it rejected Reason in favour of the mindless veneration of Mohammed, and advocated weak submission to the impulses of the flesh rather than strenuous exercise of the faculties of the mind.[11]

These are not beliefs that most people would go to the stake for; still less are they the orthodox beliefs of the Christian Church. Why then did Doughty risk his life by professing the Christian religion in 'fanatic Arabia'?

Doughty was the son and grandson of clergymen and there can be no doubt that the Christian religion occupied an important place in his early life. The way in which he clung to the appellation 'Christian' suggests that the profession of Christianity, like his vocation to serve his country, was an element of identity so early and so deeply ingrained (we do not know how) that it could never be formally abandoned. Perhaps Christianity was from his earliest years so entangled with his sense of family and race that it was, simply, the faith of his fathers, and as such could never be put aside, only betrayed.

At some time during his adolescence his intellectual seriousness and passion for truth began to lead him away from complete acceptance of traditional Christianity. As a student of geology he was exposed to ideas which made it very difficult to accept the notion that everything in the Bible was literally true. He must have been familiar with the successive editions of Lyell's *Elements of Geology*, in which the author's estimate of the age of the earth was scandalously at variance with that based on biblical evidence. Doughty the scientist could not help but follow where his intellect led him, and at some point before he went to Arabia he became convinced that truth was the prerogative of science.

The logical next step would have been agnosticism, but Doughty shrank from this: the faith of his fathers was not so easily abandoned. He clung to the moral values implicit in Christianity and infused them with religious feeling. He was by no means the first to find this solution to his difficulties – one of the by-products of nineteenth-century science was the development of ethical religions – but he could not complacently accept the compromise he had made. Just as the check to his patriotic aspirations was met by an expansion of the patriotic ideal to a devotion few naval officers would ever be required to show, so the check to his Christian belief seems to have been met by a guilty exaggeration of the desire to witness. In Arabia he was not proselytizing the Christian religion, he was witnessing to it; and he did this by putting himself in a position to be reviled for it. It was incomprehensible to Richard Burton that Doughty should tamely put up with being stoned by children, spat upon, and having his beard plucked. But Doughty put up with this and much more in the belief, as he told the Royal Geographical Society, that he was demonstrating the moral goodness enjoined by Christianity; indeed he positively invited it, for he never hesitated to air his grievances about their behaviour to the Arabs.[12] When Misshel, a great sheikh of the Anaza, showed his contempt for the Nasrany by giving Doughty only one cup of coffee instead of the two or three he gave to his tribesmen, Doughty boldly exclaimed: 'Here is billah a great sheykh and little kahwa! Is it the custom of the Auájy, O Misshel, that a guest shall sit among you who are all drinking, with his cup empty?'[13] The Blunts would never have got themselves into such a humiliating situation, but Doughty did not carry himself with the air of a man of rank: his obvious poverty combined with his air of righteousness to ensure that he would have plenty of opportunity to display stoic acceptance of humiliation.

Arabia Deserta, in spite of its length and seemingly artless digressions, possesses remarkable dramatic unity. It builds up inexorably to an emotional climax which comes towards the end, at a point when Doughty's troubles have been coming thicker and faster and considerable narrative tension has been built up. The reader anticipates a resolution, though he cannot imagine what it will be.

The crisis of his journey came at a coffee station near Mecca, to which Doughty's wanderings had brought him perilously close.[14] He had ridden over four hundred miles from Unayzah, a town where he had been received with unusual kindness and tolerance, on the first leg of his journey to Jedda and safety. It was the hottest season of the year and tempers on the journey had been short. He had had to beg his companions for food and water and when he discovered that they were keeping their water supply secret from him his protests were met with curses. When the party reached Ayn ez-Zeyma on the frontier of the Mecca district Doughty was lagging behind on his weary camel, weak with hunger, and the news went ahead that a Christian was approaching the holy city. At no other stage in his journey had he been so conspicuous. He was the only traveller in his party who was not stripped to the *ihram*, the loin cloth which is the ritual garb of the pilgrim entering Mecca; his was the only voice which had not been raised in ritual praise. There was no chance of slipping through Ayn ez-Zeyma unnoticed. His companions, who were going on to Mecca, looked for someone to take him to Jedda. With difficulty they succeeded and Doughty was mounted and trying to whip some life into his jaded beast when he heard a voice behind him say: 'Dismount, dismount! – Let me alone I say, and I will kill the kafir.' He looked round and saw a nomad coming at him with a knife. He tried to spur his dromedary to a trot, but there was no strength in the animal and he dismounted to face his attacker.

Doughty's life might have ended here and *Arabia Deserta* never been written but for the intervention of one Maabub, a respected old Negro servant of the Sherif of Mecca, who was resting at Ayn ez-Zeyma on his way to join his master at Taif. Maabub stayed the nomad's hand, and then went back to his seat in the shade. Once again Doughty's attacker rushed on him, but stopped short when his victim stood his ground. He made passes at Doughty with his knife, glaring at him horribly but uncertain what to do next. Aroused by the hullabaloo Maabub forsook his shady spot and hastened to the scene. He admonished the attacker, whose name was Salem and who was a sherif or descendant of the Prophet, to refrain from striking an Englishman. Had not the English bombarded Jedda? But Salem, intoxicated by the thought of dispatching a Christian from the face of the earth and also, Doughty thought, by the prospect of acquiring his camel and the contents of his saddle bags, was not amenable to considerations of high politics and went for Doughty again. Maabub decreed that the Christian must be taken before the Sherif of Mecca at Taif where Salem could present his case against him. He charged Salem to take Doughty safely to Taif and they set off at sunset with the Mecca caravan.

Doughty's feelings may be imagined on being entrusted to Salem's safe-keeping. He had no choice but to go, though he knew he was in the greatest danger. On the road to Taif, Salem, assisted by Fheyd, the camel master, took the opportunity to attack him again. With his knife in his hand Salem threatened to kill him unless he handed over all his possessions. Doughty drew his pistol, which was suspended from a cord inside his shirt, and

145

Fheyd advanced toward him. He had to decide quickly: whether to fire on his assailants and take a chance on getting away from them and striking out alone across the desert, or whether to abandon himself to his fate. He decided on the latter. Realizing that there was no escape for him in the wilderness he offered the fully-loaded pistol to Fheyd; there had been no time to unload. What happened next is described with biblical simplicity: 'Fheyd seized the weapon! They were now in assurance of their lives and the booty: he snatched the cord and burst it. Then came his companion Sâlem; and they spoiled me of all that I had . . .'

Now fully in command of the situation Salem told his henchman Fheyd to fire off the pistol, but to reserve one bullet for Doughty. Doughty remained calm and Salem glared at him. This would have been the moment for him to say 'dakhilak' and he sensed that Salem was angry and disconcerted that he did not do so. The camel men began to curse and threaten him but Doughty calmly replied that when they reached Taif Salem would get his just deserts from the Sherif. Fheyd then struck him hard on the nape of his neck with his camel-stick and he lost consciousness. Coming round slowly and confusedly he asked faintly, 'Why have you done this?'

'Because,' said Fheyd, 'thou didst withhold the pistol.'

'Is the pistol mine or thine? I might have shot thee dead! but I remembered the mercy of Ullah.'

Once again, the situation was saved by the arrival of Maabub, who had heard the shots as he sat resting some distance away. He was on his way to Taif and had caught up with Salem and Doughty's party during the night. The journey was resumed but before long Doughty found himself ahead of the rest of the caravan, alone again with Salem and his new companion, Ibrahim. 'Dreadest thou not to die?' jeered Salem; but Doughty replied: 'I have not so lived, Moslêm, that I must fear to die.'

Here there is a sudden release of tension in the narrative. 'Pleasant is the summer evening air of this high wilderness . . .' Doughty unexpectedly observes as they look for a place to rest and eat. The crisis is over and all that remains is for the party to proceed in relative amity to Taif, where the Sherif summarily dismisses Salem, welcomes Doughty, and gives him a safe-conduct to Jedda. The remainder of the narrative, describing the journey to Jedda, is infused with Doughty's new lightness of heart – even the face of the desert becomes suddenly benign.

The crackling and sweet-smelling watch-fire made a pleasant bower of light about us, seated on the pure sand and breathing the mountain air, among dim crags and desert acacias; the heaven was a blue deep, all glistering with stars.

that smiled to see
the rich attendance on our poverty:

we were guests of the Night, and of the vast Wilderness.[15]

Thus Doughty leaves Arabia with a benediction, at peace with the land and himself.

It is an exquisite ending to his saga, redolent of the interior peace which follows the resolution of a psychological crisis. Throughout the whole book, we now realize, Doughty had been leading up to the moment when he stood unarmed before the brutal Fheyd, ready to face calmly what he undoubtedly regarded as a martyr's death. Earlier in the narrative he had written with emotion of the death of a Christian who had accidentally strayed into Medina. This 'Christian Martyr . . . Child of Light' had been killed after refusing to profess Islam. Doughty recorded the date of his death with the symbol of martyrdom: ✝.[16] *Arabia Deserta* can be read as a passion: Doughty even used the word himself to describe his experiences in Arabia.[17] After his miraculous escape from death at the hands of Salem and Fheyd he knew that he had done as much as any man could to witness to the faith.

It was a spectacular form of witness. Travelling at the same period in roughly the same area, without any attempt at disguise, the Blunts did not go in constant fear of their lives: Doughty did so, one is driven to conclude, because his conscience demanded it. Humiliation, and possibly even death, at the hands of fanatical Moslems was a just punishment for having betrayed the simple faith of his childhood, and at the same time a testimony to his public adherence to that faith. These were the unconscious motives for travelling as he did in Arabia.

If this interpretation seems extreme it should be understood that Doughty was a man of stupendous moral seriousness who did not flinch from advocating the most gruesome acts of sacrifice for ideals he felt to be beyond question. In his poetry martyrdom is a recurrent theme. A true patriot or a true Christian is lucky to be alive at the end of one of his sombre narratives. A glorious death in the service of his country or his religion is usually in store for him – indeed the two ideals tend to become entangled in a manner ironically reminiscent of Palgrave, whom Doughty despised. 'To my mind and humble reading of Nature,' he wrote to Edward Garnett in 1912, 'a Nation without some fervent Patriotism, without Religion; that is lacking those aspirations and higher ideals which lift men above themselves: is already self-slain.'

The connection in Doughty's mind between patriotism, religion and death is brought out clearly in Part II of *The Cliffs*, which Doughty preceded with a quotation from Latimer: 'No person is born into the World, for his own sake, but for the COMMON-WEALTHS sake.' The action takes place in the temple of Britannia, whose 'august front is blindfold with a thick veil'. The words RELIGION and PATRIOTISM, engraved upon her altar, are partly effaced through neglect. An army of elves 'clad in green smocks and russet frieze coats' is summoned by an allegorical figure called 'Britain's Truth' to weigh British souls in the balance. Most of them are found wanting. One batch of souls 'of uncertain sex; that eat the fruit of others' labour' is dismissed with the savage comment: 'So might such serve to dung the common field.' In Part IV Britannia's temple has undergone some repairs as a result of panic over the imminent invasion of Britain, but Britannia is still blindfold. It is revealed that the veil may be lifted only by the hand of a male infant, his mother's only child, who in the act of lifting the veil will die. Widow Charity offers her only son, and with his death Britain is saved.

When Doughty meditated on patriotism his thoughts turned more easily than most people's in the direction of the supreme sacrifice. He wrote to Mrs Doughty Montagu on a wet winter day in 1911: 'I often comfort myself with the thought that if it was good enough for our forefathers, our grey climate should be well enough for us also; and that as patriotic English we should be ever ready to fight and die, if need were for that sunless soil which gave us birth.'

He seems to have felt of Christianity also that if it was good enough for our forefathers, it should be well enough for us; and not simply as an ethical system worth living by but as an ideal worth dying for. In *The Dawn in Britain*, a poem in which the emergence of the English national character is inextricably intertwined with the arrival of Christianity, one of the most intensely felt passages is the martyrdom of Phelles, a Roman Christian, at the hands of the druids.[18] The horror is thickly piled on. Phelles is

brought into a 'fire-blackened glade' where wounded Roman soldiers are hanging from trees with fires kindled under their feet. All
around are 'murdered wights, disembowelled carcases!' Phelles
slips and falls in the blood surrounding the sacrificial stone, stain-
ing his clothes and hair with 'abominable gore'. The druids stun
him and lay him on the stone. There they 'break the victim's chine'
and then

> One rives, with knife of flint, the mariner's chest!
> He, ah, thrust then bloody hands, in the saint's bowels,
> Pluckt forth his quivering heart-root, prophecies . . .

In *Mansoul* the Crucifixion and the martyrdom of St Stephen
('Hounds, tradition saith / Licked his gore-blood shed, in that
sinister place') are described with equal goriness. Nor is it only
martyrdom which receives this kind of treatment at Doughty's
hands. The battle scenes in *The Dawn in Britain* are full of gruesome
detail.

> Britons, like hawks, leap down, from rushing chariots:
> And, off-hewed polls, they hang, with vaunting cries,
> On hooks, round their shrill justling battle-carts . . .[19]

Doughty's imagination apparently encompassed such horrors
without difficulty, and his ability to realize them so completely in
words leaves us with a certain reserve towards him. How could
this determinedly saintly man, who revered the Christian ideal of
human brotherhood, dwell so convincingly on the worst details of
human aggression?

Here we approach the central paradox of Doughty's character, a
paradox which suggests a further reason for his wilful risking of his
life in Arabia. Though he believed in the Christian injunction to
love thy neighbour and bless them that curse thee, Doughty was
himself in the grip of strong aggressive impulses. He saw nothing
remarkable in advocating that the 'Arabian religion of the sword
must be tempered by the sword [and] the daughter of Mecca and
Medina led captive'.[20] He was to some extent aware of the strength
of his aggressive tendencies. 'I am by nature,' he wrote to his
future wife in 1886, 'self-willed, headstrong, and fierce with oppo-
nents, but my better reason and suffering in the world have bridled
these faults and in part extinguished them.' In Arabia his provoca-
tive behaviour both satisfied his aggressive impulses and invited
punishment for them. When he finally put himself at the mercy of
Salem and Fheyd he did so with the air of one facing a final spiritual

reckoning: death, if it came, would be both a chastisement and an act of witness.

It is ironic that Norman Douglas should have taken *Arabia Deserta* as a text for a sermon on individualism, for the few virtues Doughty believed the Arabs to possess were social ones, the practice of hospitality and the small civilities which were the basis of human brotherhood in the wilderness.[21] Doughty's response to the Arabs was determined by his belief that the individual existed only for the common good. This made him quite unsympathetic to any romantic notion of Bedouin freedom; on the contrary, he deplored their inability to combine together to undertake any project for the common good.[22] Nevertheless, he experienced more happiness in the tents of the Bedouin than he did among the inhabitants of towns, and when he was not vituperating against their religion, or cursing their enviousness and deceitfulness, he wrote of them with tenderness and pity.

El-Beduw *ma yetaabun*, 'toil not' (say they,) that is not bodily; but their spirits are made weary with incessant apprehension of their enemies, and their flesh with continual thirst and hunger. The necessitous lives of the Aarab may hardly reach to a virtuous mediocrity; they are constrained to be robbers. 'The life in the desert is better than any, *if there were not the Beduw*,' is said proverbially by oases' Arabians; the poor Beduins they think to be full of iniquity, *melaun el-weyladeyn*, 'of cursed kind, upon both sides, of their father and mother.' Pleasant is the sojourn in the wandering village, in this purest earth and air, with the human fellowship, which is all day met at leisure about the cheerful coffee fire, and amidst a thousand new prospects. Here, where we now alighted, is this day's rest, tomorrow our home will be yonder. The desert day returning from the East warns the Beduin awake, who rises to his prayers; or it may be, unwitting of the form, he will but murmur toward heaven the supplication of his fearful human nature, and say, 'Ah Lord my God!' and, 'Oh that this day may be fortunate; give Thou that we see not the evil!' Of daily food they have not half enough, and if any head of the cattle be taken! – how may his household yet live?[23]

One of the fascinations of *Arabia Deserta* is that passages of great tenderness such as this one lodge equally in the reader's mind with expressions of the most savage malice.

Doughty in his compassionate moments realized that the short tempers, unpredictability, and often sheer inconsequence of the Bedouin had much to do with the terrible hardness of their lives. Hungry, dirty, and ignorant, what else could they be but 'bird-witted'? Only 'the well-faring and sheykhs, men enfranchised from the pining daily carefulness of their livelihood, bred liberally and polished in the mejlis', could rise to a larger virtue. 'Human life, where the poor hardly find passage by foul and cragged ways, full of cruel gins, is spread out more evenly before them. These are the noblemen of the desert, men of ripe moderation, peacemakers of a certain erudite and subtle judgment.'[24] How many other travellers in such places have understood as Doughty did how poverty, hunger and squalor constrict the human spirit?

Doughty learned from experience that the nomads' code of hospitality transcended their natural irritability and their religious hatreds. Had this not been the case he would never have survived his Arabian experience, going among them as he did stiff-necked and cantankerous, priding himself upon his plain speaking. He must often have tested the limits of their patience, but he came through in the end. 'The sour Waháby fanaticism,' he wrote, 'has in these days cruddled the hearts of the nomads, but every Beduin tent is sanctuary in the land of Ishmael (so there be not in it some cursed Jael).' When he found himself anxious for his safety among them he reassured himself with the thought: 'But I have eaten of their cheer, and might sleep among wolves.'[25]

Sometimes the duties of hospitality were discharged with no more than a grudging consciousness that this was what was required by public opinion, but there were also times when Doughty was welcomed in a way which affected him deeply. He concluded that the instinct of hospitality which impelled poor Bedouin to give him cheerfully what little they had, though it meant going hungry themselves, was religious in origin, though it had nothing to do with the formal Islam of the towns: the nomads believed that every passing stranger was, like themselves, a guest of God in the wilderness, and must not be denied God's gifts of food and shelter.[26] The acts of hospitality which resulted from this belief were the finest expression of the nomads' 'natural religion', which Doughty perceived as a profound consciousness that their existence depended on the grace of God. 'They see but the indigence of the open soil about, full of dangers, and hardly sustaining them, and the firmament above them, habitation of the Divine salvation.'[27]

He never forgot his experience of Arabian humanity and in later life wrote movingly in his poetry of the charity of poor folk. The intolerance and fanaticism of the desert fell into perspective and as

he grew older the Bedouin seem to have become ever more frag-
rant in his memory, until his final beneficent vision of them in
Mansoul:

> Booths without fence of doors
> Or walls; but that stand open to receive;
> To surety and peace and human fellowship;
> (As they too ben Gods guests,) Gods fugitive:
> Yea, and aught forwanderd wayfarer, in their wild paths;
> Heaven sends, to their poor hearths, to try their hearts.
> Wherefore, shall not they always be forgot;
> Of the EVERLASTING FATHER of all spirits!
> Whose equal EYE is, over all the Earth.[28]

Doughty himself was moved to something like religious wonder
by the desert landscape. Here is his response to the vast lava field
of the Harra.

We look out from every height . . . over an iron desolation; what uncouth
blackness and lifeless cumber of vulcanic matter! – an hard-set face of nature
without a smile for ever, a wilderness of burning and rusty horror of unformed
matter. What lonely life would not feel constraint of heart to trespass here! the
barren heaven, the nightmare soil! where should he look for comfort? – There is a
startled conscience within a man of his *mesquîn* being, and profane, in presence of
the divine stature of the elemental world! – this lion-like sleep of cosmogonic
forces, in which is swallowed up the gnat of the soul within him, – that short
motion and parasitical usurpation which is the weak accident of life in matter.[29]

There was nothing of Romantic egoism in Doughty's response to
the desert. Like the prophets of Israel he saw it as the place where
man regained a proper sense of his own weakness and
unworthiness.[30]

Enough has been quoted to give the flavour of Doughty's English.
The immediate effect is of archaism, but all thoughtful critics of
Doughty have realized that archaism is not the defining characteristic of his style. Though he described himself as 'a disciple of the
divine Muse of Spenser and Venerable Chaucer', he was not concerned to produce a mere copy of their style. What he sought to
revive in English literature was the spirit of Chaucer and Spenser
rather than their outward form. This spirit is conceived to be 'a
justness and directness, (springing from an ingenuous disposition, and diligent searching-out and observation of natural and
human things, with knowledge and meditation of the tongue)'. By
'knowledge and meditation of the tongue' he meant the cultivation

of the ability to use words in a way which was true to their fundamental meaning, as determined etymologically and historically. 'It is idle,' he wrote, 'to imagine, that any man not a well-taught lover of his tongue, can enter into the Garden of the Muses.' These carefully chosen words, the product of a learned sensibility, were to be used for the precise, vivid, and concrete depiction of human behaviour and natural objects.[31]

In the pursuit of his ideal Doughty was not wedded to any one linguistic tradition. He was quite capable of using 'homicide' and 'manslayer' in the same paragraph.[32] But every word, whether derived from Latin, Anglo-Saxon, Suffolk dialect, the Bible, or any of the other sources Doughty used, had to have an unambiguous meaning which was apparent to an educated reader. Often, as in 'Grave is that giddy heat on the crown of the head', we are to understand a word by reference to its root, but Doughty did not disdain neologisms: later in the same description of the heat of the desert he writes of 'the hot sand-blink' in the eyes.[33] When he could not find an old word which conveyed his precise meaning he made up a new one. He also seems to have used an eccentric and very heavy system of punctuation, and unusual word order, as devices to force the reader to read slowly and appreciate the force of every word. The sentence 'What had the world been? if the tongue had not wagged, of this fatal Ishmaelite!' is a good example of the technique.[34] His punctuation seems purely arbitrary: it is difficult, for example, to find a consistent rule governing the use of single and double quotation marks, or of brackets and parentheses. But perhaps there is some subtle and elaborate Doughtean rule which escapes us.

Doughty's conception of good English had much in common with the accepted conventions of good Arabic. An Arabic stylist uses words which can be referred to a root. Like Doughty's English, classical Arabic is vivid and concrete, not easily used to convey abstractions. In the desert Doughty heard this 'pure Arabic' in the mouths of the Bedouin. He was charmed by their graceful turns of speech and admirable clarity of articulation. 'The nomads,' he wrote, 'at leisure and lively minds, have little other than this study to be eloquent. Their utterance is short and with emphasis. There is a perspicuous propriety in their speech, with quick significance.' Though his knowledge of the language was in fact meagre he had no hesitation in judging the Arabic of the

Bedouin to be superior to the 'school-taught language of the town', and in pronouncing that the finest Arabic of all was spoken in Nejd.[35]

Burton and Palgrave had also pronounced, each according to his prejudices, on this matter. Burton, who was familiar with the practice of some Arab scholars of settling linguistic disputes by reference to Bedouin usage, believed the language of the Bedouin to be 'as of yore, purer than the language of the citizens'. Palgrave, naturally, believed that only in Jebel Shammar and central Nejd was really pure Arabic, by which he meant the language of the Koran, to be found. Doughty had no patience with the Moslem convention that the language of the Koran was the model of style. He preferred tthe natural vigour of Bedouin speech.[36]

All three of these writers, of whom Burton was the only Arabic scholar, tended to attribute the 'purest' Arabic to the Arabs they liked best. All of them, especially Doughty, seem to have been influenced by the theory, a commonplace of European nationalist thought in the nineteenth century, that pure thoughts, noble actions, and pure speech go together. In a passage which could have come straight out of Fichte, Doughty made the connections explicit. It was, he wrote,

the prerogative of every lover of his Country, to use the instrument of his thought, which is the Mother-tongue, with propriety and distinction; to keep that reverently clean and bright, which lies at the root of his mental life, and so, by extension, of the life of the Community: putting away all impotent and disloyal vility of speech, which is no uncertain token of a people's decadence.

Thus it was that Doughty could regard his labours over *Arabia Deserta* as a patriotic exercise.[37]

His passion for the apt word, which he interpreted at the conscious level as his patriotic duty, was rooted at a deeper level in the fundamental dislike of ambiguity which was a central element of Doughty's character. He wanted things to be crystal clear, in life as in literature. Each painstakingly chosen word in *Arabia Deserta* represented a tiny particle of eternal truth; each painfully endured encounter with fanatical Arabians a momentary affirmation of the moral truth of the Christian religion. His intellect could not grant to Christianity the status of scientific truth, but the knowledge of betrayal was mitigated by his acts of witness in Arabia, through which he made quite unambiguous to himself and others his commitment to the Christian religion. A man without Doughty's longing for the resolution of ambiguities – of belief, of behaviour, of matters of 'fact' – would not have willingly undergone the sufferings Doughty underwent in Arabia; nor would he have written *Arabia Deserta*. His love of truth, which led him early in life into scientific pursuits, was fatally entangled with a desire for certainty which led him to be over-explicit in his Tripos examinations, profoundly accurate in his poetic diction, and compelled him to affirm through action what could not be proved by intelligence.

He hardly seemed to change in his eighty-three years of life. After *Arabia Deserta* his work showed little intellectual or emotional development. Those issues on which he permitted himself to speculate were of an order of magnitude which perhaps kept them comfortably remote from any really painful self-questioning. At the end of *Mansoul*, the magisterial inquiry into 'the Riddle of the World' which he was still revising at the time of his death, his position is the same as it was in *Arabia Deserta*: affirmation of Christian faith in the face of intellectual doubt. *Mansoul* has very little specific content. It is merely, one suspects, a public exhibition of open-mindedness of a type which close-minded people sometimes indulge in: it appears to give their unreasoning convictions a foundation of legitimate inquiry. Perhaps this seems a harsh judgement on Doughty, but it is not undeserved. He was a man capable of great pity for human frailty, but the cast of his mind was monolithic, sometimes savagely so. His own doubts and conflicts were intellectualized over a long life into a series of poetic meditations and once, unforgettably, worked out in action in a manner for which all who love books must be grateful. *Arabia Deserta* is not diminished as a work of literature by the forbidding nature of its author's character. By some mysterious process of genius every word, almost, seems as immutable as he intended it to be.

One further subject remains to be mentioned: Doughty's conception of England in relation to the Arabs. It never seems to have crossed his mind that the Arabs, even (or perhaps especially) the 'free-born, forlorn and predatory Beduw', possessed political virtues which rendered them worthy of self-government. He believed that England should take whatever steps were necessary, including the occupation of Mecca, to stamp out the Arab slave trade and to ensure the safety of Christians in Arabia.[38] He accepted British imperialism without question. In Arabia he could not refrain from pointing with pride to some sacks of Indian rice and informing the ignorant Arabs that it was

rice of the Engleys, in sacks of the Engleys; and the marks are words of the Engleys. Ye go well clad! [he continued] – though only hareem wear this blue colour in the north! but what tunics are these? – I tell you, the cotton on your backs was spun and wove in mills of the Engleys. Ye have not considered that ye are fed in part and clothed by the Engleys![39]

Only Doughty, of the four travellers discussed in this book, was capable of making such a speech. Burton cared nothing for such mundane evidence of England's glory; Palgrave was lost in the ambiguities of his own position; Blunt would have died rather than commit such a breach of good manners.

7

The Victorian Contribution

NO SINGLE STEREOTYPE of the Arab is to be found in the writings of Burton, Blunt, Palgrave and Doughty, and nothing could more clearly demonstrate the personal nature of their wanderings. Some of the familiar themes are there, but always with variations supplied by the author. They all had rather different ideas as to what constituted the finest type of Arab, but they all invested their favourite specimens with the *gravitas* and manly civility which had become his traditional attributes. Predatoriness was a feature of Bedouin life which evidently could not be evaded, but each writer treated it in a distinctive way: Burton distilled from it a code of chivalry in accordance with his own violent pursuit of honour; Palgrave and Doughty denounced it as destructive of public order; Blunt subsumed it to his theory of the aristocratic domination of the country over the town.

With the exception of the Blunts' books and articles, the conventional noble Arab was not a prominent figure in their writings. By 1850 he had become a figure of romance, a mere poetic image, a subject of after-dinner entertainment by the ladies. Victorian children declaimed *The Arab's Farewell to his Horse* and devoured *The Talisman* and the *Arabian Nights*, but ideas about Arabs derived from these sources bore little resemblance to those found in the *Narrative of a Year's Journey through Central and Eastern Arabia* or *Arabia Deserta*. The cult of Arabia as it developed in the second half of the nineteenth century was esoteric and exclusive. The run-of-the-mill reviewer confronted with Palgrave could only express delight and amazement, or disapproval and amazement, according to his bent.

The esoteric version of the noble Arab was the inhabitant of Nejd. Even Doughty felt a certain exhilaration when setting out for 'the free High Arabia!'[1] It is not hard to see how Nejd acquired its glamour. For one thing, it was almost impossible to get to, and this in itself bestowed on it an inevitable charm. It was also regarded by the Arabs themselves as the heart of Arabia, the home of the legendary hero Antar, and this increased its appeal for the well-read traveller. But mostly its charm derived from its isolation. Sealed off from the outside world by mountains and deserts, it was the one region, the cognoscenti agreed, where the true Arab was likely to be found. Speaking the purest Arabic, riding the purest horses, and being of course of the purest descent, the Nejdi had an automatic claim on the attention of anyone inclined to theorize about nationality or race.

Burton, Blunt, Palgrave and Doughty were all inclined in this direction, to a degree unusual among Englishmen. None of them possessed the complacent, uncomplicated brand of patriotism which, with all due allowance for the natural variety of human nature, might be said to be typical of Victorian England. Their patriotism was more akin to the articulate nationalism which was being expounded on the continent: emotionally intense, theoretically based, and with a strong emphasis on blood, race and language. Continental influences can hardly be held completely responsible for their untypicalness, but it is worth noting that all four of them were directly exposed to European nationalism, three of them (Burton, Palgrave, Blunt) in conditions of national, racial or social marginality which must have made these ideas, with their heroic prescriptions for self-actualization in the service of the nation, particularly interesting to them. Burton and Palgrave (and perhaps Doughty) seem to have been inspired by the German model, while Blunt was temperamentally more attuned to the Italian model.

Blunt was in many respects a Mazzini manqué. He took the Irredentist principle of Italian nationalism, absurd in an English context, and applied it to the Arabs. His problems of identity were apparently alleviated by his involvement in what he conceived as an Arab Risorgimento. If England had still been in search of political community, instead of basking in the consciousness of nationhood which was the legacy of the English Revolution, Blunt's talents would have been employed at home. Instead it was the Arabs who received the benefit of his impulse to express the principle of aristocracy in nationalist terms. In English terms Blunt was an irrelevance, in European terms he was a man of his time, and in Arab terms he was a man ahead of his time. It has been shown that the Arab nationalist, al Kawakibi, derived many of his political ideas from Blunt.[2]

Blunt and the others all had an exalted and intense idea of English nationality which led inevitably to disappointment in the face of reality. They asked the impossible of their compatriots because they had an exaggerated idea of their capacities. Burton overestimated the strength and bellicosity of the British lion, Blunt failed to understand the relation between interest and idealism in the conduct of foreign policy, Doughty never realized the extent of the Englishman's repugnance to any hysterical display of self-sacrifice, and Palgrave, with his high-minded cosmopolitanism, never understood the crudely exclusive nature of popular patriotism. They were therefore condemned to look back to the glorious past rather than forward to the glorious future. In the case of Blunt, the glorious future which is an essential part of the nationalist vision was assigned in turn to the Arabs, the Indians and the Irish.

All of them believed in England's right to interfere in the affairs of others. Burton and Doughty quite simply accepted the imperial imperative and made no exception for the Arabs. Palgrave hinted at an exception for the Arabs of Nejd. Blunt came to believe that the British Empire was a curse to mankind, but this was only the petulance of a jilted lover; in happier days he had suggested extensive (but benevolent) interference in Arab affairs. The fascination which they all felt for the Arabs did not lead to an attitude of sympathetic detachment, or even necessarily to sympathy of an intelligible sort. With the exception of Blunt they might be more accurately described, in a phrase Arnold Toynbee used of the Arabic scholar David Margoliouth, as addicts rather than enthusiasts.[3]

Their collective political legacy was not a sentimental idealism regarding Arabs but a convention that Englishmen were peculiarly good at understanding them. They did nothing themselves to encourage this idea, but the purely fortuitous appearance in rapid succession of four gifted English writers on Arabia helped to create the myth that the English 'knew the Arabs' as no one else did. A feeling of affinity was an optional extra. Peake Pasha of Transjordan used to say that an Englishman who had read *Arabia Deserta* knew more about the Bedouin than a town-bred Arab did.[4]

PART TWO

There is a nice irony in this profession of insight when we remember that what these four men wrote about the Arabs has to be read in the light of the psychological cross each one had to bear. What was insight and what was mere projection? I leave that for Arabists to decide. It is at least possible that a writer's personal obsession might occasionally illuminate his experience for him and turn out to be an aid to understanding rather than a disability.

There is an initial temptation in studying these eccentric Victorian travellers to suppose that they were turning their backs on civilization when they took off for the desert. They were, but only temporarily, and this was not the fundamental purpose of their travels. They were all highly civilized men who sought recognition in their own highly civilized society. One cannot imagine them noiselessly submerging themselves forever in the primitive societies which possessed such a fascination for them. Rather, they used these societies as a medium of self-expression. Here, where the social demands made on them were less complex than at home, they could act out their dramas of identity with virtually unimpeded self-absorption.

PART THREE

8

The Great War and the Arabists

'How do I know that you will keep your word? Perhaps to-morrow you will choose another guide?' 'The English have but one word,' said I; it is a principle that should never be abandoned in the East.

Gertrude Bell, *Amurath to Amurath*, 1911

There is no nation of Arabs.

Gertrude Bell, *Syria: the Desert and the Sown*, 1907

THE FIRST WORLD WAR was the Arabists' moment in history. Gifted amateurs of Arab history and psychology like Gertrude Bell, T. E. Lawrence and Sir Mark Sykes were precipitated by the fortunes of war into positions where they might hope to influence the course of events. They made the most of their opportunities; but it would be a mistake to credit them, either individually or collectively, with a decisive influence on British policy during the war. That policy was developed in response to political and strategic considerations by men to whom the destiny of the Arab race was not a subject of absorbing interest. Nevertheless, the local implementation of British policy gave scope for action to people who experienced in varying degrees and in various ways that fascination with the Arabs which is the subject of this book. They operated with a high degree of self-consciousness within a tradition of articulate and adventurous British interest in Arabia; the confidence with which they acted owed much to this sense of accumulated expertise.

The belief that the English were particularly qualified to meddle in Arab politics fitted in very well with the ideas of a new generation of imperial thinkers whose ideas were coming into fashion at the time. The *Round Table* group's exalted notion of an empire held together less by force than by the British genius for understanding and subtly controlling native races (while working unobtrusively in their best interests) had an inevitable appeal for those who saw themselves as following in the footsteps of Doughty and of Burton. Had not these men and others like them demonstrated beyond doubt the Englishman's unique capacity for this kind of relationship? Though neither of them was in any real sense a member of the group, both Gertrude Bell and T. E. Lawrence contributed to *The Round Table*. They subscribed to the view articulated within its pages that the legitimate national aspirations of small nations could best be served, at least for the time being, within the British Empire.

Britain's wartime involvement with the Sherif Hussein of Mecca and his family has been the subject of much scholarly attention, and crucial points of interpretation and of detail are still enthusiastically disputed. The interested reader is referred to such standard works as Elizabeth Monroe's *Britain's Moment in the Middle East*, George Antonius's *The Arab Awakening*, and Elie Kedourie's *England and the Middle East* and *In the Anglo-Arab Labyrinth*. For those unacquainted with the labyrinth the following brief guide is offered.

Until 1914 a crucial element in British foreign policy was the maintenance of friendly relations with Turkey. Ottoman territories straddled the road to India and it was therefore felt to be vital that Britain should remain on good terms with Constantinople and support as best she could its imperial authority. Throughout the nineteenth century this meant that Britain offered no material succour to secessionist movements within the Ottoman Empire, though liberal opinion at home was often sympathetic to such revolts against 'Oriental despotism'. When Turkey entered the First World War on the German side British thinking on the Middle East underwent radical revisions. Secession was now something that might be encouraged, though if possible without making promises which could prove embarrassing to any future peace settlement.

It was in this frame of mind that the British responded to requests for military assistance from the rebellious Sherif of Mecca. The Sherif's initial approaches were made through his son Abdullah to Kitchener, then British Agent in Cairo, in early 1914. Kitchener at that time naturally refused to offer any encouragement, but he kept the channel of communication open through his Oriental Secretary, Ronald Storrs. Storrs, who liked to think of himself as a beguiling combination of aesthete and man of action, was a confident amateur of Arab history and literature, well equipped in his own estimation to handle tactfully any Oriental potentate whose affairs touched on those of the British Empire.[1] It was he who in September 1914 wrote to Kitchener, then War Minister in London, to remind him of the possibility of exploiting to British advantage Arab discontent in the Hejaz, and it was he who communicated Kitchener's response to the Sherif. The message eventually sent to Mecca is worth quoting, for it nicely illustrates, with its entirely unsolicited hint about an Arab caliphate, the way in which large strategic considerations could become entangled with an enthusiastic local interest in arranging Arab affairs.

Till now we have defended and befriended Islam in the person of the Turks; henceforward it shall be in that of the noble Arab. It may be that an Arab of true race will assume the Caliphate at Mecca or Medina, and so good may come, by the help of God, out of all the evil which is now occurring. It would be well if Your Highness could convey to your followers and devotees, who are found throughout the world, in every country, the good tidings of the freedom of the Arabs, and the rising of the sun over Arabia.[2]

After receiving this message the Sherif committed himself to an alliance with the British.

In the early months of 1915 he received further gratifying evidence of a friendly British interest in his affairs, this time from General Wingate, the Governor-General of the Sudan, who moved independently to sound out the Sherif as to what assistance he might require should he decide to take up arms against the Turks. Wingate's vision of the post-war world included 'a federation of semi-independent Arab states [existing] under European guidance and supervision, linked together by racial and linguistic bonds, owing spiritual allegiance to a single Arab Primate, and looking to Great Britain as its patron and protector'.[3] It was with Britain's long-term interests in mind, therefore, that he approached the Sherif, though he was also, he said, motivated by a personal sympathy with the Arabs acquired during his long residence in the Sudan.[4] He did not seriously entertain the possibility that the forces he was proposing to unleash might prove ultimately to be beyond British control.

It was not until July 1915 that the Sherif Hussein and Sir Henry

McMahon, the British High Commissioner in Egypt, got down to serious discussion of the terms of the Anglo-Arab alliance. The correspondence between them resulted in an agreement that in the event of a British victory in the war a large area of the Middle East should be under independent Arab rule. While these negotiations were going on conversations were also taking place between the British and the French about the post-war future of Syria. The negotiators in this case were Sir Mark Sykes and M. Georges Picot, representing respectively the British and French Foreign Offices, and the result of their efforts was the document known as the Sykes–Picot agreement. This agreement divided up the Middle East into spheres of influence and areas of direct French and British control, with Palestine reserved for some form of international administration. The territory marked out for 'an independent Arab State or Confederation of Arab States' consisted mostly of the desert areas of Syria and Mesopotamia, and it was divided up into a northern part (A) in which France was to have priority of economic enterprise and sole right of supplying any foreign advisers that might be requested and a southern area (B) in which the same held for Britain.

The supposed discrepancies between the Hussein–McMahon agreement and the Sykes–Picot agreement with regard to the Arab position after the war were to be the cause of much trouble in the future. All that can be said here is that these discrepancies do not seem to have been apparent at the time. Sykes and McMahon had full knowledge of each other's doings and McMahon believed that the territories which he had excluded from the area of Arab independence in his negotiations with the Sherif were the same as the ones which had been reserved for direct French and British control in the Sykes–Picot agreement, namely the Syrian littoral and lower Mesopotamia. Where McMahon indubitably blundered was in failing to make clear to the Sherif that the future of Palestine must be a matter for multilateral agreement, an omission which was to have the most far-reaching consequences.

Though the agreement which bore his name came to be execrated by many right-thinking persons, Sir Mark Sykes was a man who loved the Arabs according to his lights. He was amiable, intelligent, and aristocratic, a late edition of the Victorian 'Travelling Gent'. Much of his life before the war was spent wandering the

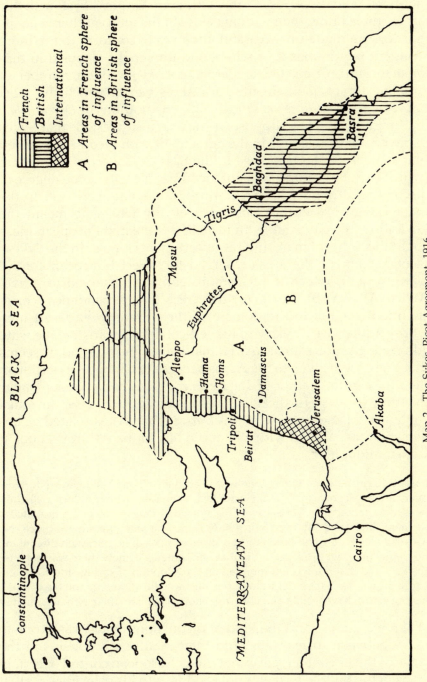

Map 2 The Sykes–Picot Agreement, 1916

highways and by-ways of the Ottoman Empire, first with his father, then alone, then with his wife. In the intervals between his journeys he made unsuccessful attempts to conform to the more stringent requirements of school and university, dabbled in diplomacy, and got elected to Parliament. He wrote a number of amusing travel books in the Kinglake style, of which the most popular was *Dar-ul-Islam* (1904). There is nothing in *Dar-ul-Islam* that might lead us to suppose, as has been suggested, that Sykes betrayed his convictions in the agreement with Picot. He believed that some inhabitants of the Middle East were worthy of freedom (which in Sykes's mind was not incompatible with some degree of discreet and friendly British control), and some were not. In the latter category was the 'Gosmobaleet', by which he meant the Levantine, the city Arab with his half-assimilated European ideas about the rights of man, and his unfortunate clothes. In the Sykes–Picot agreement the areas reserved for direct European control were those in which the 'Gosmobaleet' was observed to thrive. Areas (A) and (B), however, the areas of independence, corresponded roughly to the domain of the proud, free, desert men whose authenticity Sykes, in his self-consciously aristocratic way, admired. (As for Damascus, Homs, Hama and Aleppo, it seems that these were given to the Arabs because of Gibbon's assertion in the fifty-eighth chapter of *The Decline and Fall of the Roman Empire* that they were the furthest limit of Moslem territory after the initial conquests of the crusaders.[5]) In *Dar-ul-Islam* Sykes related a conversation he had had with a Bedouin boy in the Ashiret School in Constantinople.

I asked [him] how many years he had been there. 'Four,' he answered. 'How many more will you stay?' 'Two,' he replied. Then I asked him, 'Which are better, houses or tents?' His yellow eyes blazed with remembrance, he hesitated a moment, and cried 'By my God, tents!' There was one of a superior race. No 'Gosmobaleet'; no weak clutching at a stranger's creed; no uncertain discontent; no shame of ancient custom. From that one sentence I knew there was hope for the East and that hope is not founded on the adoption of spring-side boots and bad manners by native Christians, but on the wild, brave, manly races who, having learnt, have weight and character enough to retain their own nationality.[6]

When we understand the kind of distinctions Sykes was prone to make between 'true Arabs' and their inauthentic cousins in the cities of the Levant it is clear that direct European control of certain areas in the Middle East was not at odds with his principles at all. It is in this context that his remarks at a meeting of the war committee in July 1916, two months after the signing of the agreement, should be understood. 'In my opinion,' he observed, 'Arabs cannot be run on the lines of the "white man's" burden. The Arabs have many faults and failings, but they have physique, fire and nimbleness of mind and a sense of breed which makes it impossible to adopt the white versus coloured attitude towards them.'[7] It was of course the 'true Arabs', the ones who preferred tents to houses, to whom he was reluctant to apply the full colonial treatment, not the educated Arabs who had adopted European ideas of progress and therefore rendered themselves inauthentic in his eyes.

Sykes admired and promoted authenticity (as he saw it) wherever he found it, and he accordingly became a passionate Zionist, believing that on their own ground in Palestine the Jews' unique combination of spirituality and practicality would flower for the general good. It was an opinion from which he later retreated, after a visit to Palestine in 1918 when he saw the political and social problems that were being created by Jewish immigration.[8] He was not the only Arabist who believed that the interests of Arab and Jew were compatible, and indeed that Jewish settlement was crucial to the development of the area. Philip Graves, a journalist who worked in Cairo Intelligence during the war and later wrote quite extensively on the Middle East, believed that the Arabs, for all their attractive qualities, needed 'Jewish brains and capital . . . and British administrators' to make a go of Palestine. T. E. Lawrence also believed that the Jews would act as a beneficial economic stimulant to the Arabs. One of the few people concerned with Arab affairs who early recognized the Balfour Declaration as a catastrophe was Gertrude Bell. She believed (wrongly) that the land was incapable of development and (rightly) that the hostile Moslem majority would not sit back while the Jews moved into Palestine.[9]

The Arabism of Mark Sykes was distinctly in the minor tradition of Warburton and Kinglake; amused, ironic, even affectionate, but basically detached. If it had not been for the war Arab nationalism would have remained for him a spectator sport, something to be applauded when it appealed to his aesthetic sense. As it turned out, the war gave him an opportunity for spirited intervention in Arab affairs.

.   .   .

McMahon's final note to the Sherif of Mecca was sent off on 30 January 1916. At dawn on 10 June the Turkish barracks and garrison posts in Mecca were simultaneously attacked with rifle fire and the Arab Revolt finally began; by the end of September the towns of Jedda, Rabigh, Yanbu and Taif were in the hands of the Sherif. In October T. E. Lawrence, accompanying his colleague Ronald Storrs on a mission to the Emir Abdullah, set foot in Arabia for the first time.

Without some discussion of Lawrence – his actions, his motives, his influence on Anglo-Arab relations – this chapter would not be complete; and yet it is with some reluctance that I turn to the examination of the well-documented but still obscure personality of a man who has fascinated two generations of biographers. Statements about Lawrence's motives are full of risk. The biographer has to contend with his own biases – in my own case there is a constant struggle between dislike of a man who assiduously propagated his own legend and a desire to be fair to someone who presents too easy a target for ridicule – and those distortions and inaccuracies, many of them attributable to Lawrence himself, which appear in the primary source material. Lawrence was, firstly, a liar, and secondly, a mystic whose talent for introspection led him to believe that a man can never know his own soul. He sometimes did things for no other reason than to see what his action might reveal about himself. His own discussions of his motives, while of the greatest interest, are dangerous props for a biographer to lean on: they are all too likely to be the product either of a desire for mystification or of an effort to impose some sort of intellectual coherence on the past. The fact that his personality is so extremely well documented is a problem in itself. We are none of us blessed with the consistency of character we like to believe is normal: we all tend to respond differently to different people. But in Lawrence this tendency seems to have been exaggerated. He was more of a chameleon than most of us, partly out of curiosity about himself and his effect on people, and partly because he couldn't help it. When the friends of a man like this take the trouble to write down their recollections of him, as many of Lawrence's did in *T. E. Lawrence by his Friends*, the psychologist is confronted by information of great complexity. It is tempting to respond to this complexity by seeking the one clue that will provide the answer to the puzzle, but this is neither honest nor feasible. Lawrence is a

THE KING-MAKER

12   A photograph of Lawrence from Lowell Thomas's book,
with the original caption

rich seam to mine for anyone who is interested in the way we exist in other people's minds, but this means that any final assessment of him is probably impossible. So, in the brief space devoted to him here, no final assessment of him is attempted, only a few specula-tions (I use the word with accuracy and without embarrassment as indicating the tentative nature of my observations) about the nature of his feelings for the Arabs, and for the Sherifian family in particular.

When the Arab Revolt began Lawrence was an unimportant young staff officer whose presence on Storrs's mission to the Hejaz was the result of his own request that he should be allowed to spend his leave in Arabia. He was not entrusted with any official mission, but he nevertheless conceived his journey as having a most important purpose: 'to find the yet unknown master-spirit of the affair, and measure his capacity to carry the revolt to the goal I had conceived for it'.[10] This goal, which Lawrence intended to take a conspicuous part in achieving, was eloquently stated after the war in the book which remains the final repository of his legend, the enigmatically entitled *Seven Pillars of Wisdom*. 'I meant,' he wrote, 'to make a new nation, to restore a lost influence, to give twenty millions of Semites the foundation on which to build an inspired dream-palace of their national thoughts.'[11] It was an improbable ambition for a twenty-eight year old archaeologist turned temporary soldier – and scarcely even a soldier; in October 1916 Lawrence had yet to see active service.

On this first visit to Arabia he weighed up each of the Sherif's four sons to see if he possessed the qualities which he considered crucial to the success of the movement. Abdullah he found 'too clever', Ali 'too clean', and Zeid 'too cool'.[12] Only Feisal, the Sherif's third son, seemed to him promising material from which to fashion the armed prophet which he believed necessary for his purpose. 'I felt at first glance,' he wrote of his meeting with Feisal at Wadi Safra, 'that this was the man I had come to Arabia to seek – the leader who would bring the Arab Revolt to full glory.'[13] He communicated these assessments to his superiors in Cairo and shortly found himself back in Arabia as political and liaison officer with Feisal's forces. For the next two years, until the fall of Damas-cus, he was with the Arab army, and his activities during these years became the basis of his fame.

Noteworthy attempts have been made by Richard Aldington,

Suleiman Mousa, and John Mack to sort out from the available evidence (much of it supplied by Lawrence) just what his role in the Arab Revolt was.[14] I shall not attempt to traverse this difficult terrain again. It appears to have been fairly well established that he was a competent and imaginative guerilla leader, but his political standing with the Arabs is far less clear. In 1917, judging from an article he contributed to the *Arab Bulletin*, an intelligence news-letter circulated among Cairo officials, he conceived of himself as the power behind the scenes, a man who did not thrust himself for-ward publicly but guided the actions of those who did. The techni-que he advocated, and which he believed he had perfected, was to latch on to a member of the Sherifian family and use him as a medium for directing the course of events.

Win and keep the confidence of your leader. Strengthen his prestige at your expense before others when you can. Never refuse or quash schemes he may put forward; but ensure that they are put forward in the first instance privately to you. Always approve them, and after praise modify them insensibly, causing the suggestions to come from him, until they are in accord with your own opinion. When you attain this point, hold him to it, keep a tight grip of his ideas, and push him forward as firmly as possible, but secretly, so that no one but himself (and he not too clearly) is aware of your pressure . . . Wave a Sherif in front of you like a banner and hide your own mind and person. If you succeed, you will have hundreds of miles of country and thousands of men under your orders, and for this it is worth bartering the outward show.[15]

This supposed ability to bend Arabs secretly to his will has always been at the core of what one might term the esoteric version of the Lawrence legend, espoused by people too sophisticated to believe the vulgar version promulgated by Lowell Thomas (and secretly encouraged, it must be said, by Lawrence himself) that he was 'the leader of the Arab Army'. Whatever his role actually was, there is no doubt that at times during the revolt he permitted himself to believe that he was masterminding the whole show.[16] Unfortunately, there is no way of finding out whether he did or not: power exercised secretly is not available for historical inspec-tion. Arab contentions that Lawrence was a useful but politically insignificant member of Feisal's entourage can always be countered by Lawrence's protagonists with the retort that their hero's in-fluence was exercised with the most skilful discretion.

Although his actual position in the revolt will probably remain forever obscure, Lawrence's ideas about the Arabs and their national movement were set down by him with the utmost clarity in *Seven Pillars of Wisdom* and elsewhere. Many of them will seem familiar to readers of this book for, with one notable exception, they were derived from the works of the nineteenth-century Arabists with whose treatises we were concerned in previous chapters. The young Lawrence was saturated with Burckhardt, Doughty, Disraeli, Blunt, Palgrave (whom he thought brilliant) and Burton (whom he thought vulgar), and it therefore comes as no surprise to us to learn that the oases of Nejd are 'the true centre of Arabia, the preserve of its native spirit, and its most conscious individuality', or that the Semites possess a genius for religion which arises from their barren desert environment, or that the Bedouin fears not death and loves the desert because there he is free, or that the Arab, when inspired by an armed prophet, is a natural conqueror but a poor administrator.[17] These are the pronouncements of someone writing within a conscious tradition, though most readers of *Seven Pillars of Wisdom* are probably unaware of the fact. For a large part of the educated public the third chapter of *Seven Pillars of Wisdom*, fashioned by Lawrence with such rhetorical brilliance, is the only source of informed opinion on the character of the Arabs.

The two most important influences on Lawrence's views about Arab nationalism were undoubtedly Palgrave and Blunt. Like Palgrave he believed that the roots of Arab weakness lay in tribalism and that only when some strong leader arose who could bind the disparate elements together would a free and united Arabia arise.[18] He further believed, echoing his 'Master Arabian' Wilfrid Blunt, that the leader should come from the family of the Sherifs of Mecca, whose nomad instincts and faultless pedigree made them natural candidates for the rulership of Arabia. Blunt had been impressed by these princes who in spite of their contact with the Turkish bureaucracy and their position as hereditary rulers of Mecca still retained their nomad dress and manners and sent their children to be brought up in the tribal tents.[19] His great hope had been that the Sherif of Mecca would become, under British protection, the Caliph of Islam and that this would be the first step towards a new spiritual and cultural awakening in the Moslem world. He saw the prestige and power of an Arabian caliphate as a means of reviving Arab influence over the vast area which had grown soft and torpid without it. Lawrence cared little about the caliphate but nevertheless saw the Sherifian family as the only possible instrument for effecting a return of Arab hegemony in the East. His ideas on the subject were a creative amalgam of those of Palgrave and Blunt.

Sherifs are above all blood-feuds and local rivalries [he wrote in 1917], and form the only principle of unity among the Arabs . . . Intertribal jealousies make it impossible for any sheikh to attain a commanding position, and the only hope of union in nomad Arabia is that the Ashraf be universally acknowledged as the ruling class. Sherifs are half-townsmen, half-nomad, in manner and life, and have the instinct of command. Mere merit and money would be insufficient to obtain such recognition; but the Arab reverence for pedigree and the Prophet gives hope for the ultimate success of the Ashraf.[20]

History was to show, with its customary unkind disregard for the reputations of political pundits, that Lawrence was quite wrong in his analysis of the situation in Arabia. It was Ibn Saud the Wahhabi iconoclast who eventually brought union to Arabia, not the noble descendants of the Prophet's house. Neither in 1916 or at any time after was there any good reason for supposing that the Arab nationalist movement could only be brought to fruition through the Sherif of Mecca and his family. Lawrence was the prisoner of a preconceived idea which for a brief period during the war, as the result of Sherif Hussein's negotiations with the British, had the deceitful appearance of reflecting Arabian reality. It was a delusion which was shared for a time by others in Cairo Intelligence, but it was one which was abandoned by them when the real weakness of the Sherif's position became apparent. The Sherif was only one Arabian potentate among others who were either minding their own business, collaborating happily with the Turks, or promoting their own interests.

It is his devotion to what came to be known as the 'Sherifian cause' and his blindness to other possibilities – in the late 1920s he still thought Ibn Saud would come to nothing – that marks Lawrence off from other British officials in the Middle East.[21] Their enthusiasm for the Sherif – whose potential elevation to the caliphate undoubtedly had an appeal for the historically minded among them – tended to wane as his usefulness appeared to diminish, and by the end of the war their support for him and his family had greatly decreased as he came to be regarded by them as 'difficult'. But Lawrence was tireless in his efforts to set up the Sherifians as rulers of the lands liberated from the Turks and stuck by them through a period (1918–20) when British officials had become almost unanimously bored with Sherifian ambitions.[22] He seems to have conceived his own destiny as being intimately linked with theirs, and when his Sherifian protégés had eventually been installed on thrones specially created for them by the British he abruptly lost interest in Arab affairs, resigned from his position as Churchill's political adviser in the Middle East Department of the Colonial Office, and enlisted in the ranks of the Royal Air Force.

Lawrence has been criticized by Arab writers for his narrow conception of the nature of Arab nationalism, which resulted in the imposition of rule by an archaic Meccan aristocracy upon vast areas of the Middle East. As adviser to Churchill during the period leading up to the Cairo Conference of 1921 he clearly had great personal influence on the settlements which were made at that conference and can justly be credited with (or accused of) having considerable responsibility for the post-war configuration of the Middle East. It was agreed at that conference that Abdullah's position as ruler of what came to be called Transjordan should be recognized and upheld, and that Feisal should be made ruler of Mesopotamia. By the time the conference convened in March 1921 Abdullah's enterprising installation of himself in Amman, and the lack of suitable local candidates for ruler of Mesopotamia, had created a situation which favoured the adoption by the British Goverment of a co-ordinated 'Sherifian policy'. Lawrence was able to persuade Churchill that in one dazzling stroke he could romantically do the right thing by a noble race and make secure British interests in the Middle East. Like other British officials Lawrence believed that the Arab states which would come into being should exist under British tutelage, though the form he believed that tutelage should take was an interesting one. The future he envisaged for the Arabs was as the first 'brown dominion' in a British Commonwealth along the lines of that proposed by his friend Lionel Curtis, the leader of the *Round Table* group. He believed that by promising the Arabs dominion status within the Empire their loyalty could be secured without lavish expenditure of men or money; affiliation with a large and flourishing concern like the British Empire would offer advantages (presumably of trade and collective security) which they would not be slow to appreciate. He outlined his plan in a letter to Curzon in September 1919, adding: 'Arabs react against you if you try to drive them, and they are as tenacious as Jews: but you can lead them without force anywhere, if nominally arm in arm. The future of Mesopotamia is so immense that if it is cordially ours we can swing the whole Middle East with it.'[23]

The way in which to make it 'cordially ours', according to Lawrence, was to make a Sherifian king of it. In October 1918 he testified before the Eastern Committee of the Cabinet that Abdullah should be installed in Baghdad and Lower Mesopotamia, Zeid in Upper Mesopotamia and Feisal in Syria.[24] As the situation in the Middle East developed he proposed different permutations of this arrangement to fit the changing circumstances, but at the centre of the policies which he advocated there was always the Sherifian family.

We must ask why his vision of Arab affairs was so limited. A man as articulate as Lawrence had no trouble supplying explicit reasons for his advocacy of Sherifian primacy in the Middle East – British interests and Arab interests were cited as required – but we are left with the feeling that his association with this family had something obsessive about it. No one else in British official circles consistently saw them as providing the obvious answer to the problem of what was going to happen in the Middle East after the demise of the Ottoman Empire. Lawrence on the other hand was not deterred from supporting them even by their obvious inadequacies as the vehicle for his dreams. He told his biographer Liddell Hart in 1933 that he had consciously over-praised Feisal in his wartime reports in order to secure British support for him.[25] Was it the role of king-maker which gave him such satisfaction? Did he start out with a simply intellectual interest in the Sherifian family as part of a theory of Arab nationalism concocted from his wide reading, and then find out during the revolt that his ability (as he saw it) to control the destiny of these princes satisfied deep longings for glory and power? Did he then compulsively begin to identify their interests with his own? To attempt to answer these questions we must tackle the difficult problem of Lawrence's character and the influences which formed it.

As everyone knows, Lawrence was the illegitimate son of an Anglo-Irish baronet who had run off with the governess of his legitimate children. His mother, in spite of her one great lapse, was a woman of formidable conventional virtue, who imparted a Calvinist morality to her sons. By the time he was ten Lawrence apparently knew of his illegitimacy and the existence of his father's other family in Ireland. The influence of this knowledge has been avidly discussed by recent biographers, for it seems to provide a dramatic clue to the mystery of his personality. With sufficient adroitness it can be made to 'explain' almost anything a biographer wants it to explain and there is always a danger for any writer on Lawrence of succumbing to this temptation. The fact to be borne constantly in mind is that Lawrence had four brothers, all illegitimate, but only he became 'Lawrence of Arabia'. His extraordinary personality cannot be explained by reference to his illegitimacy alone. It seems plausible to suggest that shame at being born out of wedlock may have had something to do with the repugnance he expressed in *Seven Pillars* and his letters for sex and reproduction (he was attracted to the desert because it was sterile and therefore 'clean' – one of his favourite words); but his brother Arnold married and became the father of children. So long as we realize that speculations about the development of Lawrence's character possess no more than this kind of constricted plausibility, let us make some intelligent speculations in the hope of stumbling on to something which comes close to the truth.

In real life Lawrence found himself in a position which children often fantasize about: he discovered that he was not an ordinary suburban child but the son of a nobleman. He also realized, though not necessarily at exactly the same time, that he was a bastard. Exactly how he responded to these discoveries at the time they were made will never be known, but there is one well-documented aspect of his boyhood which perhaps gives us a clue. He developed a passionate interest in knightly romance and chivalry and read everything he could find on these subjects. He became an expert brass rubber and decorated his room with the results of his efforts. Eventually he was to write an Oxford history thesis on the Crusades and he maintained a lifelong interest in mediaeval romances. It does not seem far-fetched to suggest that, faced with his remarkable discoveries, he escaped from the newly appreciated squalor of his condition into romantic fantasies of knightly valour, with which, through his unknown knightly forebears, he felt able to identify. He always liked to think of his father as having lived a lordly and expansive life in Ireland before he was captured by his mother, and he undoubtedly came to resent being denied the place in society to which his aristocratic paternity entitled him.[26] He tells us in *Seven Pillars of Wisdom* that he had hoped 'to be a general and knighted' by the time he was thirty; and after the war, when he was famous throughout the English-speaking world, he was hurt by the fact that his father's family had not seen fit to reward him with some public recognition.[27] Under these circumstances, identification with the heroes of chivalrous romance perhaps provided a safety valve for explosive feelings.

With a head full of Malory and the *chansons de geste*, and the poignant knowledge of his own aristocratic birth, the young Lawrence was a perfect candidate for the type of Arabism personified by Wilfrid Blunt, whose disciple he became. When he began to think about promoting the Arab cause he thought about it in terms of a national revival led by aristocrats whose impeccable pedigree gave them a prestige which transcended tribal and regional loyalties; the nationalist principle was fused with the aristocratic principle in a manner which Blunt would have completely approved. This conception was always at the heart of Lawrence's interest in the revolt.

If Lawrence's ideas about the nature of Arab nationalism had an implicit connection with boyhood fantasies, which in turn had originated as a consoling response to a traumatic experience, we can begin to see perhaps why these ideas were so inflexible. The connection in Lawrence's mind between the Meccan aristocracy and the Arab nationalist movement, which seemed in 1916 to find a counterpart in reality, existed at a primitive and emotional level – though in Lawrence's case, with his unusual capacity for introspection, it would be rash to call it 'unconscious'. Participation in the revolt on the terms in which he saw it enabled him to act out chivalric fantasies. He went about dressed in the silken robes of an Arab emir and carried a dagger made of gold. In the latter part of the war, when princely fantasies seem to have acquired a melancholy grip on him, he collected around him a band of gorgeous ruffians whom he described as his bodyguard; he claimed that nearly sixty of them died for the honour of his service.[28] After the war he allowed it to be put about that he was a Prince of Mecca – a ridiculous story, but what an elevation for the illegitimate son of an Irish knight! He was too intelligent not to realize that such behaviour and such stories were absurd – and he occasionally said so – but this lordly aspect of himself during the revolt was one which he apparently found irresistible. It is quite possible that he was sur-

179

prised, and further unbalanced, by the discovery after the war that people believed in him and admired him in his role of desert prince.

The satisfaction which he obtained during the revolt not just from his association with but from his apparent control of its Sherifian leaders is evident in the unguarded report, 'Twenty-Seven Articles', which he sent to the *Arab Bulletin* in August 1917. 'Wave a Sherif in front of you like a banner' was his advice to anyone who wished to emulate his success in the act of handling Arabs. The suggestion is not so much cynical as arrogant and exuberant, the prescription of a man carried away with what he believes to be his own success. There is none of the usual laconic restraint of Englishmen in discussing such relationships, perhaps because Lawrence derived from them a kind of satisfaction more powerful and personal than that of others of his countrymen whose imperial destiny brought them into positions of power over tribal potentates. The Sherifians became his personal protégés, capable in his determined hands of providing him with un-dreamed-of – or more accurately, dreamed-of – satisfactions. His advocacy of their cause at the Peace Conference gave him access to the councils of the great, a dazzling experience for an ambitious young man who believed he was excluded from his proper rank and position in English society. Ten years after the war he wrote in a letter to the M.P. Ernest Thurtle:

Anyone who had gone up so fast as I went (remember that I was almost entirely self-made: my father had five sons, and only £300 a year) and had seen so much of the inside of the top of the world might well lose his aspirations, and get weary of the ordinary motives of action, which had moved him till he reached the top. I wasn't a King or a Prime Minister, but I made 'em, or played with them, and after that there wasn't much more, in that direction, for me to do.[29]

Lawrence wanted power and rank and public recognition of his inherent distinction, and his association with the Sherifians brought him those things. Churchill's admiration for him knew no bounds and great positions were in his gift. But Lawrence was oppressed by what he knew to be the vulgar absurdity of the legend he had helped to create and by the chronic sense of worth-lessness which was the obverse of his desire for glory; and so he hid himself in the ranks, though he could never bring himself to sever completely his connections with his powerful friends. On the contrary, he was an assiduous correspondent of the mighty and could not resist putting out rumours of the great positions he had been offered and refused. He maintained a vigorous interest in Arab affairs until his Sherifian emirs had been installed on their respective thrones. After that he lost interest.

I have tried to discover an explanation of Lawrence's attachment to the Sherifian family, a subject on which comparatively little ink has been spilled but which seems to me to be the most politically significant aspect of his role in Anglo-Arab relations. In a book like this there is scarcely room for more, but it is difficult to leave the subject of Lawrence without saying something about two other aspects of his character: the sense of his own singularity which he shared with that other aspiring leader of the Arabs, Wilfrid Blunt; and the obsession with suffering which is so vivid a part of *Seven Pillars of Wisdom* and which distorted his perception of the Arabs.

Throughout his life Lawrence behaved as though he was one of that small group of people singled out for special attention by the gods, liable at any moment to be called on to perform some heroic task – or suffer some special degradation. Like Wilfrid Blunt he seems to have responded to what he perceived as his extraordinary situation in part by deciding that he was an extraordinary person. Indeed his situation was almost a caricature of that of Blunt. There was some mysterious flaw in the older man's sense of his social position; in Lawrence's case the knowledge that by right of birth he was above the common herd was compromised by the shaming knowledge of his illegitimacy. The strange pattern of his life, with its succession of wild flights from the ordinary (disguised sometimes as a search for the ordinary), seems inexplicable unless we assume the existence of a powerful but ambiguous feeling of singularity which on some days made him feel like a hero and on other days like a worm. It is not enough to say, as has often been said, that he was driven by contradictory impulses of self-aggrandizement and self-destruction, for it is clear that he acted out these impulses in ways commensurate with his sense of his own unusualness. In his own eyes he was like the little girl in the nursery rhyme – when he was good he was very, very good and when he was bad he was horrid; but never ordinary. It may be that by the end of his life, after years in the ranks, he finally purged himself of the burden of singularity.[30]

The belief that he had an extraordinary destiny enabled him to conceive of himself as the leader of a national movement. There was little scope for this in England so he had to look elsewhere. He claimed that since the age of sixteen he had been 'filled with [the] idea of freeing a people and had chosen Arabs as only suitable ones left'. It is tempting to be sceptical about this extraordinary remark, but he also said, at the end of *Seven Pillars of Wisdom*, that '"Super flumina Babylonis", read as a boy, had left me longing to feel myself the node of a national movement', and this is convincing.[31] Swinburne's poem about the Risorgimento, with its emphasis on the idea of redemption through suffering and its erotico-religious exaltation of pain endured for the sake of the cause, is precisely the sort of thing which would have appealed to Lawrence, in adolescence and after. The psychiatrist John Mack has explored with great delicacy the element of personal redemption (from the shame of his illegitimacy and his beloved mother's fall from grace) in Lawrence's conception of his role in the revolt and has stressed the extent to which he conceived the redemption as taking place through suffering as well as through fantastic acts of heroism. He had a desire to suffer, and to suffer extremely, beyond what any normal person would be called upon to do. Participation in the revolt provided him with legitimate outlets for this desire, as well as his longings for glory and power.

In the conditions of the revolt such a desire could be amply fulfilled. Lawrence endured the terrible climate of Arabia, the constant hunger of the nomad, and the strain of battle. He underwent hardships which he regarded as a systematic chastisement of the flesh and he persuaded himself that the Arabs also so regarded the hardships which they endured. In *Seven Pillars of Wisdom* he described them as exulting in the mortification of the flesh.[32] Of all Lawrence's ideas about the Arabs this is the only one that has no discernible literary ancestor. It is patently the result of his projection on to the Arabs of his thirst for physical degradation and his horror of his own body, that body which had been brought into existence through sin. He experienced a purgation through suffering and he assumed, absurdly, that the Arabs felt the same. (He was quick to sense the element of masochism in Doughty: there was a genuine affinity between the two men, though Lawrence was conscious of it and Doughty was not.)[33] The fact that he perceived his most intimate bond with the Arabs as being a common delight in pain may explain some of the shame which he later expressed about his connection with them. 'For an Englishman to put himself at the disposal of a red race,' he confessed to an acquaintance at the Peace Conference, 'is to sell himself to a brute . . .'[34] His experiences in the desert, that sounding box for tortured psyches, apparently revealed to him rather more about himself than he cared to know, that pain was not only redeeming but, in the melancholy Freudian sense of the reduction of unbearable tension, pleasurable. The massacre of Turkish prioners at Tafas, which Lawrence ordered and may even have taken part in, seems further to have revealed to him that the infliction as well as the endurance of pain fulfilled some horrible craving. The incident at Tafas and the assault experienced by Lawrence at Deraa – about which the full truth will never be known – seem to have made these aspects of his nature plain to him. He accepted the knowledge, but was tormented by it.

It is time to recall that Lawrence was not sent to Arabia to lead a movement for the regeneration of the Arab race. He went to Arabia as a British liaison officer – one among others – with an army of Arab irregulars which happened to find itself on the same side as the British in a world war. The rather prosaic reality of the Arab campaign, which was virtually unknown to the British public before 1919, bore little resemblance to the 'crusade' which became world famous. It was Lawrence, through his own books and those of his mouthpieces Robert Graves and Liddell Hart, and through his encouragement of the activities of the journalist Lowell Thomas, who invested it with an air of high romance and the great and tragic working out of the destiny of nations. His involvement in the Arab war was of enormous psychological importance to him, and for reasons which will be discussed in a later chapter, he succeeded in making it important to the world.

Before his translation to the Hejaz and immortality Lawrence was one of a group of officials in Cairo who formed what was known as the Arab Bureau. This was a group of (mostly young) men supposedly expert in the care and feeding of Arabs. They were brought together in February 1916 for the purpose of co-ordinating British policy in Arabia. It was a group of rather fluid composition but its members included D. G. Hogarth, Gilbert Clayton, Stewart Symes and Kinahan Cornwallis. Others who drifted into its orbit at various times were George Lloyd (who became British High Commissioner in Egypt in 1925), Aubrey Herbert, and A. C. Parker.

Ronald Storrs, who shared Mark Sykes's sophisticated aesthetic approach to the Arab (both were wittily pained at the sight of elastic-sided boots peeping out from under flowing robes), was not a member of the Bureau but was always an influential presence. After the war he was the Emir Feisal's impresario in London, persuading him to wear his robes to society functions at which he might hope to find support for the Arab cause.[35]

This group of officials is usually described as 'Arabophile', but they were not Arabophile in any way that makes sense to the simple post-imperial mind. D. G. Hogarth, the director of the Bureau and Lawrence's patron and mentor, was a shrewd imperialist who coolly played the odds on the Sherif's usefulness to Great Britain during the war and then with equal coolness watched him go under to Ibn Saud in 1925. In a paper read at the Royal Institute of International Affairs in January 1925 he explained that 'we' (Cairo Intelligence) knew from the beginning of the British involvement with the Arab Revolt that 'sooner or later . . . Hejaz must go under for a while', but decided to support Hussein, because of his prestige in the Moslem World as Keeper of the Holy Places, and to fend off Ibn Saud with subsidies until such time as Hussein had outlived his usefulness as an ally.[36] This may not be a completely true picture of the complex situation with regard to British support for the revolt, but it shows the extent of Hogarth's regard for Arab nationalism, as represented by the Sherif of Mecca or anyone else. He was an Oxford archaeologist whose views about the Arabs had been formed from his experience in the Middle East before the war and from his extensive reading. He regarded the Arab of the desert as an attractive but useless animal, and the inhabitants of Nejd, whom contact with the oases had raised from the level of the Bedouin, as fine but still primitive specimens whose major talent was for an oppressive and puritanical monotheism. He entertained no illusions about their political capacities, but believed that Arab states under European tutelage must be set up to fill the political vacuum which would be created by the imminent collapse of the Ottoman Empire.[37]

Clayton, Symes and Cornwallis were all old Sudan hands who had imbibed their ideas about Arabs from Wingate in Khartoum.[38] They shared Wingate's dream of an Arab revival under British guidance and control. Clayton was Director of Intelligence in Cairo during the war and in 1915 and 1916 he was corresponding with his old friend Wingate in Khartoum. They were of like mind about the advantages of supporting the Sherif against the Turks and about the ease with which Arab ambitions could be controlled after the war.[39] Like Hogarth, Clayton regarded the singling out of the Sherif of Mecca for British support as a happy stroke of policy which entailed no obligations to the Sherif beyond liberation from the Turks. He persuaded himself that the Arab nationalists whom the British were encouraging for their own ends aspired to no more than 'a fair measure of self-government in the countries concerned under the guidance and with the help and support of England'.[40] Symes's views differed little from Clayton's. He too regarded the Sherif as a pawn in a diplomatic and strategic game, a potential instrument of post-war British hegemony in the Middle East.[41] Cornwallis also was committed to the promotion of British interests via the Sherif, and then, when the old man began to look too much like a liability, via his son Feisal, who, he believed in 1921, 'would serve us loyally and well'.[42] Cornwallis went on to become Chief Adviser to Feisal after he was elected King of Iraq, and British Ambassador to Baghdad during the Second World War. He was one of the pillars of the Anglo-Sherifian alliance in its palmiest days.

All these men were concerned to use the Arabs to promote British imperial interests, preferably at the expense of those of France. To say that they 'used' the Arabs is not to ignore the fact that they often enjoyed their company: it is merely to put the element of friendship into its proper political perspective. Elie Kedourie has argued convincingly that their collective unease about the Sykes–Picot agreement was partly due to their belief that it gave too much to France.[43] A French Syria was not part of their grand design. Cornwallis, who in 1918 was British liaison officer with Feisal in Damascus, was the subject of official complaints from the French authorities because of his anti-French behaviour.[44] T. E. Lawrence, for all his admiration of the *chansons de geste,* was a notorious Francophobe who wanted to 'biff the French out of all hope of Syria'.[45]

This anti-French attitude was the result not merely of imperial greed but of a genuine conviction that the British were by temperament and tradition better equipped to be the arbiters of Arab destiny than were the French. When the French evicted Feisal from Damascus in July 1920 Gertrude Bell wrote home from Mesopotamia:

Whatever initial success the French may have, they're bound to go under in the end, just as surely as we're bound to come to the top here if we carry out the programme we say we're going to carry out, because there's a fundamental sympathy between us and the people here and there's a fundamental hatred between the Syrians and the French.[46]

Such was the stuff imperial dreams were made of in 1920.

While Lawrence was blowing up railway tracks in the Hejaz a very different sort of war was being fought in Mesopotamia. In 1914 British troops were landed in Basra in a show of force designed to protect the South Persian oil-fields and to stiffen the resolution of the friendly leaders of the Gulf sheikhdoms, with whom Britain had treaties of long standing. As the Turks fled an advance from Basra aimed at Baghdad seemed irresistible and the prolonged disaster of the Mesopotamian campaign began. It was later described by Curzon as the worst piece of British incompetence since the Crimea. Many lives were lost in futile attempts to relieve the British troops besieged in Kut-el-Imara from the beginning of 1916 to 1917. The great unknown factor in the war was the allegiance of the local tribes, whose goodwill was crucial to an orderly British advance. It was the job of the political officers with the British Expeditionary Force to 'bring in' the tribes, which they did with varying degrees of success.

At the beginning of 1917, with the arrival of General Maude, the British advance at last gained momentum. Kut was recovered and Baghdad was occupied. It became imperative to provide the occupied territory with an efficient peacetime administration, without allowing it to appear that the British were settling in for good. It fell to Sir Percy Cox, the Chief Political Officer with the British expedition and a former Political Resident in the Persian Gulf, to perform this delicate task. He did so by importing political officers from India: there was at that time and in the urgent conditions which prevailed nowhere else to turn. The result was that, despite nervous injunctions from the Foreign Office that occupied Mesopotamia was not to be regarded as a convenient extension of India, the administration inevitably took shape on Indian lines.

From Baghdad the Arab world looked rather different than it did from Cairo: Ibn Saud of Nejd and the Government of India loomed much larger and the revolt in the Hejaz seemed considerably less significant. The claims of the Sherif of Mecca and his family did not at first enter into the calculations of Cox's Indian 'politicals'. In 1918 none of them supposed that in 1921 the Emir Feisal would be crowned King of Iraq.

The brilliant amateur among these Mesopotamian officials was Gertrude Bell, and though she cannot be accused of having an 'Indian' cast of mind there was little that was unconventional in her political ideas. Compared to Lawrence, she was a relatively simple soul. She had no axe to grind for the Sherifians or anyone else, no grand theory about the Arabs, simply an unremitting delight in their company and the glories of their past, and when the opportunity arose, an itch to interfere in their affairs.

The first months of the war found her cataloguing wounded in Boulogne, but in November 1915, at the request of Hogarth, she was summoned to Cairo to give Military Intelligence the benefit of her knowledge of the tribes of northern Arabia. Her reputation as an Arabist had already been established by two books published before the war (*Syria: The Desert and the Sown*, 1907, and *Amurath to Amurath*, 1911), and Hogarth knew from long personal acquaintance with her that she was a woman of formidable energy and intelligence. Her views on Anglo-Arab cooperation were at this time very similar to his and may possibly have been influenced by him.[47] She saw the opportunity for an English presence in the Middle East after the war (though she realized that 'colonisation would have to be very carefully and delicately handled') and appreciated the value of keeping the Sherif in play. She assumed that whatever independent Arab states emerged after the war would be eager for the help and advice of Great Britain, and though the French might not like it they would have to put up with it. It went almost without saying that the Arabs, while admirable in many ways, 'can't govern themselves'.[48]

Her earliest writings on the Arab East show her bursting with imperial confidence and eager to impart to the Arabs the benefits of British rule which the Egyptians had already received from the wise and benevolent Cromer – 'how far beyond all praise,' she wrote to him of *Modern Egypt* in 1908, 'like turning over the pages of the Recording Angel – though we have no reason to believe his phrases will be as felicitous as yours'.[49] The extravagance of her admiration for Cromer was typical of her. Throughout her life, beginning with her father, she formed admiring attachments to strong men. Sir Percy Cox, Arnold Wilson (for a while),

From Trebizond to Tripolis
She rolls the Pashas flat
And tells them what to think of this
And what to think of that

13   Gertrude Bell in her natural element

and Kinahan Cornwallis were all in turn the objects of her devotion.

On her Eastern journeys before the war she developed a romantic attachment to the Arabs and a profound and scholarly admiration for their literature and ancient civilization. She loved to be received as a personage in their tents and felt keenly the exhilaration of desert life as Burton, Kinglake and others had done before her.[50] There was much about her of Lady Hester Stanhope and as she got older the resemblance, unfortunately, became more marked. Both women consoled themselves with Eastern travel for tragic love affairs and both found, or thought they found, positions in the East which were denied to them as mere women at home.

She believed throughout her life that the English were loved and admired by Orientals and went out of her way to record tributes to her race. In this respect she was quite unfitted for the proconsular duties to which she aspired: such duties required a toughness of mind and spirit she did not possess. Always she longed for her efforts to be rewarded with grateful affection. She barely managed, during the latter part of her life, to keep her craving for affection under control and eagerly accepted the worthless compliments of those who sought to use her for their own needs. Her capacity for self-delusion was enormous: in 1922 she wrote to her father that she was 'happy in feeling that I've got the love and confidence of a whole nation'.[51] There may have been an unconscious sexual element in the delight she took in courtly expressions of regard from Arab notables, for she was a passionate woman whose two major love affairs ended in frustration and misery.

In 1916, when she arrived in Basra to take up first intelligence work and then political duties with Sir Percy Cox, she was at the height of her powers and was able to turn her capacity for friendship to brilliant use. She revived her pre-war contacts with the tribes and in 1917 was rewarded by the defection to the British of her old acquaintance Fahad Bey, the paramount sheikh of the Amara. The practical value of these desert alliances was not always apparent to the British officers whose lot it was to lead undisciplined Bedouin troops, whose thoughts were mostly of booty and whose loyalty was uncertain, into battle against the Turks; but to the politicals at headquarters resounding declarations of sheikhly support were always welcome. After the war military bitterness about the unedifying way in which Britain's Arab 'allies' had behaved in the field was a factor in the agitation against further heavy expenditure of British manpower and money in the country.[52]

In December 1916 Gertrude Bell met Ibn Saud of Nejd and the meeting confirmed her impression that he was the coming man in Arabia. She would have liked to take him in hand and instruct him in the arts of government, but by the end of 1916 some of the old imperial confidence had gone. She permitted herself to wonder whether 'we don't do these people more harm than good . . . [especially] now that our civilisation has broken down so completely. But,' she concluded, 'we can't leave them alone, they won't be left alone anyway . . .'[53] The war had a shattering effect on her. By the end of 1917 she was writing to Valentine Chirol: 'My England has gone.' She had no wish to return to a society which she believed to be changed beyond recognition and eventually she came to regard Mesopotamia as her home.[54]

During her first two years in Mesopotamia her chief was Sir Percy Cox, a man who combined massive personal dignity with a ruthless appreciation of the techniques of indirect rule. He had a strait-laced charm which Gertrude Bell believed no Arab could resist. She was devoted to him. In March 1918 he was called home to London for talks on Mesopotamia and then sent to Teheran to take up the post of British Minister. He was succeeded as Civil Commissioner by his deputy, Arnold Wilson, a very different sort of man from the imperturbable Cox. Gertrude Bell's relations with Wilson were at first harmonious. At Versailles the two of them went into battle together against Lawrence's belief that Sherifian rule could be imposed on Mesopotamia with its Shia majority, its Kurdish minority, and Ibn Saud knocking on its back door.[55] But initial good relations evaporated when their views on the administration of Mesopotamia began to diverge.

Wilson was a brilliant and dynamic organizer who never grasped the idea of indirect rule. Unable to tolerate any whiff of muddling through, he wanted to establish an efficient Indian-style administration in Mesopotamia, seeing no need, as some of his colleagues did, to modify Indian methods to suit local conditions: anything less would have constituted a dereliction of imperial duty in his eyes. To his credit it must be said that he had a belief in England's civilizing mission and was prepared to stand by it. He loathed the Bedouin, largely because of their treacherous and savage behaviour during the war.[56] Unlike Gertrude Bell and T. E. Lawrence he was unable to resign himself to their incorrigible individualism; he took too seriously the moral lessons of his upbringing, which derived in undiluted form from Dr Arnold. His father, a former science master at Rugby, had sent him to Clifton whence he emerged, after a brief period of rebellion, the Arnoldian public schoolboy par excellence. He was the unusually perfect product of a public school ethos from which every scrap of aristocratic dilettantism and individualism had been purged. He was no more capable of admiring the predatory Bedouin than Richard Burton was of becoming a Quaker. In later life he found much to admire in Nazi Germany – its classlessness, its sense of purpose, its Spartan emphasis on physical fitness.[57]

His complete inflexibility in the face of nationalist demands resulted in a violent rebellion against British rule which broke out in the summer of 1920. Local patriots throughout the country expressed their discontent through the murder of British officials, including the enigmatic Colonel Leachman whose bravery, brutality, and knowledge of the Bedouin were legendary. Faced with a crisis requiring unpopular and expensive military operations in Mesopotamia the British government turned to Sir Percy Cox, who was sent out to replace Wilson in August.

Throughout 1918 and 1919 Gertrude Bell had been dead against the idea of an Arab government ('There is no one here who could run it'), but the violence of the uprising shook her deeply. She had not really believed it possible.[58] In a remarkable *volte face* which seems to have been inspired by panic at the thought that the British might be forced out of Mesopotamia she advocated setting up a purely Arab administration under a Sherifian emir, with herself and her British colleagues reduced to a genuinely advisory status. She was converted to Lawrence's and Clayton's views that such concessions were an indispensable condition of Britain's continued presence in the area.[59] It was unthinkable to her, for personal as well as patriotic reasons, that Britain should get out of Mesopotamia. She had come to feel a sense of personal destiny in her involvement with its sheikhs and notables and had begun to entertain the fatal notion that her advice was indispensable to them.

When Cox returned to Baghdad with instructions to set up an Arab Council of Ministers she threw herself with enthusiasm into the task of selecting suitable candidates for the posts. The following spring she and Cox attended the Cairo Conference at which it was agreed that after a decent show of consulting public opinion the Emir Feisal should be installed as ruler of Mesopotamia. An election was set in progress but when the Sherifian candidate arrived at Basra in a British battleship the Council of Ministers realistically decided to dispense with democratic formalities and welcome Feisal as their new king. Gertrude Bell was jubilant. 'It's not at all true,' she wrote home in September 1921, 'that I've determined the fortunes of Iraq but it is true that with an Arab Govt. I've come into my own.'[60] In this she was mistaken. Feisal proved more independent than she had supposed. More in sorrow than in anger she went to remonstrate with him and was rewarded by a display of affection which soothed her for a while.[61] Gradually her political influence declined and she spent the last years of her life devotedly employed in the creation of a national museum in Baghdad.

With the creation of thrones for two of the Sherif's sons in Mesopotamia and Transjordan Lawrence felt able to declare that 'we were quit of the wartime Eastern adventure, with clean hands'.[62] It did not seem that way to everyone. In the Anglo-French Declaration of 1918, a glibly Wilsonian document hurriedly produced a few days before the armistice, the Arabs had been assured that the governments of Great Britain and France wished only to assist them in the 'establishment of national governments and administrations deriving their authority from the initiative and free choice of the indigenous populations'. The installation in Amman and Baghdad of Sherifian emirs whose independence was clearly intended to be nominal fell far short of this promise given so lightly in the euphoria of victory. Over the next forty years the British struggled to control the Middle East through the aristocrats with whom they had allied themselves. It is wrong to suppose that they were blind to the nature of Arab nationalism, which owed far more to mission schools than to Bedouin tents; but they naturally worked with the people who were willing to work with them, and these were the desert potentates who shot and rode and sent their sons to Harrow. Nor was the manipulation all on one side: Arab statesmen like King Abdullah of Transjordan and Nuri Pasha of Iraq proved to be remarkably adept at binding British interests inextricably to theirs.

9

Hail and Farewell

Referring to the relations between Ibn Sa'ud and 'Iraq, there was no doubt that the former . . . had great difficulty in keeping his distant tribes under control; but as to their right to roam the desert towards 'Iraq, there was so much misinformed talk in the papers sometimes on this point, that he would like to remind his hearers that we were no longer living in the days of Abraham but of the League of Nations.

Sir Percy Cox, commenting on a paper read by Sir Gilbert Clayton at the Royal Institute of International Affairs, 4 December 1928

THIS CHAPTER records briefly how Britain's moment in the Middle East coincided with the demise of Arabia as a happy hunting ground for the imagination. The Englishmen who stayed on after the war to administer the peace helped to usher in changes which some of them lived to deplore. But there was period of about ten years immediately after the war when the itch to administer and improve could be combined with the enjoyment of Bedouin society in its still primitive state.

The officials whose job it was to administer the desert lands for which Britain had acquired responsibility after the war soon realized that some of the traditional ways of the Bedouin constituted a threat to public order. In this they were at one with the leaders of the Arab governments which they nominally served. When F. G. Peake (Peake Pasha) took up administrative duties in Transjordan in 1918 he found that the Bedouin, as was their wont, were taking advantage of unsettled conditions to prey on the cultivators. In spite of his partiality for the Bedouin, with whom he had fought during the war, he decided that if the country were ever to attain a level of prosperity which would enable it to pay its own way the cultivators must be protected from the nomads.[1] He therefore began to recruit Arab villagers for a police force to control the incursions of the nomads into settled lands. Eventually this force was to become the Arab Legion.

At first no attempt was made to prevent the Bedouin from preying on each other. English officials frequently regarded inter-tribal raiding as a form of sport and it went on as before. But after 1926, when Ibn Saud extended his dominions up to the frontiers of Transjordan, it became apparent that raids across frontiers were a potential source of international incidents. In 1930 Major J. B. Glubb was brought to Transjordan from Iraq to form a Desert Police Force to control raiding. Unlike the Arab Legion this was a force recruited from Bedouin and herein perhaps lay its remarkable success. In 1934 Glubb was able to announce that 'bedouin forces in armed cars [had] accomplished what no government had succeeded in for centuries, the complete subjugation of the bedouin tribes of Northern Arabia'.[2] By offering Bedouins with a taste for novelty the opportunity for what amounted to unlimited raiding with superior weapons, Glubb was able to bring the others into line.

Glubb was, and remained, an ardent Bedouinophile. His writings are full of illustrations, drawn from his own experience, of their poetic qualities, their courtesy, generosity and chivalry. After his dismissal from the command of the Arab Legion by King Hussein in 1956, he described how he had gone to Iraq in 1920 as a young officer in the British army, and how after five years he had decided to resign his commission and devote his life to the Arabs. 'My decision was largely emotional,' he wrote, 'I loved them.'[3] He threw himself enthusiastically into the task of bringing peace and security to the desert. Years later he came to believe that the suppression of raiding had meant the beginning of the end for the Bedouin society he admired.[4] Raids had helped to equalize wealth between the tribes and had given every man a chance to recoup his fortunes. Without this equalizing mechanism differences in wealth among the Bedouin had become more marked. The richer tribesmen had begun to take to politics or agriculture and the poorer Bedouin to decline into mere poverty-stricken wanderers. It is hard to escape the feeling when reading Glubb that he came to believe that with the decline of raiding much of the poetry went out of Bedouin life. Without it there were no longer the same opportunities for the pursuit of glory and the practice of chivalry.

This was not what Glubb had envisaged at all. He had hoped

that the pacification of the tribes would be the first stage in a process of controlled modernization: the Arabs would acquire the European skills necessary for holding their own in the modern world without losing their fine traditional qualities.[5] The suppression of raiding, in which he had taken a conspicuous part, seemed to have contributed to the frustration of this hope; but there was never much possibility that modernization would take place in the orderly fashion he had imagined. Like their counterparts in other Asian countries young Jordanians of advanced ideas were eager for Westernization at a pace which scandalized Glubb, a Christian moralist who had turned his back on the materialism of his own society. He had the unhappy experience of being ridiculed by educated Arabs for his attachment to the Bedouin.[6]

Though he did not realize it at the time Glubb was merely an agent of an inevitable change which was taking place all over the Arab world. There was no room for Bedouin, who respected only tribal law and showed a fine disregard for government officials, in the nations of taxpayers which forward-looking Arabs aspired to lead. One of the first items on their agenda was the settlement of the tribes in permanent agricultural settlements, a process which came to be known in sociological jargon as sedentarization. The most conspicuously successful in this aim was the Bedouin king himself, Ibn Saud. Watched with admiration by his English friend St John Philby, Ibn Saud efficiently consolidated his Arabian empire by settling his fanatical Wahhabi warriors on the land, where the demands of agriculture and the pursuit of godliness kept them out of mischief. Few of these agricultural settlements were long-term successes – the warriors knew little about farming and cared less – but Ibn Saud had begun the process of reducing tribal autonomy before the power of a centralized state.

To St John Philby, the last of that peculiar group of English men and women who identified their own destiny with that of the Arabs, Ibn Saud's activities seemed to herald a new dawn for Arabia. Freed from the curse of tribalism, he believed, a united Arabian nation could take its place among the great ones of the earth.[7] He was echoing the traditional Arabist belief, expounded by Voltaire and Carlyle and their successors, that the Arabs could only become great when their warring elements were united under a charismatic leader. Ibn Saud, Philby believed, was that leader.

It was natural to Philby to admire a reforming autocrat like Ibn Saud. They had much in common. Philby's own brief reign as captain of Westminster School was long remembered for its combination of reforming zeal and autocratic methods. Determined to live up to his high office – he later described his election as the greatest thrill of his life – he had set out to restore to the school 'some of her pristine vigour and discipline'.[8] Ibn Saud set out upon a similar enterprise but brought to it more tact and statesmanship than Philby had shown.

In 1915 Philby found himself in the Arab East as a result of Sir Percy Cox's urgent request to India for political officers for Mesopotamia. For the next two years his great energies were deployed in Basra, but then came an opportunity which was to change his life. The British government wished to induce Ibn Saud, who was extending his control over the central Arabian tribes, to attack his rival, Ibn Rashid of Hail, an ally of the Turks; or failing that, to refrain from attacking his other rival, the Sherif of Mecca, who was an ally of the British. Ronald Storrs was sent to talk to Ibn Saud, but he collapsed from sunstroke and had to turn back. Philby was sent to replace him and not only reached Riyad without incident but discovered on the way his great aptitude for desert travel. His meeting with Ibn Saud changed his whole attitude towards the Arabs: for the first time he met an Arab whom he could regard as his equal and he went back to Mesopotamia in November 1918 full of ideas about an independent future for the Arabs. He welcomed the Anglo-French Declaration but it quickly became obvious to him that it was mere window-dressing by the European powers who were anxious to make some gesture in keeping with President Woodrow Wilson's Fourteen Points. Like Arnold Wilson, whom he resembled in his temperament though not his ideas, Philby had an exalted conception of Britain's imperial duty; but he believed that this duty with respect to the Arabs lay in giving them the freedom which the Anglo-French Declaration had promised them. He was disappointed in Mesopotamia when the British installed a puppet emir who seemed to him to cut a sorry figure in comparison to Ibn Saud, and again in Transjordan when the real extent of that country's independence became apparent. His resignation from British government service took effect in 1925 after a disastrous attempt at unauthorized mediation between King Ali of the Hejaz (the eldest son of the Sherif of Mecca) and Ibn Saud. Thereafter his fortunes were bound up with those of Ibn Saud. He went to live in Riyad, where he was to witness the birth of a new Arabia unlike anything he had dreamed of.

At the age of forty Philby, due partly to his indiscretions in the service of what he believed to be Ibn Saud's and Britain's common interests, had found himself without a career. For a man of his ambition this was intolerable. There was no choice but to throw in his lot with Ibn Saud and hope to influence events through his friendship with the King. It is clear from Elizabeth Monroe's biography that this hope did not substantially materialize. There remained to satisfy his ambition a career in Arabian exploration, for which he seemed to be admirably placed.

But in this respect his friendship with the King turned out to be a mixed blessing. His journeys, when they were finally made, were made with the King's invaluable backing, but Ibn Saud often kept him on tenterhooks for months, even years, before giving his blessing. It was the King's reluctance to allow him to venture into the Empty Quarter, the last great challenge of Arabian exploration, which cost him the great prize of being the first to cross it. Instead the palm went to Bertram Thomas, the least flamboyant of Arabian explorers, and, unfortunately, a former subordinate of Philby's in Iraq and Transjordan. Nevertheless, Philby did cross the Empty Quarter in 1932 and by a more difficult route than Thomas. For years he had regarded the great desert as an enemy and also (using an image which came naturally to a man who was highly sexed) as 'the bride of my constant desire'.[9] In the book he later wrote he demonstrated his complete subjugation of it by describing it remorselessly, stone by stone.

The fame which his journeys brought provided some balm for his soul but did not solve the practical problem of earning a living. He had children in England for whom he wished to provide an expensive education. His import business in Jedda, Sharqieh Ltd, had not been a success, and did not begin to be one until 1934 when he secured a monopoly on the import of Fords. But in 1932 the door to affluence, if not riches, was opened to him when he was approached by Standard Oil of California with a request to act as their intermediary in negotiations with the King. This was the beginning of a mutually profitable association. Standard Oil got their concession and Philby was taken on permanently at a salary of £1,000 a year. Thus Philby, by an irony it would be crude to underline, made his contribution to what he came to regard as the tragedy of Arabia.

He was, as it happened, one of a number of British officials and ex-officials who were involved in the development of Middle East oil. Brigadier Stephen Longrigg for the Iraq Petroleum Company, Arnold Wilson for the Anglo-Persian Oil Company, and Harold Dickson in Kuwait were others. Dickson was a Bedouinophile to compare with Glubb, the author of a detailed work on the Bedouin of Kuwait, but he seems to have had no misgivings about joining in the oil bonanza. No one in the early days foresaw the size of the revenues which would accrue from oil and the rapidity with which Arabia would change as a result. Saudi Arabian oil revenues were about two million dollars a year between 1939 and 1944. They increased to $5 million in 1950, $334 million in 1960, $1.25 billion in 1970 and over $3 billion in 1973.

Before the impact of oil revenues was felt the introduction of the motor car began to change the face of the desert. All over the Middle East a drop in the price of camels brought about by the advent of motorized transport was robbing Bedouins of their traditional livelihood. The result, especially in Transjordan, was a great deal of voluntary settlement on the land, quite unrelated to government programmes designed to achieve this end. As land was brought under cultivation some of the remaining nomads were deprived of grazing grounds and forced to supplement their income by doing some cultivation. For many this was a first step towards settlement.

As it began to appear that nomadism was on its way out some division of opinion became apparent among British officials. Those who regarded the Bedouin as a useless (though perhaps charming) anachronism welcomed the decline of nomadism and worried only about how to turn the settled Bedouin into a really efficient cultivator. C. S. Jarvis, who spent twenty years in the deserts of Libya, Sinai and Southern Palestine, publicized this point of view.[10] Citing archaeological evidence that in late Roman times these areas had supported a much larger population, he argued that there was no reason why they should not do so now. He set about repairing some of the disused Roman cisterns, constructing new concrete reservoirs, and planting olives and vines. Who could argue with the common sense of this? Few could, and those who hated to see the Bedouin disappear had to find pressing reasons why he should not. Some of these were supplied in an article published by Colonel W. S. Elphinston in 1945.[11] He argued that the Bedouin were an indispensable part of the economy of the Middle East, for the meat, milk and wool which their flocks and herds provided could only be produced under nomadic conditions. He advocated increasing the desert's efficiency as a grazing ground by such measures as sinking new wells.

In 1945 Elphinston's voice was in a minority. There were many who felt a romantic regret that such colourful folk should disappear from the face of the earth but accepted it as inevitable that nomadic pastoralism would die out, to be succeeded by settled agriculture. They were influenced by the views of early anthropologists who believed, in the best tradition of Victorian ideas about progress, that there was an inevitable human progression, onward and upward, from hunting and gathering, through nomadic pastoralism, to agriculture. Thus nomadism was seen as an archaic, inefficient and inferior mode of life. Governments who have to deal with nomads still justify repressive measures against them with this belief, but the failure of many settlement schemes and the more detailed research of anthropologists is leading to a revision of opinion on this subject. Anthropologists and ecologists now believe that nomadism and agriculture are both forms of adaptation to differing conditions, neither being superior or inferior to the other. They distinguish between areas which can be productive only under a system of nomadic pastoralism and areas which are climatically suited for settlement and cultivation. In a sense both Jarvis and Elphinston were right. Some desert areas can doubtless be reclaimed, with patient effort, but there are others which probably never will be; they will remain the preserve of men and animals who through centuries of adaptation have learned to survive there.

In the 1940s the elegiac note began to predominate in the writings of English travellers in the Middle East. The inroads of Western civilization and the tide of nationalism (which like the middle class is always rising) brought home to introspective travellers that it would soon be time to say goodbye to all that. The noble Arab enjoyed a final brilliant revival at the hands of writers who despaired of the growing greyness and uniformity of their own civilization and were horrified to see it spreading over the wild places of the earth. Not even Wilfrid Blunt painted the Bedouin in such glowing colours as Gerald de Gaury, Freya Stark and Wilfred Thesiger. Oddly enough, their eulogies are often convincing. Brave, generous and godly, the Bedouin of the Empty Quarter spring vividly to life in Thesiger's *Arabian Sands*. Only the most jaded reader could fail to share the author's anguish at the thought of these repositories of primitive virtue being transformed into a proletariat by the lure of easy money in the oil-fields. Perhaps these writers are persuasive because they are almost entirely free from that knowingness, that easy assumption of understanding, which is such an unattractive feature of the minor travel writers of the nineteenth and early twentieth centuries. There is some genuine humility in their approach to another culture and way of life, a belief in their own private values combined with a readiness to learn.

Thesiger was a man who turned his back on civilization in a way which would have been inconceivable to Richard Burton, or Wilfrid Blunt; but then the civilization he was renouncing was rather different from theirs, and his perspective on it different also. The circumstances of his upbringing rendered him completely unfit for life in the welfare state, and rather than make the best of it he turned his back on it. He was born in 1910 in a mud hut in Addis Ababa, where his father was British Minister, and at the age of nine months was initiated into the art of rough travel by his mother, who took him with her on a camel journey across Abyssinia. As a child he lived in its barbaric mediaeval world and witnessed its feudal wars. He was one of those Englishmen, the product of empire, whose only prolonged exposure to English life was at school, and for Thesiger it was not at first a happy experience. The boys at his preparatory school called him a liar when he told them of the things he had seen and done in Abyssinia, and in his isolation he dreamt of Africa. Later he went to Eton, for which he acquired a great affection.

During his early manhood the British Empire provided him with wild and lonely outposts in which to live, but after the war he turned, as others with a taste for the primitive were to do, to the international organizations that were taking up the civilizing mission where the Empire had left off. He was offered a job with the Food and Agriculture Organization of the United Nations, collecting information about locust movements in the Empty Quarter.

His first crossing of the Empty Quarter was made under their aegis. His second crossing was made under his own steam and attracted the suspicious interest of local potentates and American oil-men, neither of whom believed he was travelling for his own pleasure. He left Arabia in 1949 realizing that he had made his last journey in the Empty Quarter. There was no question of returning permanently to England and he wandered around looking for a primitive haven in which to settle down. He found one among the Marsh Arabs of Iraq, a people hitherto despised by conventional Arabists as being on a par with the Egyptian fellahin. But shortly after he left Iraq to write a book about his experiences the last Sherifian king of Iraq was killed in the coup of 1958 and he realized that Iraq too was a place to which he would never be able to return. A man undaunted by the prospect of brigands or physical hardship in any form, he had to confess defeat at the hands of bureaucrats.

His motives for his journeys, while quite simple, were articulated with a degree of self-analysis appropriate to the final, self-conscious phase of exploration in which he found himself. There was no more glory to be had from discovery, no more imperial urges to be satisfied: the only motive left for arduous travel was escape. This was Thesiger's motive. He loathed machines and the materialist civilization which had produced them; he loathed the bureaucratic state which robbed men of their self-reliance. Determined to test his own capacity to endure, he made his journeys on foot or with animal transport, and sought out primitive people who supported themselves without benefit of technology, and who were not afraid to be generous, reckless and loyal.[12]

The wheel had come full circle, back to Niebuhr's admiration of the noble savage. But the admiration now was less playful than Niebuhr's, and less detached, because after two world wars the doubts about the value of European civilization went so much deeper, and because shortly, it appeared, the noble savage was doomed to disappear as the result of the inexorable spread of that civilization.

Even St John Philby, who had greeted with delight the opportunity for mechanized exploration and had promoted to the best of his ability the development of oil, came to regret the simpler life of the past. He was not a man who despised material things, but he was never ruled by them. The Arabs' reaction to riches appalled him. Like postmen who had won the pools the Saudi Arabian elite were enjoying undiscerningly all the gimcrackery of the West. To Philby's disgust, Ibn Saud succumbed to the charms of a sedentary life in an invalid chair, a gift from President Roosevelt. But Philby's real fury was reserved for the corruption rampant in the Saudi Arabian government. He could not stand by and see the ideals of administrative probity which he had cherished all his life disgraced by the people with whom he had publicly identified himself. With Ibn Saud's death in 1953 his inhibitions about public criticism of the regime vanished, and in *Sa'udi Arabia* he informed the world that: 'The traditional anarchy of the Bedouin tribes now yields pride of place to the selfish irresponsibility of a new bureaucracy, whose thin veneer of education has done in a couple of decades more harm to the reputation of a great country than the wild men of the desert ever did in thousands of years.'[13] The reaction came in March 1955: he was asked to pack up and leave.

The great days of Arabian travel were over, and with them the role of Britain in Middle Eastern politics. By 1958 Britain counted for very little in the Arab states and any notions of affinity or manifest destiny had been painfully dispelled. By the end of his life Philby had abandoned his belief that the English and the Arabs were natural partners in the modern world: it was a belief only too obviously being contradicted by events, though not everyone saw it as clearly as he.

The mapping of Arabia was completed by the oil companies, and their representatives began to replace the old Political Agents and Residents who had watched over British interests in the Arabian states. But there was still one aspect of Arabia which remained imperfectly known: its people. Much had been written about them, but until 1975 there was no book available which described the nomads of Arabia from the perspective of a trained observer who had lived with them for a long period in peace and amity, able to watch them go about their normal business and record his observations openly and without fear.

The first anthropologist to obtain permission from the Saudi Arabian government to carry out research was Donald Powell Cole, an American doctoral student at Berkeley. He decided to study the Al Murra Bedouin, one of the remotest and most traditional of Arabian tribes. They were pure camel nomads living deep in the Empty Quarter, as yet very little touched by the changes going on elsewhere in Arabia. For eighteen months between 1968 and 1970 Cole lived with the Al Murra as a permanent guest in the tent of Ali ibn Salem ibn al-Kurbi of the Al Azab lineage.

His first contact with the Al Murra was in an abandoned workers' barracks near the oil processing plant at Abqaiq. This was the headquarters of the tribe's emir, whose position as intermediary between the tribe and the government required that he should live apart from his tribesmen in a place conveniently close to the towns of Abqaiq, Dammam and Hofuf. Here he was visited by scores of Al Murra who came to do their monthly stint in the National Guard or to bring their problems to their emir. In the past the Al Murra emirs had been powerful military leaders but in the peaceful days of the Al Saud they had developed into human links between the new bureaucracy and the formerly autonomous tribes. The present Al Murra emir had access to high government officials and even, for important matters, to the King himself.

It was at the emir's headquarters that Cole found the man who was to be his guide and friend for the eighteen months he lived with the Al Murra. This was al-Kurbi, a young man in his early thirties who had just returned from working in Kuwait. He had been working for wages away from the tribe since he was a youth but he had not lost contact with it or lost status within it. On the contrary, he was highly respected among the Al Murra because of his success in the outside world. With his savings he had bought a truck and was about to set himself up in a desert haulage business.

During the next year and a half Cole got to know al-Kurbi's family well, for he saw virtually no other. The nearest tents were over fifteen miles away and his hosts had no petrol to waste on gadding about. He chafed at his isolation from the rest of the tribe which he had come to study, but in the end he realized that he was experiencing a central fact of Bedouin life. Dispersal was an adaptive necessity for the Al Murra. The Rub al Khali could not support large concentrations of people and the tribe was broken down for most of the year into small, highly mobile household groups. The remarkable thing was that the Al Murra, scattered as they were, still had a strong conception of themselves as members of a tribe. They spoke constantly of their 'brothers' whom they scarcely saw.

One of the most ambitious of the Saudi Arabian government's settlement projects had been initiated in Al Murra territory and had been a complete failure. The most advanced technology was used to make the desert bloom, and vast sums of money were spent, but no one bothered to ask the Al Murra what they thought about these proposed innovations in their mode of subsistence. A few Al Murra tribesmen – only about twenty – went to work on the demonstration farm for wages which were about 40 per cent of that of their Bedouin foreman and many times less than their foreign supervisors. They were housed in concrete barracks with the other labourers, mostly lower class villagers from South Arabia. No man of standing in the tribe ever had anything to do with the project. They were unimpressed by the government's claim that the new water supply would last for at least a hundred years: had they not managed quite well without it for several thousand years?

The response of planners to this kind of failure is frequently to sigh and point to the nomad's well-known conservatism. The stereotype of the unchanging, and unchangeable, Bedouin is confirmed. But Cole found that the Al Murra were not mindlessly conservative but showed a high degree of realism in their reaction to the changes they saw happening in their environment. Their response was cautiously adaptive, in the present as it had been in the past. Anyone who knows something of the history of rural development projects in poor countries will know just how wrong the planners can be in their judgement as to what the results of their innovations will be. The objects of their attentions are frequently entirely justified in deciding to wait and see, or keep something in reserve. Cole found that the Al Murra retained their basic commitment to pastoralism but were spontaneously adapting it to modern conditions in ways which seemed to them reasonable and relatively free of risk. The drilling of deep wells in the desert has made it possible for many Arabian Bedouin to change from herding camels for their own subsistence to herding sheep and goats for subsistence and for sale. Sheep and goats need to drink more often than camels and formerly it was not possible to keep them in the deep desert; but when it was made possible the Bedouin were not slow to grasp the opportunity for income and an improved standard of life. The Rub al Khali, with its vast distances between patches of vegetation, is still not suitable for anything but camels, but Al Murra outside the Rub al Khali have begun the change over to sheep and goats. Another innovation adopted with enthusiasm has been trucks. The Al Murra love their camels, some of the finest in Arabia, but much prefer to make long journeys by truck. For those who are adopting sheep and goat herding, trucks prove very useful for taking the herds to the wells, or taking water to the herds. Mechanized transport has not proved necessarily inimical to a pastoral way of life, but is being used by these people to modernize it.

The Al Murra do not look back with nostalgia on the life of the past. They are thankful for the peace brought by Ibn Saud and the money from the oil business which makes their lives a little easier. Many families have one member who has settled in a town, working for wages while his animals are taken care of by those at home. He contributes money to the family and is a link with the modern world, like al-Kurbi who came back with a truck. The tribe is poised at a very important moment in its existence as a tribe. They could be encouraged in their tentative efforts to modernize their nomadic pastoralism, or they could be written off by the government and their advisers as people who are beyond help.

Whatever the government in its wisdom decides to do, the odds are that the Al Murra, along with other Bedouin all over the Middle East, will continue to demonstrate a capacity for survival. For it is becoming clear that the Bedouin and their way of life are not on the verge of extinction. Donald Cole estimates that there are just as many animals and tents in the Saudi Arabian desert as there were before the discovery of oil, and the American Arabist Raphael Patai believes that the Bedouin population of Jordan has not declined even with the large amount of settlement there.[14] Settlement has merely skimmed off the surplus population which the desert continually produces. It seems that announcements of the demise of nomadism have been premature.

But what are the nomads really like? Does the anthropologist breathe life into the myths of the past, or does his work sweep them away forever? There is no simple answer to this question. An anthropologist can only study one group at a time, and nomadic societies are as diverse as agricultural and industrial societies. Donald Cole found the Al Murra among whom he lived to be lovable people whose hard lives were illuminated by their capacity for generosity and their simple faith in God. They displayed a humanity in their dealings with each other which made him ashamed of his own civilization.

We cannot dismiss Cole as merely another in that long line of sentimental Europeans who have apostrophized the primitive, for he lived with the Al Murra under conditions which would have destroyed facile sentiment. What he discovered was that, given the right conditions, people can be good. Exactly what those conditions are remains a mystery; certainly it is not enough to be primitive: hatred and meanness are found as often among primitive peoples as they are among civilized ones. Nor is it enough to be a nomad or to live in a desert. When we understand why the Al Murra welcomed the young anthropologist into their midst with 'brotherly love' we shall understand something important about human nature.[15] Meanwhile, we can wish the Al Murra well in coping with the many changes which are about to enter their world.

Epilogue
To Know Them was to Love Them

THE MIDDLE EASTERN MANDATES were acquired at a time when Englishmen had been mesmerized by their own charisma into believing that whole populations could be controlled by moral influence and very little else. The extent to which the British were prepared to go in their Middle Eastern mandates in the direction of indirection was quite remarkable. Under the watchful eye of the League of Nations, and with apparent confidence in their ability to carry off this experiment in new model imperialism, they steadily reduced the number of their civilian personnel and assigned them to posts which were explicitly advisory. The backbone of the British administration in Iraq was a handful of British Administrative Inspectors who were supposed to carry out British policy without giving direct orders to the Iraqi officials they 'advised'. As T. E. Lawrence had pointed out in *The Round Table*, this was a form of control which was highly exacting; it required strength of character and a sure touch with the natives.[1] In their own estimation the British possessed these qualities in abundance: they had a sense of mission and an implicit faith in the psychological ascendancy they derived from knowledge, a knowledge which seemed all the more powerful because it was believed to be unilateral. The legendary ability of certain Englishmen to pass as Arabs constituted ultimate proof of this knowledge. Reciprocity was inconceivable – no Arab ever would or could attempt to pass as an Englishman.

To say that we 'know' a person is to imply that, other things being equal, we can assume a certain power over him because of our ability to predict what he will do. Events which can be predicted can also be controlled: this is a fundamental axiom of applied science and also an implicit assumption underlying many human actions. Whether or not we use the power we believe knowledge gives us is determined in part by the nature of the moral constraints which apply to the exercise of that power. Where moral values point to the use of power rather than towards abstention from its use knowledge is perceived as a legitimate instrument of control. The confident belief that they 'knew' the Arabs helped to make it psychologically possible for the British over several decades to maintain a commanding position in an area where international public opinion made it difficult to contemplate the use of force.

We have seen that the ideas about Arabs which could be acquired from a study of English writers on the subject were confused and contradictory – there was no clear, well-integrated stereotype of the Arab but a number of possible mini-stereotypes which could be bandied about with supporting references to one authority or another. The fact that the best known of these authorities were English had given rise to a tradition of English expertise on the Arabs which came to be regarded as almost a racial characteristic: it was in the nature of Englishmen to understand Arabs, and it was in the nature of Arabs to be understandable to Englishmen.

The essential vagueness of this idea, its lack of specific content, made it almost indestructible. It was so amorphous that it allowed for great flexibility in assimilating new information. Simple, concrete and specific stereotypes, e.g. all Arabs are hospitable, are constantly liable to be contradicted by experience, with consequent loss of confidence in the ability to predict and control; but the much vaguer notion that the English are good at interpreting the behaviour of Arabs is far less likely to be proven false by events. It is therefore a very useful idea for an administrator to have. It encourages a flattering image of himself as a wise old bird with an instinctive faculty for understanding the native mind; and this belief gives him the confidence he needs to impose his will on those whom fate has appointed him to rule. Faced by unanticipated developments, he can always resort to a refusal to be surprised by human oddness, because he believes that somehow (he is not always sure how) these oddities conform to a system to which he has been given the key.

Though a belief of this type, vague but powerful, can endure for a long time in spite of the existence of facts which do not support it, it cannot endure indefinitely without strain. There is a limit to the capacity of any belief to withstand the facts, even when a great deal of self-esteem is invested in it. Under sufficient strain, efforts to resist the truth must finally be abandoned; but it is still possible to retire in good order, psychologically speaking, if some face-saving formula can be found. Though the British were eventually forced to conclude that the behaviour of Arabs had passed beyond their understanding, they consoled themselves with the thought that the Arabs had changed. Men like Sir Alec Kirkbride, accustomed to grey eminence in the Arab world, ended their careers with the realization that what they had supposed to be their massive personal influence had vanished, but they held on to the comforting belief that once things had been different. It had become 'more difficult', Kirkbride wrote with masterly understatement, 'to establish with the newcomers the sympathetic co-operation which had marked my relations with their fathers'.[2] The new generation of Arabs was indeed different from their fathers, though the difference was not as great as the British supposed. The product of universities at which they were exposed to a heady combination of socialist and nationalist ideas, the newcomers were not about to accommadate themselves to British fantasies of benevolent omniscience, as their parents, astutely sizing up the weakness of their masters, had done.

There is a natural tendency to like people we think we can control, though it is, as Albert Hourani noticed, 'a queer sort of liking, not very similar to love or friendship'.[3] It undoubtedly played its part in prompting English officials to write of their fondness for the Arabs whose sympathetic co-operation they had enjoyed. But there were other reasons why these men could claim quite truthfully to have experienced a feeling of affinity for the Arabs.

The ease with which many British officers and gentlemen during and after the First World War took to Bedouin life when circumstances demanded it was quite remarkable. A host of memoirs and travel books testify to this. These people found that they felt at home in Bedouin society, and they rationalized this feeling by pointing to the existence of shared values. The tradition of Arab gentlemanliness had survived, sometimes in attenuated and barely recognizable form, throughout the nineteenth century and provided a convenient peg to hang rather inchoate feelings on, though it is noticeable that those who really felt the fascination of Bedouin life rarely explained it in this way. John Glubb, who claimed to find many similarities between Bedouin chivalry and English gentlemanliness, knew that the Bedouin warrior was in reality very far from the English gentleman; he would slit your throat as easily as peeling an orange and was as different as could be imagined from Chaucer's 'parfit gentle knight'. 'The nomad warrior was anything but modest,' Glubb wrote 'indeed he would have struck any Englishman as unpleasantly arrogant and boastful.'[4]

The feeling of affinity, which certainly existed, was experienced at a much more primitive level than the conscious perception of a common gentlemanliness. If this had not been so, the very slender and ambiguous evidence of shared values would not have counted for much. Some Englishmen who were otherwise partial to primitive nomad life found the notion of Bedouin gentlemanliness so unconvincing that they could not enjoy their company at all. Arnold Wilson delighted in the hardy, abstemious life of the Bakhtiari of southern Persia but found the Iraqi Bedouin repulsive. Their unconcern for larger loyalties and predatory habits were things he was quite unable to tolerate. Others, less morally consistent than he, did not allow evidence of Bedouin failings to spoil their enjoyment of Bedouin life.

Their response perhaps had much to do with a sense of lives structured in a common fashion. Most of the Englishmen who became involved with the Bedouin as officers in the Hejaz campaign and as administrators after the war had undergone the formative experience of public school, and the life of an English public school and the life of a Bedouin camp have certain things in common: hardship, male comradeship, a delight in sports and outdoor pursuits, and the frequent recital of epic poetry, to name but a few. Schoolboy loyalty to school and house is mirrored in the Bedouin's loyalty to his tribe and clan, and in both societies there is a delicate combination of egalitarianism and respect for authority. Both practice a form of conciliar government, through elders among the Bedouin and prefects among the schoolboys, with a sheikh or head boy as *primus inter pares*. Englishmen accustomed to the half-serious, half-playful local patriotism required by inter-house and inter-school sports found themselves inclined to sympathize with Bedouin raiding, which they regarded as on a par with the harmless trophy hunting of schoolboys. There was even a common element of nomadism, in the English boy's repeated treks between home and school and the Bedouin's regular movements between dry-season wells and wet-season grazing grounds. The comparison is more than merely entertaining: it almost certainly helps to explain why Lord Winterton, a veteran of Eton and the Hejaz, believed that 'there are only two places where one can enjoy life – in the desert and in this country'.[5] Participation in Bedouin life was in some respects like a prolongation of adolescence, a period of life at which many Englishmen of that time and class appear to have been permanently fixated. Who can read English autobiographies of the last thirty or forty years without noticing the disproportionate amount of space allocated to schooldays? The personality of boys and their relationship to each other and to the social and political institutions of the school are delineated with a precision which would do credit to an anthropologist.

According to Harold Nicolson the English practice of sending boys away from home and a certain brutality in their approach to child-rearing long pre-date the public school.[6] Clearly the public school was largely an institutionalization of an existing belief that it was good for boys to be knocked into presentable shape by persons other than their parents. One of the consequences of the peculiar mode of education which arose from this belief was that boys spent their formative years, the years in which Erikson claims with some justice that our 'identity' is acquired, in miniature self-contained societies which in many respects can be described as tribal. They had their own dialects, their own myths, their own initiation rituals, and above all their pride in their own institution's uniqueness. Isolated from the larger world of ordinary human society and the smaller world of the family, boys were wholly absorbed, at a time when the appeal of groups and cliques as experiments in self-definition is naturally very strong, in the life of the school. Afterwards they recognized each other wherever they went, for the experience put its indefinable stamp on them. They recognized themselves too in certain of the primitive peoples, usually nomads with strong group feelings and traditions of superiority, with whom the Empire brought them into contact. The Bedouin were one of these peoples – the Masai were another – and the ease which Englishmen felt in Bedouin company, combined with a tradition of English interest in Arabia, produced a feeling that the English presence in Arab lands had something quite natural and inevitable about it.

The appeal of the Bedouin for Englishmen was almost wholly confined to members of the officer class. Other ranks tended to regard them as savages.[7] This was not simply because private soldiers had not shared their officers' tribal experience of adolescence and so were less susceptible to feelings of affinity; it was also because Bedouin life was best savoured from a commanding position. The English private soldier, as a person of low degree, was regarded with no particular respect by the Bedouin and suffered at their hands what he felt were unpardonable liberties. An officer was far less likely to be practically inconvenienced by their presumption and could enjoy what he might choose to regard as their charming independence of manner.

As long ago as 1826 an Englishwoman in Muscat had noticed that 'good order and subordination' remained fundamentally unaffected by the frank and uncompromising demeanour adopted by Arab tribesmen towards their ruler.[8] Beneath the Bedouin's wildness of manner there was a respect for legitimate authority which upper class Englishmen instinctively recognized. Wilfrid Blunt, with his sensitivity to the subject of respect for traditional authority, had seen it immediately and had consequently felt at home. This seemingly paradoxical combination of sturdy independence and acquiescence in the status quo had a strong appeal for English officers and officials in the Middle East. In the world of the Bedouin they could enjoy the very subtle, and very English, pleasure of being treated as an equal by the very people over whom fate had given them a measure of control.

When John Glubb first encountered the Bedouin in the shape of the Juwasim tribe of Iraq there was 'something about them' which attracted him: in spite of their poverty and filth they seemed 'unaware of any desire to be richer' and did not at all feel that their mode of life was inferior; 'on the contrary, they believed themselves to be the élite of the human race'.[9] Ronald Storrs, in many respects a very different man from Glubb, reported similar feelings. When he found himself, after long service in the Middle East, 'appointed to the rule of a million and half blacks, of whom one only, the Paramount Chief of Barotseland, could have his hand shaken by a white', he found the contrast, 'after lands where you gave your hand to and shared the food of the poorest Bedu camel-driver (or his eyes wondered where you had been bred) almost overwhelmingly disagreeable'.[10] In trying to sum up the attraction of the Bedouin for people like himself Glubb wrote:

The great attraction which they exercised on the occasional Europeans who met them lay in the fact they they lived in a different world, which was neither class-conscious nor race-conscious, and so suffered neither from the agressiveness nor from the alternative servility of those communities whose members were constantly obsessed by doubts as to their own value in comparison with the other groups with which they came in contact. A complete lack of self-consciousness – to be perfectly natural, as we say – was one of the most attractive human qualities. The bedouins thirty or forty years ago were unaware of the existence of class or race inequalities. As a result, they unconsciously treated all men as equals, without any mental embarrassments or reservations.

Even that very day, a bearded and ragged ruffian seated in the tent, striking the ground in front of him with his cane for emphasis, had shouted at me: 'O man. What is the use of your government? They do not defend their subjects.'

Was it this straightforward and open frankness which constituted their charm?[11]

It was indeed, and not simply because Bedouin manners were a flattering caricature of English manners, of that 'naturalness' on which an English gentleman prided himself. Neither Glubb nor Storrs questions the legitimacy of their own domination – that too is perfectly natural; nor does the outspoken Bedouin question the fact that Glubb represents the government of which he is a 'subject'. There is no challenge to legitimate authority implied in the straightforward and open frankness Glubb finds so pleasing. He even suggests that the Bedouin's pride in himself is actually conducive to the maintenance of good order. Being conscious of his own value, the Bedouin is not servile, but neither is he aggressive: only those, it is implied, who do not have a proper consciousness of their own value – presumably in the sight of God – feel the need to assert themselves by challenging the status quo.

The response of men like Glubb to people who appeared to be 'unaware' of class or race inequalities, that is to say, unaware of the nature of their relationship with the English officials in their midst, was enthusiastic compliance with what they took to be the appropriate social conventions. They relished a situation which allowed for, even demanded, the appearance of equality between people who were manifestly unequal. In Glubb's desert patrols officers and men ate from the same dish and discipline was maintained through appeals to a man's honour or threats of expulsion from the group.[12] Kinahan Cornwallis, who played a prominent role in Anglo-Arab diplomacy for over twenty years, advised that if you treat the Arab 'as a friend and an equal . . . you get the best out of him', that is to say, he would serve you 'loyally and well', as Cornwallis had hoped Feisal would do.[13]

It has long been commonplace in England to ridicule class-consciousness without implying any criticism of the class system. Many a lord who would have been aghast at an attempt to effect a genuine levelling has expected his inferiors to look him steadily in the eye, and even to display a certain truculence. So long as the foundations of human society were not perceived to be threatened, asseverations of equality in the sight of God have not gone amiss with the English governing class, have in fact even been welcomed as demonstrations of the liberty of every true-born Englishman. When Oliver Cromwell said of the Quaker members of his household: 'Shall I disown them because they will not put off their hats?', and then refused to abolish tithes, he was being, as so often, quintessentially English. The reasons for this situation are to be found in English history and go back long before the English Revolution. For economic reasons a class of independent peasant farmers and merchants emerged much earlier in England than it did in Europe, and centralization and autocracy did not develop in England as they did on the continent. Tendencies in this direction under the Stuarts were brought to an end by Cromwell's revolution. By the end of the seventeenth century 'the liberty of the English people' was an established political concept, and though the people were usually defined in such a way as to exclude what would now be called the working class, the idea was none the less powerful for that. Liberty is an idea which defies the exercise of proprietary rights – a genie which once let out refuses to go back in the bottle. Political actions justified by appeals to the rights of Englishmen, no matter how limited or selfish in intention, kept alive the idea that the nation consisted of free men linked together by a voluntary compact. This very dangerous idea was accepted by many people who had much to lose if it was carried to its logical conclusion, a phenomenon more common in politics than Marxists would have us suppose. These people resisted the logical implications of the idea because their interests were at stake, but made concessions they deemed to be politic and which they might not have made if the idea had not had a genuine hold on them. The presence of this unassimilated vein of radical sentiment has meant that though upper class Englishmen have rarely demonstrated an active commitment to human equality they have often expected people to behave as though it already existed.

This kind of behaviour implies some recognition, however fleeting and uneasy, of the degradation experienced by someone who submits to the will of a privileged class. An Englishman who reacts to obsequious behaviour with inarticulate embarrassment or articulate misery at the sight of another's shame is making at least a minimal acknowledgement of the interchangeability of human destinies, without which there can be no foundation for a real belief in human equality. In so far as his behaviour suggests a capacity for empathy it does the English gentleman credit, but it also suggests a desire not to be reminded of the human consequences of the system which provides him with his special privileges. He hankers after dominance without tears, for a form of acquiescence on the part of those dominated which reassures him that their personal integrity remains intact.

When the English acquired some power in the Middle East they found a traditional society which seemed to offer the possibility of dominance with a good conscience. The egalitarian demeanour of even the most miserable Bedouin assured them that the natives retained a dignified sense of their own value. If a man knew he was your equal in the sight of God, what possible harm could you be doing him?

This power over the Arabs was acquired at a time when the English class system appeared to be in danger from the newly organized working class. The illusion of social consensus, of familyhood, had become increasingly difficult to sustain. Perhaps it was consoling to find a corner of the earth where the old balancing trick could still be performed, where political illusions long cherished could be cherished a little longer. The English working man might be showing distressing signs of getting above himself, but the unreconstructed Bedouin seemed ready to settle for equality before God without worrying about equality before man.

The decline of British influence in the Middle East was paralleled by a decline in the reputation of T. E. Lawrence. While he was alive, and for two decades after his death, he was worshipped as an imperial hero, exemplifying for part of his enormous public the special relationship between the English and the Arabs; but his eventual posthumous fate was to provide a focus for the collective embarrassment of a people whose imperial glory had abruptly departed.

The story of the creation of the Lawrence legend is well known: how it was launched (with Lawrence's connivance) by the American journalist Lowell Thomas; how it was confirmed by the idolatrous biographies of Robert Graves and Liddell Hart; how it was debunked by Richard Aldington in 1955. At its peak the Lawrence mania produced such absurdities as Douglas Glen's *In the Steps of Lawrence of Arabia* (1941), in which the author's attempts to retrace Lawrence's steps were recounted with ludicrous solemnity. (When he asked local Arabs if they remembered El Auruns they usually looked blank; but awkward facts like this have never been allowed to get in the way of myth.)

In 1918 the British public were ready for Lawrence. After four years of unprecedentedly horrible war they welcomed the emergence of a glamorous hero, his white robes unspotted by Flanders mud, who, it was said, had princes and potentates of Arabia at his command. They were informed by Robert Graves that Lawrence could have made himself Emperor of the Arabs, but instead he 'came away and left [them] to employ the freedom that he had given them, a freedom unencumbered by his rule which, however just and wise, would always have been an alien rule'.[14] It seems incredible that such rubbish could have been believed less than fifty years ago, but it was. Lawrence's exploits (real or imaginary) appealed to millions whose dreams of effortless domination found expression through identification with the British Empire and its heroes.

For an understanding of the mass reaction to Lawrence we must look, not to the writings of such esoteric figures as Wilfrid Blunt, but to the popular literature of imperialism, to the kind of story in which unassuming but intrepid Englishmen halt whole regiments of hostile natives with a single word. The French psychiatrist O. Mannoni has suggested that the archetype of all such stories is *The Tempest*, a play whose hero, having ignominiously left his native land, exerts a magical sway over the natives of a faraway island. Mannoni identifies the motive spring of European colonialism as the impulse to triumph over feelings of inferiority (an inevitable feature of a competitive and individualistic society) through

domination over creatures less real, and therefore, less deman-
ding, than those at home.[15] This is an over-simplification of a very
complex historical phenomenon, but it seems to explain something
of the nature of imperial dreams, if less perhaps of imperial
realities.[16] The enormous popularity of 'Lawrence of Arabia' is
made more comprehensible if we assume that his audience identified with him as a Prospero figure, a magician capable of control-
ing effortlessly the destinies of both good natives and bad. In the
particular imperial romance in which Lawrence played the leading
role the Arabs were assigned the part of Ariel (the archetypal 'good
native' who according to Mannoni is the personification of infantile
wishes for a compliant companion) and the Turks, naturally,
played the part of Caliban, the 'bad native' who personifies the
infantile terrors which only magic can keep at bay. To his adoring
public Lawrence seemed to possess that magic.

Lawrence as a Prospero figure comes through very clearly in a
book by S. C. Rolls, an enlisted man who served in the Hejaz
campaign as an armoured car driver. Rolls described how Lawrence's arrival in Feisal's camp restored a feeling of ease and
well-being to the British enlisted men who had just spent months
in the desert with Arab 'allies' whom they hated and feared. (It is
apparent from Rolls's book that it required a certain distance for
ordinary Englishmen to perceive Arabs as Ariel-like. At close quar-
ters they seemed more like Caliban.) When the Englishmen saw
the courtesy with which Lawrence was received by Feisal and the
other leaders they concluded that he was a hero whom the Arabs
instinctively worshipped. They ceased to be ordinary blokes living
in uncomfortable proximity with people they regarded as incomprehensible savages, and took pride once more in their country's
imperial destiny. Their self-confidence was restored.[17]

Many people, including some very able ones, testified to the
awesome impression Lawrence made on them. These testimonies
are of course tainted by the fact that most of them were committed
to print after 'Lawrence of Arabia' had become a legend; but it is
conceivable that through some mystery of personality Lawrence
managed to convey the suggestion of almost magical powers. 'It is
said,' wrote Peake Pasha in an apocalyptic mood, 'that when the
Emperor Napoleon lay dying at St. Helena a great storm swept
over the island, and, strangely, just as Lawrence stood up to say
good-bye, and leave Deraa and Syria for the last time, an earth-

quake shook the house and left us awed.'[18] Prospero himself could hardly have managed it better.

The more closely one looks at Lawrence's life and personality the more ideally suited he seems to be for his role as Prospero. Erik Erikson has developed a theory that men who are perceived as great by their contemporaries are often suffering from, and at the same time creatively coping with, what might be termed a representative neurosis. Lawrence seems a case in point. He experienced in particularly intense form the unresolved feelings of inferiority which Mannoni claims are at the root of the European dream of colonialism. Because he was also convinced of his own extraordinariness he attempted to overcome these feelings in ways which other people only dreamed about. Unlike ordinary men he went from daydream to firm intention: he, Lawrence, would lead a great national movement; he, Lawrence, would be king, in reality if not in name, over thousands of natives. The war provided him with an amazing opportunity to cast himself in the role he had marked out for himself. Whether he actually succeeded in doing so or not is immaterial; what mattered was that he managed, in fleeting moments free from the hyper-consciousness of the workings of his own mind which both crippled and stimulated him, to overcome his feelings of inferiority through action. This was an aspect of Lawrence's story to which the public instinctively responded; and Lawrence, with the kind of sixth sense possessed by those who create their own legend, stressed those aspects of his life and personality which contributed to the potency of his myth. He made much of his lack of military experience, his previous 'insignificance' in civilian life and the army hierarchy, his youth (a form of natural inferiority), his rather puny body and his deliberate 'hardening' of it – in short the manifold disadvantages he had so gloriously overcome. The vast public which was waiting for him took heart from his triumph and through identifying with him felt they could share it.

When Lawrence broke his staff and threw away his books to go and merge himself penitentially in the ranks the legend was complete. By choosing not to wield his awful powers he had provided ultimate proof of their reality. Liddell Hart was of the opinion in 1934 that he might be called upon to emerge from his solitude in order to set his own country to rights, but fortunately he was neither called nor chosen.[19]

The Aldington biography, which first appeared in French as *Lawrence, l'imposteur,* was greeted with pious horror by English reviewers. The notices it received were astoundingly vicious; they finished Aldington. But his book turned out to be only the first of several exercises in debunking. Ten years later it was the fashion to attack Lawrence as a pervert and a poseur.

The reason was that his magic had not worked. Britain no longer had any control, effortless or otherwise, over what was happening in the Middle East. With the loss of empire the claim to possess mysterious influence over Eastern races – a claim which Lawrence had personified – could only be embarrassing. Therefore he was violently disowned. His reputation reached its nadir in Alan Bennett's play *Forty Years On*, a work suffused with suppressed nostalgia for empire.

There are signs that Lawrence's reputation may be due for some rehabilitation. He was after all, though deeply flawed, a gifted, shrewd and interesting man. But the myth of England's special relationship with the Arabs will be left on the scrap heap of history, where it belongs.

Notes

1 A Sometimes Noble Savage

1. William of Tyre, *A History of Deeds Done Beyond the Sea*, Vol. I, p. 433; Joinville, *Chronicle of the Crusade of St Lewis*, p. 197.
2. William of Tyre, *A History of Deeds Done Beyond the Sea*, Vol. I, p. 445.
3. *Mandeville's Travels*, Vol. I, p. 47.
4. Lithgow, *Totall Discourse*, p. 262.
5. Plaisted, *A Journal from Busserah to Aleppo*, p. 94; Carmichael, *A Journey from Aleppo to Basserah*, p. 177. Excellent secondary sources for English travellers in the East at this and later periods are Fedden, *English Travellers in the Near East*; Searight, *The British in the Middle East*; Brent, *Far Arabia*; Nasir, *The Arabs and the English*.
6. Plaisted, *A Journal from Busserah to Aleppo*, pp. 70–3.
7. D'Arvieux, *Travels in Arabia the Desart*, p. 91.
8. D'Arvieux, *Travels in Arabia the Desart*, pp. 9–10.
9. D'Arvieux, *Travels in Arabia the Desart*, p. ii.
10. D'Arvieux, *Travels in Arabia the Desart*, pp. 95–146.
11. D'Herbelot, *Bibliothèque orientale*, p. 120.
12. Strabo, Vol. VII, p. 211; Diodorus Siculus, Vol. II, p. 41 and Vol. X, pp. 87–8; Herodotus, Vol. II, p. 11.
13. *Dictionary of National Biography*, entry on George Sale.
14. Sale, 'Preliminary Discourse' to the Koran, pp. 10, 23.
15. B. G. Niebuhr, *Life of Carsten Niebuhr*, p. 30. See also Thorkild Hansen's excellent account of the Danish expedition, *Arabia Felix*.
16. Niebuhr, *Travels in Arabia*, p. 79.
17. Niebuhr, *Travels in Arabia*, pp. 84–6, 133.
18. Niebuhr, *Travels in Arabia*, p. 65.
19. Hansen, *Arabia Felix*, pp. 112–14.
20. Carmichael, *A Journey from Aleppo to Basserah*, p. 139; Bruce, *Travels to Discover the Source of the Nile*, Vol. I, p. 145; Hill, *With the Bedouins*, p. 225.
21. Gibbon, *Decline and Fall*, pp. 216–17.
22. Jones, 'Discourse on the Arabs', p. 69.
23. Jones, 'Discourse on the Arabs', p. 50.
24. Arberry, 'New Light on Sir William Jones'.
25. Jones, 'Discourse on the Arabs', p. 59.
26. Clarke, *Travels in Various Countries of Europe, Asia and Africa*, Vol. IV, pp. 234–55, 423, 428.

27. Lord Valentia, *Voyages and Travels*, Vol. II, pp. 354–6.
28. Irwin, *The Bedouins;* and *A Series of Adventures in the Course of a Voyage up the Red Sea*, pp. 56–7.
29. Erikson, *Childhood and Society*, pp. 247–51.
30. Bruce, *Travels to Discover the Source of the Nile*, Vol. I, p. lxx.
31. Sim, *Desert Traveller*, p. 46.
32. Burckhardt, *Travels in Arabia*, pp. 160–1.
33. Burckhardt, *Travels in Arabia*, pp. 51, 202, 466–7; and *Notes on the Bedouins and Wahabys*, pp. 204–5 and passim.
34. Burckhardt, *Notes on the Bedouins and Wahabys*, p. 18.
35. Burckhardt, *Notes on the Bedouins and Wahabys*, p. 193.
36. Burckhardt, *Travels in Arabia*, p. 462; and *Travels in Nubia*, p. lxxi.
37. *Edinburgh Review*, 1829, 50, p. 177.
38. Burckhardt, *Travels in Arabia*, p. 229.
39. Nicolson, *Good Behaviour*, p. 202.
40. Heude, *A Voyage up the Persian Gulf*, p. 63.
41. T. P. Thompson, 'Arabs and Persians', pp. 206, 210.

2 'Oh! that the Desert were my dwelling-place . . .'

1. B. G. Niebuhr, *The Life of Carsten Niebuhr*, p. 15.
2. Sim, *Desert Traveller*, p. 99.
3. Chateaubriand, *Travels in Greece, Palestine, Egypt and Barbary* (English translation of *Itinéraire de Paris à Jérusalem*), p. i.
4. Chateaubriand, *Travels in Greece, Palestine, Egypt and Barbary*, p. 272.
5. Chateaubriand, *Travels in Greece, Palestine, Egypt and Barbary*, pp. 274–5.
6. Chateaubriand, *Travels in Greece, Palestine, Egypt and Barbary*, p. 393.
7. Chateaubriand, *Travels in Greece, Palestine, Egypt and Barbary*, p. 274. See also Burton, *Pilgrimage*, Vol. II, pp. 118–19.
8. Byron, *Childe Harold*, pp. 200–1.
9. Shelley, 'The Deserts of Dim Sleep', in *Poetical Works*, p. 633.
10. Hunt, 'The Nile', in *Poetical Works*, p. 248.
11. Burton, *The Gold Mines of Midian*, p. 357.
12. Burton, foreword to *Arabian Nights*, Vol. I, pp. vii–viii.
13. Sadlier, *Diary of a Journey across Arabia*, p. 40.
14. Strachey, 'Lady Hester Stanhope', p. 217.
15. See e.g. Lamartine, *A Pilgrimage to the Holy Land* (English translation of *Voyage en Orient*), Vol. I, pp. 133–45; Kinglake, *Eothen*, Chapter VIII.
16. Kinglake, *Eothen*, p. 109.
17. Duchess of Cleveland, *The Life and Letters of Lady Hester Stanhope*, pp. 159–60.
18. Duchess of Cleveland, *The Life and Letters of Lady Hester Stanhope*, p. 401; Meryon, *Memoirs*, Vol. I, p. 52.
19. Disraeli, *Tancred*, pp. 149, 150.
20. Disraeli, *Tancred*, p. 253.
21. Lawrence, *Seven Pillars of Wisdom*, pp. 36–41; Renan, *De la part des peuples sémitiques dans l'histoire de la civilisation*, p. 28.
22. Disraeli, *Tancred*, pp. 171, 260.
23. Disraeli, *Tancred*, pp. 262–3.
24. Voltaire, *Essai sur les mœurs*, pp. 212–13; and *Mahomet*. For English interest in the Arab Empire see e.g. Crichton, *History of Arabia*.
25. Anon., 'The Arabian Empire'; Anon., 'What the Arab is and is not'.

26. Carlyle, 'The Hero as Prophet', pp. 278–82; Watt, 'Carlyle on Muhammad', p. 247.
27. D'Arvieux, *Travels in Arabia the Desart*, p. 124.
28. Burton, *Pilgrimage*, Vol. II, pp. 109–10; Palgrave, *Narrative*, Vol. I, pp. 8, 68–9.
29. Carlyle, 'The Hero as Prophet', pp. 279, 284, 302.
30. Hardwick, 'Jane Carlyle', pp. 32, 34.
31. De Gaury, *Travelling Gent*, p. 25.
32. Kinglake, *Eothen*, p. xi.
33. De Gaury, *Travelling Gent*, p. xi. See also Kinglake, *Eothen*, p. 24.
34. Kinglake, *Eothen*, pp. 25–6.
35. Kinglake, *Eothen*, p. 234.
36. Kinglake, *Eothen*, pp. 175–7, 218.
37. Kinglake, *Eothen*, pp. 290, 293.
38. Warburton, *The Crescent and the Cross*, p. xiv.
39. Warburton, *The Crescent and the Cross*, Part I, p. 3.
40. Warburton, *The Crescent and the Cross*, Part I, p. 25.
41. Warburton, *The Crescent and the Cross*, Part I, p. 72.
42. Warburton, *The Crescent and the Cross*, Part I, pp. 37, 244, and Part II, pp. 235–6.
43. Duff Gordon, *Letters from Egypt*, p. 300.
44. Burton, *Pilgrimage*, Vol. I, pp. 111–12.
45. Warburton, *The Crescent and the Cross*, Part II, Chapter XII.
46. Warburton, *The Crescent and the Cross*, Part I, pp. 65, 74.
47. St John, *Adventures in the Libyan Desert*, p. 22; Anon., 'Military Expedition into Arabia Felix', p. 377.
48. De Gaury, *Arabian Journey*, p. 5.
49. Thackeray, *Cornhill to Grand Cairo*, p. 396.
50. Thackeray, *Cornhill to Grand Cairo*, p. 401.
51. Thackeray, *Cornhill to Grand Cairo*, p. 455.
52. Thackeray, *Vanity Fair*, p. 661.
53. Thackeray, *Vanity Fair*, p. 488.

3   Richard Burton (1821–1890)

1. Biographical references, except as otherwise noted, are from Fawn Brodie, *The Devil Drives*. I have followed closely Mrs Brodie's interpretation of the effect of Burton's early experiences on his adult character, which seems to me consistently plausible. The analysis of the relation between Burton's character and his attitude to the Arabs is my own. A useful study of Burton is also to be found in Thomas J. Assad, *Three Victorian Travellers*.
2. Erikson, *Identity, Youth and Crisis*, pp. 172–6.
3. Quoted in Brodie, *The Devil Drives*, pp. 49–50.
4. Burton, *Sindh*, pp. 234, 239, 255, 283.
5. Quoted in Brodie, *The Devil Drives*, pp. 166–7.
6. Burton, *First Footsteps in East Africa*, p. 205.
7. Burton, *Kasidah*, pp. vii, 100.
8. Isabel Burton, *Life*, Vol. II, p. 442.
9. Burton, preface to *First Footsteps in East Africa*, p. 22.
10. Burton, *Lord Beaconsfield: a Sketch*; Stisted, *The True Life of Capt. Sir Richard F. Burton*, p. 182.
11. Burton, *Pilgrimage*, Vol. I, p. 40 and Vol. II, p. 267.
12. *Edinburgh Review*, 1856, 104, p. 200.

13. Burton, foreword to *Arabian Nights*, Vol. i, p. xxiv.
14. Burton, *Pilgrimage*, Vol. ii, p. 87.
15. Burton, *Pilgrimage*, Vol. i, p. 258 and Vol. ii, pp. 263–4; Burton and Tyrwhitt-Drake, *Unexplored Syria*, Vol. ii, p. 191; Isabel Burton, *Life*, Vol. ii, p. 270.
16. *Dictionary of National Biography*, entry on Burton.
17. Burton, *Pilgrimage*, Vol. i, p. 45.
18. Burton, *Pilgrimage*, Vol. i, pp. 143–4, 148.
19. Burton, *Pilgrimage*, Vol. i, p. 141.
20. Burton, *Pilgrimage*, Vol. i, p. 149; and *The Gold Mines of Midian*, p. 356.
21. Burton, *Pilgrimage*, Vol. ii, p. 161.
22. Burton, *Pilgrimage*, Vol. ii, pp. 86–7.
23. Burton, *Pilgrimage*, Vol. ii, p. 10.
24. Cited in Brodie, *The Devil Drives*, p. 365.
25. Burton, *Pilgrimage*, Vol. ii, p. 102.
26. Brodie, *The Devil Drives*, pp. 143–4; Burton, *First Footsteps in East Africa*, p. 143.
27. Brodie, *The Devil Drives*, pp. 334–6; Burton, 'The Jew' in *The Jew, the Gypsy, and El Islam*; and *The Highlands of Brazil*, Vol. i, p. 403.
28. Burton, *Pilgrimage*, Vol. i, pp. 149, 205; and foreword to *Arabian Nights*, Vol. i, p. viii.
29. Burton, *Pilgrimage*, Vol. i, pp. 258–9.
30. Burton, *Pilgrimage*, Vol. ii, p. 268.
31. Burton, *The Gold Mines of Midian*, p. 155; Burton and Tyrwhitt-Drake, *Unexplored Syria*, Vol. i, p. 151.
32. Isabel Burton, *Life*, Vol. i, pp. 21, 70.
33. Burton, *Pilgrimage*, Vol. ii, p. 80.
34. Burton, *Pilgrimage*, Vol. ii, pp. 80–4.
35. Burton, *Pilgrimage*, Vol. ii, pp. 13–14.
36. Burton, *Zanzibar*, Vol. i, pp. 375–6.
37. Stanley, *Through the Dark Continent*, p. 29.
38. Hardinge, *A Diplomatist in the East*; Ingrams, *Zanzibar*.
39. Burton, *Zanzibar*, Vol. i, pp. 416–20; and *The Lake Regions of Central Africa*, Vol. i, p. 36.
40. Burton, *A Mission to Gelele*, Vol. ii, Chapter xix.
41. Burton, *A Mission to Gelele*, Vol. ii, pp. 183, 198.
42. Prichard, *The Natural History of Man*, Vol. i, pp. 134–5; and *Researches into the Physical History of Mankind*, Vol. iv, pp. 547–96.
43. Prichard, *The Natural History of Man*, Vol. i, pp. 137–45; Sladen, *Egypt and the English*, p. 89; Polson Newman, *Great Britain in Egypt*, pp. 10–19; Lane, *Manners and Customs of the Modern Egyptians*, Vol. i, p. 247; Cromer, *Modern Egypt*, Vol. ii, p. 173.
44. Burton, *The Gold Mines of Midian*, p. 10.
45. Quoted in Brodie, *The Devil Drives*, pp. 31–2.
46. Burton, *Pilgrimage*, Vol. i, pp. 146–8, and Vol. ii, pp. 77–8.
47. Isabel Burton, *Life*, Vol. ii, p. 324.
48. Burton, 'Terminal Essay' to *Arabian Nights*, Vol. x, pp. 63–5.

4 Gifford Palgrave (1826–1888)

1. *Athenaeum*, 13 October 1888, p. 483.
2. Sir Francis Palgrave, *The English Commonwealth*, p. 26.

3. Biographical sources for Sir Francis Palgrave and William Gifford Palgrave are the *Dictionary of National Biography*; Mea Allen, *Palgrave of Arabia*; and Benjamin Meir Braude, 'The Spiritual Quest of William Gifford Palgrave'.
4. Palgrave, *Narrative*, Vol. I, pp. 181–2.
5. *Proceedings of the Royal Geographical Society*, 1888, *10*, p. 713; *Times*, 16 June 1865, p. 10.
6. Palgrave, *Narrative*, Vol. I, pp. 119, 241.
7. Burton, *Pilgrimage*, preface to third edition, Vol. I, p. xxi.
8. Quoted in Allen, *Palgrave of Arabia*, p. 156.
9. Palgrave, 'From Montevideo to Paraguay', in *Ulysses*, p. 270.
10. Palgrave, preface to *Narrative*, Vol. I, p. vii.
11. Palgrave, *Narrative*, Vol. I, pp. 258–65; Hogarth, *The Life of Charles M. Doughty*, p. 152.
12. Palgrave, *Narrative*, Vol. I, pp. 92–3.
13. Palgrave, 'Notes of a Journey from Gaza, through the Interior of Arabia, to El Khatif on the Persian Gulf, and thence to Omàn, in 1862–63'; anonymous review of Palgrave's *Narrative* in *Quarterly Review*, 1866, *119*, pp. 182–215.
14. Allen, *Palgrave of Arabia*, pp. 206–9; Philby, *The Heart of Arabia*, Vol. II, pp. 117–56, and 'Palgrave in Arabia'; Cheesman, 'The Deserts of Jafura and Jabrin'.
15. Palgrave, *Narrative*, Vol. I, p. 201.
16. Palgrave, 'Mahometanism in the Levant', in *Essays on Eastern Questions*, p. 62.
17. Palgrave, 'Eastern Christians', in *Essays on Eastern Questions*, p. 212.
18. Cited in Braude, 'The Spiritual Quest of William Gifford Palgrave', p. 53.
19. Palgrave, 'The Mahometan Revival', in *Essays on Eastern Questions*, p. 126.
20. Braude, 'The Spiritual Quest of William Gifford Palgrave', p. 44.
21. George, *Lamartine and Romantic Unanism*, pp. 14–15.
22. Lamartine, *A Pilgrimage to the Holy Land* (English translation of *Voyage en Orient*), Vol. II, pp. 129–30.
23. Palgrave, *Hermann Agha*, pp. 130–4.
24. See the reviews in the *Athenaeum*, *Blackwood's*, *Chambers' Edinburgh Journal*, *Edinburgh Review*, *Fortnightly Review*, *Littell's Living Age* and *The Times*.
25. Palgrave, *Narrative*, Vol. I, Chapter I.
26. Palgrave, *Narrative*, Vol. I, p. 22.
27. Palgrave, *Narrative*, Vol. I, pp. 119–20.
28. Palgrave, *A Vision of Life*, pp. 13, 49, 52.
29. Palgrave, *Narrative*, Vol. II, pp. 162–3.
30. Palgrave, *Narrative*, Vol. I, p. 137.
31. Blunt, *My Diaries. Part II*, p. 130.
32. Palgrave, *Narrative*, Vol. I, pp. 241–2, 344.
33. Palgrave, *Narrative*, Vol. I, p. 70.
34. *Westminster Review*, 1865, *84*, p. 400.
35. Palgrave, *Narrative*, Vol. I, p. 128.
36. Palgrave, *Hermann Agha*, pp. 311–13; 'Arabia', p. 246; and *Narrative*, Vol. I, p. 34.
37. Palgrave, *Narrative*, Vol. I, pp. 142–3.
38. *Westminster Review*, 1865, *84*, p. 401; *Blackwood's*, 1865, *98*, p. 737.
39. Palgrave, *Narrative*, Vol. I, pp. 119, 175–6.
40. Palgrave, *A Vision of Life*, p. 319.
41. Quoted in Allen, *Palgrave of Arabia*, p. 257.
42. Palgrave, 'Phra-Bat', in *Ulysses*, p. 171; and 'The Three Cities', in *Ulysses*, p. 216.

43. Palgrave, 'Kioto', in *Ulysses*, pp. 219, 243–4.
44. Palgrave, *A Vision of Life*, p. 97 and passim.
45. Palgrave, *A Vision of Life*, p. 400.

5 Wilfrid Scawen Blunt (1840–1922)

1. Blunt, *Esther*, Sonnets xxii and xxv, in *Poems*, pp. 14, 15.
2. Biographical references in this chapter, except as otherwise noted, are from Edith Finch, *Wilfrid Scawen Blunt*. Elizabeth Longford's biography (*A Pilgrimage of Passion: The Life of Wilfrid Scawen Blunt*), which is based on previously inaccessible papers in the Fitzwilliam Museum in Cambridge, appeared as this book was going to press. Longford states that Francis Blunt 'died of a chill contracted while cub-hunting at Crabbet' (p. 6); other biographers do not specify the cause of death.
3. Quoted in Finch, *Wilfrid Scawen Blunt*, p. 19.
4. Blunt, *My Diaries. Part I*, p. 337.
5. Blunt and Meynell, *Proteus and Amadeus*, p. 23.
6. Blunt, *My Diaries. Part I*, p. 292.
7. Blunt, *Esther*, Sonnet xxiii, in *Poems*, p. 14.
8. Blunt, *Esther*, Sonnet xxiv, in *Poems*, p. 15.
9. Blunt, *Esther*, Sonnet xxiv, in *Poems*, p. 15.
10. Blunt and Meynell, *Proteus and Amadeus*, p. 25.
11. Blunt and Meynell, *Proteus and Amadeus*, p. 28.
12. Blunt and Meynell, *Proteus and Amadeus*, p. 161; Assad, *Three Victorian Travellers*, p. 67.
13. Blunt and Meynell, *Proteus and Amadeus*, p. 2.
14. Blunt and Meynell, *Proteus and Amadeus*, pp. 5–6.
15. Blunt, *Love Sonnets of Proteus*, Sonnet xc, in *Poems*, p. 84.
16. Blunt, *Esther*, Sonnet xxi, in *Poems*, p. 13.
17. Blunt, *My Diaries. Part II*, p. 231.
18. Blunt, 'The Old Squire', in *Poetical Works*, Vol. ii, p. 13.
19. MacCarthy, *Memories*, p. 222; Anthony Lytton, *The Desert and the Green*, p. 30; Neville Lytton, *The English Country Gentleman*, p. 242.
20. Manuscript letter from Blunt to Father Gerard, 13 October 1904. Found in the British Museum's copy of *Proteus and Amadeus*.
21. Blunt, *My Diaries. Part II*, p. 422.
22. Blunt, *Secret History*, p. 27.
23. Lady Anne Blunt, *Bedouin Tribes of the Euphrates*, p. 228. Wilfrid Blunt wrote the preface (pp. 7–10), the postscript (pp. 441–5), and Chapters xxiii to xxviii (pp. 361–440).
24. Lady Anne Blunt, *Bedouin Tribes of the Euphrates*, pp. 179–81.
25. Lady Anne Blunt, *Bedouin Tribes of the Euphrates*, pp. 137, 188–9, 411.
26. Lady Anne Blunt, *Bedouin Tribes of the Euphrates*, p. 234.
27. Lady Anne Blunt, *Bedouin Tribes of the Euphrates*, pp. 399, 402.
28. Lady Anne Blunt, *Bedouin Tribes of the Euphrates*, p. 387.
29. Lady Anne Blunt, *Bedouin Tribes of the Euphrates*, pp. 404–5.
30. Blunt, 'Arabian Poetry of the Days of Ignorance', pp. 627–9.
31. Lady Anne Blunt, *Bedouin Tribes of the Euphrates*, p. 409; Blunt, *Secret History*, p. 5.
32. Lady Anne Blunt, *Bedouin Tribes of the Euphrates*, p. 408.

33. Lady Anne Blunt, *Bedouin Tribes of the Euphrates*, p. 411.
34. Quoted in Finch, *Wilfrid Scawen Blunt*, p. 212.
35. Lady Anne Blunt, *Bedouin Tribes of the Euphrates*, p. 410.
36. Blunt, *Secret History*, pp. 28–9.
37. Lady Anne Blunt, *A Pilgrimage to Nejd*, Vol. I, p. x. Wilfrid Blunt wrote the preface (pp. ix–xxviii) and Chapter XI (pp. 257–73) in Vol. I and Chapter XII (pp. 1–17) and an appendix (pp. 251–68) in Vol. II.
38. Blunt, *Secret History*, p. 58.
39. Blunt's chapters in Vol. I of *A Pilgrimage to Nejd*; Blunt, *Secret History*, p. 57.
40. Blunt, *Secret History*, p. 58; Lady Anne Blunt, *A Pilgrimage to Nejd*, Vol. I, p. 270.
41. Blunt, *Secret History*, pp. 58–9.
42. Quoted in Finch, *Wilfrid Scawen Blunt*, p. 273.
43. Blunt, *Secret History*, p. 89.
44. Blunt, *Secret History*, p. 89.
45. Blunt, 'The Future of Islam', Part V, p. 44.
46. Lawrence, foreword to Bertram Thomas, *Arabia Felix*, p. xv; list of Lawrence's books given as an appendix in A. W. Lawrence, ed., *T. E. Lawrence by his Friends*.
47. Blunt, *Secret History*, pp. 97–8.
48. Blunt, *Secret History*, pp. 62–3, 91–2.
49. Blunt, *The Shame of the Nineteenth Century*, p. 5.
50. Blunt, 'Recent Events in Arabia', p. 719.
51. Blunt, *Secret History*, p. 139.
52. Blunt, *Secret History*, p. 171.
53. Blunt, *Secret History*, p. 385.
54. Blunt, 'Ideas about India', Parts I and II.
55. Blunt, 'Ideas about India', Part IV, p. 234.
56. Blunt, *The Land War in Ireland*, p. 300.
57. Blunt, *The Land War in Ireland*, pp. 373, 378.
58. Blunt, *My Diaries. Part I*, p. 271.
59. Judith Lytton, *The Authentic Arabian Horse*, Chapter II.
60. Blunt, 'Satan Absolved', in *Poems*, p. 164.
61. Blunt, 'The By-Law Tyranny and Rural Depopulation'.
62. Blunt, *Gordon at Khartoum*, p. 58; letter from Wilfrid Blunt to Syed Mahmud, 28 July 1913, reproduced in Anthony Lytton, *Wilfrid Scawen Blunt*, pp. 182–190.
63. Blunt, *India under Ripon*, p. 233.
64. Biddiss, 'Gobineau and the Origins of European Racism'.
65. Elizabeth Longford suggests that Blunt's detestation of Jews may have originated with his discovery that he shared Skittles with a wealthy Jew. (Longford, *A Pilgrimage of Passion*, pp. 49–50.)
66. Lawrence, foreword to Bertram Thomas, *Arabia Felix*, p. xv.
67. Blunt, 'Ambition', in *Poems*, p. 237.

6   Charles M. Doughty (1843–1926)

1. Biographical references and quotations from Doughty's letters are from D. G. Hogarth, *The Life of Charles M. Doughty*. Other book-length studies of Doughty are Barker Fairley, *Charles M. Doughty: A Critical Study*; Annette M. McCormick, 'The Origin and Development of the Style of Charles M. Doughty's

Travels in Arabia Deserta'; Anne Treneer, *Charles M. Doughty*. See also Thomas J. Assad, *Three Victorian Travellers*.

2. Letter from Doughty to Cambridge University Syndics, published in *London Mercury*, 1926, 14, p. 187.
3. Doughty, *Arabia Deserta*, preface to first edition, Vol. I, p. 29. All references to *Arabia Deserta* are to the 1936 edition, in which Doughty's prefaces to the three previous editions are reprinted.
4. Doughty, *Arabia Deserta*, preface to third edition, Vol. I, p. 35, and Vol. I, p. 306.
5. Doughty, *Arabia Deserta*, preface to second edition, Vol. I, p. 31; preface to third edition, Vol. I, p. 35; and *Adam Cast Forth*.
6. Doughty, *Arabia Deserta*, Vol. I, p. 143.
7. Burton, review of *Arabia Deserta*, in *Academy*, 1888, 34, pp. 47–8.
8. Doughty, *Arabia Deserta*, preface to first edition, Vol. I, p. 29.
9. Doughty, *Mansoul*, pp. 114–15.
10. Doughty, *Arabia Deserta*, preface to second edition, Vol. I, p. 33; Hogarth, *The Life of Charles M. Doughty*, p. 204.
11. Doughty, *Arabia Deserta*, Vol. I, pp. 95, 141–2, 342, and Vol. II, pp. 406–7, 409.
12. Doughty, 'Travels in North-Western Arabia and Nejd', p. 387.
13. Doughty, *Arabia Deserta*, Vol. I, p. 618. See also Vol. I, pp. 508, 583–4, and Vol II, p. 135 and passim.
14. Doughty, *Arabia Deserta*, Vol. II, pp. 518–36.
15. Doughty, *Arabia Deserta*, Vol. II, p. 561.
16. Doughty, *Arabia Deserta*, Vol. II, pp. 177–8.
17. Doughty, *Arabia Deserta*, Vol. II, p. 68.
18. Doughty, *The Dawn in Britain*, Vol. VI, pp. 217–22.
19. Doughty, *Mansoul*, pp. 97, 104–5; and *The Dawn in Britain*, Vol. III, p. 225.
20. Doughty, *Arabia Deserta*, Vol. II, p. 406.
21. Douglas, review of *Arabia Deserta*, in *London Mercury*, 1921, 4, pp. 60–70.
22. Doughty, *Arabia Deserta*, Vol. I, p. 393.
23. Doughty, *Arabia Deserta*, Vol. I, pp. 285–6.
24. Doughty, *Arabia Deserta*, Vol. I, p. 302.
25. Doughty, *Arabia Deserta*, Vol. I, pp. 95, 551.
26. Doughty, *Arabia Deserta*, Vol. I, pp. 256, 269, 447, and Vol. II, pp. 83, 259–260.
27. Doughty, *Arabia Deserta*, Vol. I, pp. 283, 306.
28. Doughty, *Mansoul*, pp. 73–4. See also *Adam Cast Forth* and Doughty's review of D. G. Hogarth's *Arabia*, in *The Observer*, 19 March 1922, pp. 13–14.
29. Doughty, *Arabia Deserta*, Vol. I, pp. 451–2.
30. See Flight, 'The Nomadic Idea and Ideal in the Old Testament'.
31. Doughty, *Arabia Deserta*, preface to the second edition, Vol. I, p. 31; and *The Dawn in Britain*, postscript, Vol. VI, pp. 241–4.
32. Doughty, *Arabia Deserta*, Vol. I, pp. 206–7.
33. Doughty, *Arabia Deserta*, Vol. I, p. 367.
34. Taylor, *Doughty's English*, p. 35; Doughty, *Arabia Deserta*, Vol. I, p. 141.
35. Doughty, *Arabia Deserta*, Vol. I, pp. 168, 276, 307, 632; Gibb, *Arabic Literature*, pp. 7–10, 29; Taylor, *Doughty's English*, pp. 4–10.
36. Burton, *Pilgrimage*, Vol. II, p. 98; Palgrave, *Narrative*, Vol. I, p. 311; Doughty, *Arabia Deserta*, Vol. I, p. 307.
37. Doughty, *The Dawn in Britain*, postscript, Vol. VI, p. 243. For an excellent discussion of nationalist theories of language see Kedourie, *Nationalism*.

38. Doughty, *Arabia Deserta*, Vol. I, p. 394, and Vol. II, pp. 68, 187.
39. Doughty, *Arabia Deserta*, Vol. II, pp. 525–6.

7 The Victorian Contribution

1. Doughty, *Arabia Deserta*, Vol. I, p. 566. See also Vol. I, p. 179.
2. Haim, 'Blunt and Al-Kawakibi'.
3. Toynbee, *Acquaintances*, p. 46.
4. Jarvis, *Arab Command*, p. 60.

8 The Great War and the Arabists

1. See his *Orientations*.
2. Kedourie, *In the Anglo-Arab Labyrinth*, p. 19.
3. Kedourie, 'Cairo and Khartoum on the Arab Question', p. 284.
4. An unexpected result of the British campaigns against the Sudanese Mahdiya was the emergence of the Arab of the Sudan as a heroic figure – the noble enemy. See Churchill, *The River War*, Chapters I, II and XV; Gordon, *Khartoum Journal*, p. 120; Magnus, *Kitchener*, pp. 171–2; Wingate, *Mahdism and the Egyptian Sudan*, p. 9; *Spectator*, 1885, 58, pp. 415–16. A general discussion of British attitudes towards the Mahdiya is to be found in Norman Daniel, *Islam, Europe and Empire*, Chapter XV.
5. Marmorstein, 'A Note on Damascus, Homs, Hama and Aleppo'. Marmorstein assumes that the idea of this boundary originated with Sykes, but Kedourie (*In the Anglo-Arab Labyrinth*, p. 87) argues that it originated with Storrs.
6. Sykes, *Dar-ul-Islam*, p. 256.
7. Beloff, *Imperial Sunset*, Vol. I, p. 256.
8. Leslie, *Mark Sykes: His Life and Letters*, pp. 271, 284.
9. Philip Graves, *Palestine, the Land of Three Faiths*, p. 3; Lawrence, 'The Changing East', p. 769; Burgoyne, *Gertrude Bell*, Vol. II, p. 75. See also Chaim Weizmann's essay in A. W. Lawrence, ed., *T. E. Lawrence by his Friends*.
10. Lawrence, *Seven Pillars of Wisdom*, p. 68.
11. Lawrence, *Seven Pillars of Wisdom*, p. 23.
12. Lawrence, *Seven Pillars of Wisdom*, p. 64.
13. Lawrence, *Seven Pillars of Wisdom*, pp. 68, 92.
14. Richard Aldington, *Lawrence of Arabia*; Suleiman Mousa, *T. E. Lawrence: An Arab View*; John Mack, *A Prince of our Disorder: The Life of T. E. Lawrence*.
15. Lawrence, 'Twenty-seven Articles', pp. 127, 128. Reprinted from the *Arab Bulletin* in Lawrence, *Secret Despatches from Arabia*.
16. See e.g. *Seven Pillars of Wisdom*, pp. 193, 331; and letter to Lionel Curtis, 19 March 1923, in *Letters of T. E. Lawrence*, pp. 411–12.
17. Garnett, ed., *Letters of T. E. Lawrence*, p. 768; Lawrence, *Letters to his Biographers, Robert Graves–Liddell Hart*, Part I, p. 67; *Seven Pillars of Wisdom*, pp. 32, 36–44; introduction to Doughty's *Arabia Deserta*, Vol. I, pp. 21–8; and 'The Changing East', p. 765; Graves, *Lawrence and the Arabian Adventure*, p. 22.
18. Lawrence, *Seven Pillars of Wisdom*, pp. 103, 149, 181.
19. Blunt, 'The Future of Islam', Part III, p. 446.
20. Lawrence, 'Twenty-Seven Articles', p. 128.
21. Garnett, ed., *Letters of T. E. Lawrence*, p. 577.
22. See Klieman, *Foundations of British Policy in the Arab World* for a detailed study

of the Cairo Conference and Lawrence's promotion of a Sherifian policy.

23. Garnett, ed., *Letters of T. E. Lawrence*, pp. 291–2. See also Lawrence, 'The Changing East'.
24. Klieman, *Foundations of British Policy in the Arab World*, p. 96.
25. Lawrence, *Letters to his Biographers, Robert Graves–Liddell Hart*, Part II, p. 189.
26. Mack, *A Prince of our Disorder*, pp. 6–7.
27. Lawrence, *Seven Pillars of Wisdom*, p. 579; Liddell Hart, '*T. E. Lawrence*' in *Arabia and After*, p. 14. (The account of his family in Liddell Hart's book was written by Lawrence. See Aldington, *Lawrence of Arabia*, p. 55.)
28. Lawrence, *Seven Pillars of Wisdom*, p. 476.
29. Garnett, ed., *Letters of T. E. Lawrence*, p. 653.
30. For a tortured expression of his feeling of singularity, see *Seven Pillars of Wisdom*, Chapter CIII.
31. Lawrence, *Letters to his Biographers, Robert Graves–Liddell Hart*, Part II, p. 24; and *Seven Pillars of Wisdom*, p. 684.
32. Lawrence, *Seven Pillars of Wisdom*, pp. 28–9, 40, 475 and passim.
33. Lawrence, introduction to Doughty's *Arabia Deserta*, Vol. I, p. 18.
34. Knightley and Simpson, *The Secret Lives of Lawrence of Arabia*, pp. 156–7.
35. Storrs, *Orientations*, p. 382.
36. Hogarth, 'Wahabism and British Interests', p. 71.
37. Hogarth, *The Nearer East*, pp. 256–68; and *Arabia*, pp. 21, 99–100; Kedourie, *England and the Middle East*, p. 93.
38. Symes, *Tour of Duty*, p. 50.
39. Kedourie, 'Cairo and Khartoum on the Arab Question', p. 285.
40. Clayton, 'Arabia and the Arabs', p. 13; Kedourie, 'Cairo and Khartoum on the Arab Question', p. 285.
41. Kedourie, 'Cairo and Khartoum on the Arab Question', p. 296.
42. Klieman, *Foundations of British Policy in the Arab World*, pp. 98, 101–2.
43. Kedourie, 'Cairo and Khartoum on the Arab Question', passim.
44. Aldington, *Lawrence of Arabia*, p. 284.
45. Garnett, ed., *Letters of T. E. Lawrence*, p. 196.
46. Burgoyne, *Gertrude Bell*, Vol. II, p. 151.
47. Garnett, ed., *Letters of T. E. Lawrence*, p. 543.
48. Burgoyne, *Gertrude Bell*, Vol. II, pp. 31–3.
49. Bell, *Syria: The Desert and the Sown*, p. xi; and preface to *Amurath to Amurath*; Daniel, *Islam, Europe and Empire*, p. 471.
50. Bell, *Syria: The Desert and the Sown*, p. x; and *Amurath to Amurath*, p. 116.
51. Burgoyne, *Gertrude Bell*, Vol. II, p. 262. See also Seton Dearden, 'Gertrude Bell: a Journey of the Heart'.
52. George Buchanan, letter to *The Times*, 21 June 1920, p. 10.
53. Burgoyne, *Gertrude Bell*, Vol. II, p. 48. See also Lady Richmond, ed., *Selected Letters of Gertrude Bell*, p. 253.
54. Burgoyne, *Gertrude Bell*, Vol. II, pp. 71, 77.
55. Burgoyne, *Gertrude Bell*, Vol. II, p. 111.
56. Wilson, *Loyalties*, pp. xiv, 54, 118–19, 206–7, 213.
57. Marlowe, *Late Victorian*, passim.
58. Burgoyne, *Gertrude Bell*, Vol. II, pp. 78, 162.
59. Burgoyne, *Gertrude Bell*, Vol. II, pp. 113, 178, 204.
60. Burgoyne, *Gertrude Bell*, Vol. II, p. 245.
61. Burgoyne, *Gertrude Bell*, Vol. II, pp. 271–2.
62. Lawrence, *Seven Pillars of Wisdom*, p. 283.

9 Hail and Farewell

1. Jarvis, *Arab Command*, pp. 60–1.
2. Glubb, 'The Bedouins of Northern 'Iraq', p. 30.
3. Glubb, *A Soldier with the Arabs*, p. 5.
4. Glubb, *War in the Desert*, p. 26.
5. Glubb, *A Soldier with the Arabs*, p. 6.
6. Glubb, *Britain and the Arabs*, pp. 389–92; and *War in the Desert*, pp. 94–5.
7. Philby, *The Heart of Arabia*, Vol. i, pp. 299–300; and *Arabia*, pp. 180–3.
8. Monroe, *Philby of Arabia*, pp. 19–20; Philby, *Arabian Days*, p. 28.
9. Philby, *The Empty Quarter*, pp. xvii, xxi.
10. Jarvis, 'The Desert Bedouin and his Future'; and 'Southern Palestine and its Possibilities for Settlement'.
11. Elphinston, 'The Future of the Bedouin of Northern Arabia'.
12. Thesiger, *The Marsh Arabs*, pp. 6, 50.
13. Philby, *Sa'udi Arabia*, p. xviii. See also his *Arabian Jubilee*.
14. Cole, *Nomads of the Nomads*, p. 158; Patai, *The Kingdom of Jordan*, p. 196.
15. Cole, *Nomads of the Nomads*, p. 12.

Epilogue
To Know Them was to Love Them

1. Lawrence, 'The Changing East'.
2. Kirkbride, *A Crackle of Thorns*, p. 196.
3. Hourani, 'The Decline of the West in the Middle East', pp. 33–4.
4. Glubb, *War in the Desert*, p. 31; 'The Bedouins of Northern 'Iraq', p. 23; and 'Arab Chivalry'.
5. Winterton, comment on Glubb, 'Arab Chivalry', *Journal of the Royal Central Asian Society*, 1937, 24, p. 26.
6. Nicolson, *Good Behaviour*.
7. Rolls, *Steel Chariots in the Desert*.
8. T. P. Thompson, 'Arabs and Persians', p. 210. (See Chapter 1, p. 31.)
9. Glubb, *War in the Desert*, p. 94.
10. Storrs, *Orientations*, p. 494.
11. Glubb, *War in the Desert*, p. 95.
12. Glubb, 'Arab Chivalry', p. 26.
13. Cornwallis, foreword to Stark, *A Winter in Arabia*, p. 2; Klieman, *Foundations of British Policy in the Arab World*, p. 102.
14. Graves, *Lawrence and the Arabian Adventure*, p. 35.
15. Mannoni, *Prospero and Caliban*.
16. Kinglake's friend Eliot Warburton might be regarded as an unusually perfect specimen of Mannoni's colonial type. See Chapter 2, p. 48.
17. Rolls, *Steel Chariots in the Desert*, p. 238.
18. Jarvis, *Arab Command*, p. 53.
19. Liddell Hart, 'T. E. Lawrence' in Arabia and After, p. 448.

Bibliography

I have not attempted to provide a complete bibliography of the subject. The following is simply an alphabetical list of works referred to in the text.

Aldington, Richard. *Lawrence of Arabia*. Penguin edition, London, 1971. First published 1955.

Allen, Mea. *Palgrave of Arabia*. London, 1972.

Anon. 'The Arabian Empire'. *Blackwood's*, 1838, *43*, pp. 661–76.

Anon. 'Military Expedition into Arabia Felix'. *Littell's Living Age*, 1852, *34*, pp. 375–9. Reprinted from *United Services Magazine*.

Anon. 'What the Arab is and is Not'. *Edinburgh Review*, 1905, *201*, pp. 386–409.

Antonius, George. *The Arab Awakening*. London, 1938.

Arberry, A. J. 'New Light on Sir William Jones'. *Bulletin of the School of Oriental and African Studies*, 1946, *11*, pp. 673–85.

Assad, Thomas J. *Three Victorian Travellers: Burton, Blunt, Doughty*. London, 1964.

Bashford, Major Lindsay. 'Egypt and Palestine'. *Edinburgh Review*, 1920, *231*, pp. 115–33.

Bayle, Pierre. *A General Dictionary, Historical and Critical*. London, 1734–41.

Belhaven, The Master of. *The Kingdom of Melchior*, London, 1949.

Bell, Gertrude. *Syria: The Desert and the Sown*. London, 1908. First published 1907. *Amurath to Amurath*. New York, 1911.
Selected Letters of Gertrude Bell. Lady Richmond, ed., London, 1953.

Beloff, Max. *Imperial Sunset. Vol. I: Britain's Liberal Empire, 1897–1921*. London, 1969.

Bennett, Alan. *Forty Years On*. London, 1969.

Biddiss, Michael. 'Gobineau and the Origins of European Racism'. *Race*, 1966, *7*, pp. 255–70.

Blunt, Lady Anne. *Bedouin Tribes of the Euphrates*. New York, 1879. The preface (pp. 7–10), the postscript (pp. 441–5), and Chapters xxiii to xxviii (pp. 361–440) are by Wilfrid Blunt.
A Pilgrimage to Nejd. London, 1881. The preface (Vol. i, pp. ix–xxviii), Chapter xi of Vol. i (pp. 257–73), and the appendix of Vol. ii (pp. 251–68) are by Wilfrid Blunt.

Blunt, Wilfrid. 'Recent Events in Arabia'. *Fortnightly Review*, 1880, *27*, pp. 707–19.
'The Future of Islam'. Appeared in five parts in *Fortnightly Review*, 1881, *30*, pp. 204–23, 315–32, 441–58, 585–602; and *Fortnightly Review*, 1882, *31*, pp. 32–48.
'Ideas about India'. Appeared in five parts in *Fortnightly Review*, 1884, *36*, pp. 165–78, 445–59, 624–37; and *Fortnightly Review*, 1885, *37*, pp. 234–48, 386–98.
'Arabian Poetry of the Days of Ignorance'. *New Review*, 1896, *14*, pp. 626–35.

The Shame of the Nineteenth Century. Pamphlet, reprinted from *The Times*, 24 December 1900.

'The By-Law Tyranny and Rural Depopulation'. *The Nineteenth Century*, 1904, 56, pp. 643–51.

Secret History of the English Occupation of Egypt. London, 1907.

India under Ripon. London, 1909.

Gordon at Khartoum. London, 1911.

The Land War in Ireland. London, 1912.

The Poetical Works of Wilfrid Scawen Blunt. London, 1914.

My Diaries. Part I (1888–1900). New York, 1921. First published 1919.

My Diaries. Part II (1900–1914). New York, 1921. First published 1920.

Poems. New York, 1923.

Blunt, Wilfrid and Meynell, Charles. *Proteus and Amadeus: A Correspondence*. London, 1878. Published pseudonymously.

Braude, Benjamin Meir. 'The Spiritual Quest of William Gifford Palgrave'. Unpublished honours thesis, Harvard College, 1967.

Brent, Peter. *Far Arabia: Explorers of the Myth*. London, 1977.

Brodie, Fawn M. *The Devil Drives. A Life of Sir Richard Burton*. Penguin edition, London, 1971. First published 1967.

Bruce, James. *Travels to Discover the Source of the Nile*. Edinburgh, 1790.

Buchan, John. *Greenmantle*. London, 1967. First published 1916.

Burckhardt, J. L. *Travels in Nubia*. London, 1819.

Travels in Arabia. Frank Cass reprint, London, 1968. First published 1829.

Notes on the Bedouins and Wahabys. London, 1830.

Review of *Travels in Arabia*: Anon., *Edinburgh Review*, 1829, 50, pp. 164–81.

Burgoyne, Elizabeth. *Gertrude Bell: from her Personal Papers*. London, 1958–1961.

Burton, Isabel. *The Life of Capt. Sir Richard F. Burton*. London, 1893.

Burton, Richard. *Goa and the Blue Mountains*. London, 1851.

Scinde; or The Unhappy Valley. London, 1851.

Sindh, and the Races that Inhabit the Valley of the Indus. London, 1851.

Falconry in the Valley of the Indus. London, 1852.

Personal Narrative of a Pilgrimage to Al-Madinah & Meccah. Dover reprint of the Memorial Edition, New York, 1964. First published 1855–6.

First Footsteps in East Africa. Gordon Waterfield, ed., London, 1966. First published 1856.

The Lake Regions of Central Africa. Alan Moorehead, ed., New York, 1961. First published 1860.

A Mission to Gelele, King of Dahomey. University Microfilms reprint, Ann Arbor, 1962. First published 1864.

The Highlands of Brazil. London, 1869.

Zanzibar; City, Island and Coast. London, 1872.

The Gold Mines of Midian and the Ruined Midianite Cities. London, 1878.

The Kasidah. New York, 1926. First published 1880.

A Plain and Literal Translation of the Arabian Nights' Entertainments. London, 1885–8.

The Jew, the Gypsy, and El Islam. W. H. Wilkins, ed., London, 1898.

Lord Beaconsfield: A Sketch. Pamphlet, no date.

Review of *Pilgrimage*: Anon., *Edinburgh Review*, 1856, 104, pp. 186–204.

Burton, Richard and Tyrwhitt-Drake, Charles. *Unexplored Syria*. London, 1872.

Bibliography

Byron, Lord. *Childe Harold's Pilgrimage, and Other Romantic Poems*. Samuel Chew, ed., New York, 1936.

Carlyle, Thomas. 'The Hero as Prophet'. In *Heroes and Hero-Worship*, Centennial Memorial Edition, Boston, no date, pp. 273–306. First published 1840.

Carmichael, John. *A Journey from Aleppo, over the Desert, to Basserah*. In Douglas Carruthers, ed., *The Desert Route to India*, London, Hakluyt Society, 1929, pp. 129–79. First published 1772.

Carruthers, Douglas, ed. *The Desert Route to India*. London, Hakluyt Society, 1929.
Arabian Adventure. London, 1935.

Chateaubriand, F.-R. de. *Travels in Greece, Palestine, Egypt, and Barbary, during the Years 1806 and 1807*. English translation by F. Shoberl of *Itinéraire de Paris à Jérusalem*, New York, 1814. First published in French in 1811.

Cheesman, R. E. 'The Deserts of Jafura and Jabrin'. *Geographical Journal*, 1925, *65*, pp. 112–40.

Churchill, Winston. *The River War*. London, 1951. First published 1899.

Clarke, Edward. *Travels in Various Countries of Europe, Asia and Africa*. Fourth edition, London, 1816–24. First published 1810–23.

Clayton, Gilbert. 'Arabia and the Arabs'. *Journal of the Royal Institute of International Affairs*, 1929, *8*, pp. 8–20.

Cleveland, The Duchess of. *The Life and Letters of Lady Hester Stanhope*. London, 1914.

Cole, Donald Powell. *Nomads of the Nomads: The Āl Murrah Bedouin of the Empty Quarter*. Chicago 1975.

Crichton, Andrew. *History of Arabia, Ancient and Modern*. Edinburgh, 1834.

Cromer, Lord. *Modern Egypt*. London, 1908.

Daniel, Norman. *Islam, Europe and Empire*. Edinburgh, 1966.

D'Arvieux, Laurent, *The Chevalier d'Arvieux's Travels in Arabia the Desart*. English translation of *Voyage en Palestine* by M. de la Roque, London, 1718.

Dearden, Seton. 'Gertrude Bell; a Journey of the Heart'. *Cornhill*, 1969, *177*, pp. 457–509.

De Gaury, Gerald. *Arabia Phoenix*. London, 1946.
Arabian Journey. London, 1950.
Travelling Gent: Life of Alexander Kinglake, 1809–1891. London and Boston, 1972.

D'Herbelot, Bartholomeo. *Bibliothèque orientale*. Paris, 1697.

De la Mare, Walter. *The Complete Poems of Walter de la Mare*. London, 1969.

Dickson, H. R. P. *The Arab of the Desert*. London, 1949.

Diodorus Siculus. *Diodorus of Sicily*. Loeb edition, London, 1933.

Disraeli, Benjamin. *Tancred, or The New Crusade*. Collected edition of the *Novels and Tales by the Rt. Hon. B. Disraeli*, Vol. iv, London, 1896. First published 1847.

Doughty, Charles M. 'Travels in North-Western Arabia and Nejd'. *Proceedings of the Royal Geographical Society*, 1884, *6*, pp. 382–99.
Travels in Arabia Deserta. Definitive edition with introduction by T. E. Lawrence, London, 1936. First published 1888.
Under Arms. London, 1900.
The Dawn in Britain. London, 1906.
Adam Cast Forth. London, 1908.
The Cliffs. London, 1909.
The Clouds. London, 1912.
The Titans. London, 1916.
Mansoul (or, the Riddle of the World). London, 1920.
Review of D. G. Hogarth's *Arabia*. *The Observer*, 19 March 1922, pp. 13–14.

Letter to Cambridge University Syndics. Published in *London Mercury*, 1926, *14*, p. 187.

Reviews of *Arabia Deserta*: Burton, Richard, *Academy*, 1888, *34*, pp. 47–8; Douglas, Norman, *London Mercury*, 1921, *4*, pp. 60–70.

Duff Gordon, Lady Lucie. *Letters from Egypt*. Gordon Waterfield, ed., London, 1969. First published 1865.

Elphinston, W. G. 'The Future of the Bedouin of Northern Arabia'. *Journal of the Royal Institute of International Affairs*, 1945, *21*, pp. 370–5.

Erikson, Erik. *Childhood and Society*. Second edition, New York, 1963.
Identity, Youth and Crisis. New York, 1968.

Fairley, Barker. *Charles M. Doughty: A Critical Study*. London, 1927.

Fedden, Robin. *English Travellers in the Near East*. London, 1958.

Finch, Edith. *Wilfrid Scawen Blunt*. London, 1938.

Flight, J. W. 'The Nomadic Idea and Ideal in the Old Testament'. *Journal of Biblical Literature and Exegesis*, 1923, *42*, pp. 158–226.

George, A. J. *Lamartine and Romantic Unanism*. New York, 1940.

Gibb, H. A. R. *Arabic Literature: An Introduction*. Revised edition, Oxford, 1963.

Gibbon, Edward. *Decline and Fall of the Roman Empire*. Christopher Dawson, ed., Everyman edition, London, 1957. First published 1776–88.

Glen, Douglas. *In the Steps of Lawrence of Arabia*. London, 1941.

Glubb, J. B. 'The Bedouins of Northern 'Iraq'. *Journal of the Royal Central Asian Society*, 1935, *22*, pp. 13–31.
'Arab Chivalry'. *Journal of the Royal Central Asian Society*, 1937, *24*, pp. 5–26.
A Soldier with the Arabs. London, 1957.
Britain and the Arabs. London, 1959.
War in the Desert. London, 1960.

Gobineau, Comte de. *Gobineau's Selected Political Writings*. Michael Biddiss, ed., London, 1970.

Gordon, Charles. *General Gordon's Khartoum Journal*. Lord Elton, ed., London, 1961.

Graves, Philip. *Palestine, the Land of Three Faiths*. London, 1923.

Graves, Robert. *Lawrence and the Arabian Adventure*. New York, 1928. (Published in England in 1927 as *Lawrence and the Arabs*.)

Haim, S. G. 'Blunt and Al-Kawakibi'. *Oriente Moderne*, 1955, *35*, pp. 132–43.

Hansen, Thorkild. *Arabia Felix: The Danish Expedition of 1761–1767*. London, 1964.

Hardinge, Arthur. *A Diplomatist in the East*. London, 1928.

Hardwick, Elizabeth. 'Jane Carlyle'. *New York Review of Books*, 14 December 1972, pp. 32–4.

Herodotus. *Herodotus*. Loeb edition, London, 1921.

Heude, William. *A Voyage up the Persian Gulf and a Journey Overland from India to England*. London, 1819.

Hill, Gray. *With the Bedouins*. London, 1891.

Hogarth, D. G. *The Nearer East*. New York, 1902.
Arabia. Oxford, 1922.
'Wahabism and British Interests'. *Journal of the Royal Institute of International Affairs*, 1925, *4*, pp. 70–9.
The Life of Charles M. Doughty. New York, 1929.

Hourani, Albert. 'The Decline of the West in the Middle East'. *International Affairs*, 1953, *29*, pp. 22–42, 156–83.

Hunt, Leigh. *The Poetical Works of Leigh Hunt*. Oxford, 1923.

Ingrams, W. H. *Zanzibar: Its History and People*. London, 1931.

The Interpreter's Dictionary of the Bible. New York, 1962.

Irwin, Eyles. *A Series of Adventures in the Course of a Voyage up the Red Sea, on the Coasts of Arabia and Egypt.* Dublin, 1780.

The Bedouins, or, Arabs of the Desert. Dublin, 1802.

Jarvis, C. S. 'The Desert Bedouin and his Future'. *Journal of the Royal Central Asian Society*, 1936, 23, pp. 585–93.

'Southern Palestine and its Possibilities for Settlement'. *Journal of the Royal Central Asian Society*, 1938, 25, pp. 204–18.

Arab Command: The Biography of Lt Col F. G. Peake Pasha. London, 1942.

Joinville, Sire Jean de. *Chronicle of the Crusade of St Lewis.* In *Memoirs of the Crusades*, London, Everyman's Library, no date.

Jones, Sir William. 'Discourse on the Arabs'. In *Works of Sir William Jones*, Lord Teignmouth, ed., Vol. III, London, 1807.

Kedourie, Elie. *England and the Middle East. 1914–1920.* London, 1956.

Nationalism. London, 1960.

'Cairo and Khartoum on the Arab Question, 1915–1918'. *The Historical Journal*, 1964, 7, pp. 280–97.

In the Anglo-Arab Labyrinth. Cambridge, 1976.

Kinglake, Alexander. *Eothen, or Traces of Travel Brought Home from the East.* London, 1904. First published 1844.

Kirkbride, Alec. *A Crackle of Thorns.* London, 1956.

Klieman, A. S. *Foundations of British Policy in the Arab World: The Cairo Conference of 1921.* Baltimore, 1970.

Knightley, Philip and Simpson, Colin. *The Secret Lives of Lawrence of Arabia.* London, 1969.

Lamartine, Alphonse de. *A Pilgrimage to the Holy Land.* English translation of *Voyage en Orient.* New York, 1848. First published in French in 1835.

Lane, E. W. *Manners and Customs of the Modern Egyptians.* Fifth edition, London, 1904. First published 1836.

Lawrence, A. W., ed. *T. E. Lawrence by his Friends.* London, 1937.

Lawrence, T. E. 'The Changing East'. Unsigned article in *The Round Table*, 1919–20, 10, pp. 756–72.

Seven Pillars of Wisdom: A Triumph. Penguin edition, London, 1965. First published 1935.

The Letters of T. E. Lawrence. David Garnett, ed., New York, 1939.

Secret Despatches from Arabia. London, 1939. A collection of wartime articles reprinted from the *Arab Bulletin.*

Letters to his Biographers. Robert Graves–Liddell Hart. London, 1963.

Leslie, Shane. *Mark Sykes: His Life and Letters.* London, 1923.

Liddell Hart, B. H. *'T. E. Lawrence' in Arabia and After.* London, 1934.

Lithgow, William. *The Totall Discourse of the Rare Adventures and Painefull Peregrinations of Long Nineteene Years Travayles from Scotland to the Most Famous Kingdoms in Europe, Asia and Affrica.* Glasgow, 1906. First published 1632.

Longford, Elizabeth. *A Pilgrimage of Passion: The Life of Wilfrid Scawen Blunt.* London, 1979.

Lytton, Anthony. *The Desert and the Green.* London, 1957.

Wilfrid Scawen Blunt: A Memoir by his Grandson. London, 1961.

Lytton, Judith. *The Authentic Arabian Horse.* London, 1945.

Lytton, Neville. *The English Country Gentleman.* London, 1925.

MacCarthy, Desmond. *Memories.* New York, 1953.

McCormick, Annette M. 'The Origin and Development of the Style of Charles M.

Doughty's *Travels in Arabia Deserta'*. Unpublished Ph.D. thesis, London University, 1951.

Mack, John E. *A Prince of our Disorder: The Life of T. E. Lawrence*. Boston and Toronto, 1976.

Magnus, Philip. *Kitchener: Portrait of an Imperialist*. London, 1964.

Mandeville, Sir John. *Mandeville's Travels*. London, Hakluyt Society, 1953.

Mannoni, O. *Prospero and Caliban: The Psychology of Colonization*. London, 1956.

Marlowe, John. *Late Victorian: The Life of Sir Arnold Talbot Wilson*. London, 1967.

Marmorstein, E. 'A Note on Damascus, Homs, Hama and Aleppo'. *St Antony's Papers*, 1961, *11*, pp. 161–5.

Meinertzhagen, Richard. *Middle East Diary, 1917–1956*. London, 1959.

Meryon, Charles. *Memoirs of Lady Hester Stanhope*. Second edition, London, 1846.

Monroe, Elizabeth. *Britain's Moment in the Middle East: 1914–1956*. University Paperback edition, London, 1965.

Philby of Arabia. London, 1973.

Mousa, Suleiman, *T. E. Lawrence: An Arab View*. New York, 1966.

Nasir, Sari J. *The Arabs and the English*. London, 1976.

Nicolson, Harold. *Good Behaviour: Being a Study of Certain Types of Civility*. London, 1955.

Niebuhr, B. G. *The Life of Carsten Niebuhr, the Oriental Traveller*. Edinburgh, 1836.

Niebuhr, Carsten. *Travels in Arabia*. Abridged version in John Pinkerton, ed., *A General Collection*, Vol. x, pp. 1–221. First published in English 1792.

Norton, Caroline. 'The Arab's Farewell to his Horse', pp. 269–72. In *The Undying One, and Other Poems*, London, 1830, pp. 269–72.

Ockley, Simon. *The History of the Saracens*. 1708–18.

Palgrave, Sir Francis. *The Rise and Progress of the English Commonwealth: Anglo Saxon Period*. In *Collected Historical Works*, Vol. vi, Cambridge, 1921. First published 1832.

Palgrave, William Gifford. 'Notes of a Journey from Gaza, through the Interior of Arabia, to El Khatif on the Persian Gulf, and thence to Omàn, in 1862–63'. *Proceedings of the Royal Geographical Society*, 1864, *8*, pp. 63–82, 97–107.

Narrative of a Year's Journey through Central and Eastern Arabia (1862–63). London and Cambridge, 1865.

Essays on Eastern Questions. London, 1872.

Hermann Agha: An Eastern Narrative. London, 1878. First published 1872.

'Arabia'. *Encyclopaedia Britannica*, ninth edition, 1875, Vol. ii, pp. 234–65.

Ulysses, or Scenes and Studies in Many Lands. London, 1887.

A Vision of Life: Semblance and Reality. London, 1891.

Reviews of *Narrative of a Year's Journey*:
   Anon., *Athenaeum*, 1865, pp. 773–5.
   Anon., *Blackwood's*, 1865, *98*, pp. 723–42.
   Anon., *Chambers' Edinburgh Journal*, 1865, *42*, pp. 536–66.
   Anon., *Edinburgh Review*, 1865, *122*, pp. 244–62.
   Anon., *Littell's Living Age*, 1865, *87*, pp. 529–42.
   Anon., *The Times*, 19 September 1865, p. 4.
   Anon., *Westminster Review*, 1865, *84*, pp. 381–401.
   Anon., *Quarterly Review*, 1866, *119*, pp. 182–215.
   Poole, R. S., *Fortnightly Review*, 1865, *1*, pp. 459–71.
Obituaries of Palgrave:
   Anon., *Athenaeum*, 1888, pp. 483–4.
   Anon., *Proceedings of the Royal Geographical Society*, 1888, *10*, pp. 713–15.

Patai, Raphael. *The Kingdom of Jordan*. Princeton, 1958.

Philby, H. St J. B. *The Heart of Arabia*. New York and London, 1923.
   Arabia. London, 1930.
   The Empty Quarter. London, 1933.
   'Palgrave in Arabia'. *Journal of the Royal Geographical Society*, 1947, *109*, pp. 282–5.
   Arabian Days. London, 1948.
   Arabian Jubilee. London, 1952.
   Sa'udi Arabia. New York, 1955.

Pinkerton, John. *A General Collection of the Best and Most Interesting Voyages and Travels in All Parts of the World*. London, 1808–14.

Plaisted, Bartholomew. *A Journal from Busserah to Aleppo*. In Douglas Carruthers, ed., *The Desert Route to India*, London, Hakluyt Society, 1929, pp. 49–128. First published 1757.

Polson Newman, E. W. *Great Britain in Egypt*. London, 1928.

Prichard, James Cowles. *Researches into the Physical History of Mankind*. 5 vols., third edition, London, 1836–43. This edition is the same as the second edition (1826), a greatly expanded and revised version of the first (1813) edition.
   The Natural History of Man. Fourth edition, London, 1855. First published 1843.

Renan, Ernest, *De la part des peuples sémitiques dans l'histoire de la civilisation*. Seventh edition, Paris, 1875. First published 1862.

Rolls, S. C. *Steel Chariots in the Desert*. London, 1937.

Sadlier, G. F. *Diary of a Journey across Arabia, from El Khatif in the Persian Gulf to Yambo on the Red Sea, during the Year 1819*. Bombay, 1866.

Said, Edward W. *Orientalism*. New York and London, 1978.

St John, Bayle. *Adventures in the Libyan Desert and the Oasis of Jupiter Ammon*. London, 1849.

Sale, George. *The Koran*. London, Frederick Warne & Co, no date. First published 1734.

Scott, Walter. *The Talisman*. London, 1832.

Searight, Sarah. *The British in the Middle East*. London, 1969.

Shelley, P. B. *The Poetical Works of Shelley*. Oxford, 1905.

Sim, Katherine. *Desert Traveller: The Life of Jean Louis Burckhardt*. London, 1969.

Sladen, Douglas. *Egypt and the English*. London, 1908.

Stanley, H. M. *Through the Dark Continent*. London, 1880. First published 1878.

Stark, Freya. *The Southern Gates of Arabia*. London, 1936.
   A Winter in Arabia. London, 1940.
   The Journey's Echo. New York, 1964.

Stisted, Georgiana. *The True Life of Capt. Sir Richard F. Burton*. Ward Lock reprint, London, 1970. First published 1896.

Storrs, Ronald. *Orientations*. London, 1939. First published 1937.

Strabo. *The Geography of Strabo*. Loeb edition, London, 1917.

Strachey, Lytton. 'Lady Hester Stanhope'. In *Biographical Essays*, New York, no date, pp. 211–18.

Swinburne, A. C. *The Complete Works of A. C. Swinburne*. London, 1925.

Sykes, Mark. *Dar-ul-Islam*. London, 1904.

Symes, Stewart. *Tour of Duty*. London, 1946.

Taylor, Walt. *Doughty's English*. Pamphlet issued by the Society for Pure English, Oxford, 1939.

Tennyson, Alfred. *The Poems of Tennyson*. London, 1969.

Thackeray, W. M. *Notes of a Journey from Cornhill to Grand Cairo*. In *The Works of*

    William Makepeace Thackeray, Vol. xiv, pp. 345–514, London, 1869. First published 1846.

  Vanity Fair. New York, 1899. First published 1848.

Thesiger, Wilfred. *Arabian Sands*. London, 1959.

  The Marsh Arabs. New York, 1964.

Thomas, Bertram. *Arabia Felix*. London, 1932.

Thomas, Lowell. *With Lawrence in Arabia*. Arrow edition, London, 1964. First published 1924.

Thompson, T. P. 'Arabs and Persians'. *Westminster Review*, 1826, 5, pp. 202–48.

Toynbee, Arnold. *Acquaintances*. London, 1967.

Treneer, Anne. *Charles M. Doughty*. London, 1935.

Valentia, Lord. *Voyages and Travels to India, Ceylon, the Red Sea, Abyssinia and Egypt*. London, 1809.

Voltaire, F. M. A. de. *Mahomet the Prophet, or Fanaticism*. New York, 1964. First published 1742.

  'Essai sur les mœurs'. In *Oeuvres complètes de Voltaire*, Vol. ii, Paris, 1878. First published 1756.

Warburton, Eliot. *Travels in Egypt and the Holy Land: or The Crescent and the Cross. Comprising the Romance and Realities of Eastern Travel*. Philadelphia, 1859. First published 1845.

Watt, W. Montgomery. 'Carlyle on Muhammad'. *The Hibbert Journal*, 1954–5, 53, pp. 247–54.

William of Tyre. *A History of Deeds Done Beyond the Sea*. New York, 1943.

Wilson, A. T. *Loyalties. Mesopotamia. 1914–1917*. London, 1930.

Wingate, Reginald. *Mahdism and the Egyptian Sudan*. London, 1891.

Index

Abdullah, son of Emir Feisal of Nejd, 92–3

Abdullah, son of Sherif Hussein of Mecca (later King of Transjordan), 164, 170, 172, 176, 177, 192

Abqaiq, 203

Abu Yemama, 128

Aden, 65, 73, 99, 102, 141

Afghans, 61, 127

Aldington, Richard, 172, 216, 219

Aleppo, 8, 26, 28, 93, 118, 168

Alexandria, 33, 48, 129

Algeria, 118, 138

Algiers, 99

Ali, son of Sherif Hussein of Mecca (later King of the Hejaz), 172, 196

al Kawakibi, 159

Allen, Mea, 89, 93

All the Year Round, 53

Al Murra tribe, 202–6

Amara tribe, 189

Amman, 176, 192

Anaza tribe, 28, 81, 118, 122, 144

Anglo-French Declaration (1918), 192, 196

Anglo-Persian Oil Company, 198

Antar, 87, 158

Antonius, George, 164

Arab Bulletin, 173, 180

Arab Bureau, 183

Arab Empire, 6, 21, 42–3

Arabi, Ahmed, 128–9

Arabia, 5, 11, 13, 20–1, 36–7

Arabian Nights, 36–7, 50, 64, 82, 138, 157

Arabic language, 10–11, 153–4

Arabic poetry, 11, 121

Arab Legion, 194

Arabs (*see also* Bedouin)
  as exception to White Man's Burden, 106, 128, 159, 169
  English affinity with, 30–1, 43, 100–1, 159, 185–6, 202, 209–11, 215–16, 219

tradition of English expertise on, 1, 159, 163–4, 207–9

Arab's Farewell to his Horse, The, 157

Asquith, Herbert Henry, 134

Athenaeum, 84

Ayn ez-Zeyma, 145

Badger, Rev. G. P., 87, 93

Baghdad, 93, 177, 185, 186, 191, 192

Bahrein, 93

Bakhtiari tribe, 210

Baldwin I of Jerusalem, 7

Balfour Declaration, 169

Baluchis, 61

Basra, 21, 93, 99, 186, 189, 191, 196

Baurenfeind, Georg Wilhelm, 15, 16

Bayle, Pierre, 12

Beckx, Father, 94

Bedouin
  as subjects of English humour, 47, 52, 53
  biblical associations of, 16, 36, 50, 138
  bravery, 17, 20, 22, 30, 40, 121, 168, 200
  capacity for endurance, 139–40, 182
  chivalry, 49, 72–3, 121, 194, 210
  divisive, individualistic tendencies, 42–3, 98, 150, 174, 195
  faithfulness to pledges, 9, 11, 23–4, 31
  first anthropological study of Arabian Bedouin, 202–6
  good manners, 9, 17–18, 22, 30–1, 33, 118, 194
  hospitality, 9, 12, 18, 23–4, 49, 97, 121, 151–2
  idealization of, 11–12, 16, 19–20, 23–4, 29–30
  liberty of, 11, 12, 16, 17, 19, 20–1, 28, 49, 155, 174
  love of poetry, 11, 18
  mediaeval European attitudes towards, 7

Index

Index